THE LIFE AND TIMES OF
CHARLES THEOPHILUS HAHN

A JOLLY LIFE

John Odling-Smee

Mereo Books

2nd Floor, 6-8 Dyer Street, Cirencester, Gloucestershire, GL7 2PF
An imprint of Memoirs Books. www.mereobooks.com
and www.memoirsbooks.co.uk

A Jolly Life

ISBN: 978-1-86151-976-4

First published in Great Britain in 2021
by Mereo Books, an imprint of Memoirs Books.

The address for Memoirs Books can be found at www.mereobooks.com

Mereo Books Ltd. Reg. No. 12157152

Typeset in 11/15pt Century Schoolbook by Wiltshire Associates.
Printed and bound in Great Britain

CONTENTS

ABOUT THE AUTHOR

John Odling-Smee is a retired economist who taught economics at Oxford University, advised the governments of Ghana and the UK on economic policy and headed the department at the International Monetary Fund responsible for relations with the fifteen countries of the former Soviet Union. In retirement he has collected the journals, sketches and paintings of his great uncle Charles Theophilus Hahn and used them to write Charles' biography in his own words and with his own illustrations. He and his wife divide their time between homes in Washington DC and the Cotswolds.

PREFACE

In February 2002 my cousin Peter Odling-Smee was contacted by John Tinker, a retired civil servant. His grandfather had collected books and had acquired some journals written by Charles Theophilus Hahn in the 1890s and 1900s, together with sketches and watercolours. John Tinker had inherited them from his father and aunt. He and his wife read the journals, which, to them, read more like novels than diaries and gave a fascinating insight into daily life at the time. They felt that they would be of interest to the family and set about finding Charles' closest living relatives. This was not easy because Charles had no children and had changed his name from Hahn to Headley during World War I. Through skilled genealogical detective work John Tinker found that Charles' sister Emma had married George Smee Odling, who changed his name to Odling-Smee. He was then able to find Peter Odling-Smee, Emma and George's grandson. John and Peter met, and John kindly handed over the collection of Charles' papers to Peter.

A second set of journals and watercolours came down through the family. Charles' wife Marion was the godmother of Emma and George's only daughter Barbara. She passed the journals and watercolours on to Barbara, who in turn left them to her daughters Sally Oliver and Barbara Oates, my (and Peter's) cousins.

My cousins Peter, Sally and Barbara have let me use Charles' papers as the basis for this biography. Apart from these, and a few family anecdotes and public records, we do not have other information about Charles. He died in 1930 and no relative now living knew him. Much of this story is therefore written in Charles' words. Wherever it made sense, I have quoted him directly. While his style was not always elegant, it was direct and clear (as was his handwriting). The idioms and expressions he used themselves recall the times in which he was writing. Taken together, his writings provide a fascinating picture of an interesting life in England and Southern Africa in turbulent times.

In addition to my cousins and John Tinker, I would like to thank Tony Berrett, Martha Kaplan and David Odling-Smee. Their comments and encouragement improved the book and kept me going.

Charles was my great uncle. My father, Charles William Odling-Smee (known as Bill), was fairly close to him, and always referred to him as Uncle Charlie. I shall call him Charles.

INTRODUCTION

Charles Theophilus Hahn was born in 1870 and grew up in a moderately prosperous family in a village in Hampshire. With his sister Emma, his only sibling, he enjoyed outdoor activities; both energetic ones, such as tennis, rowing, ice skating and cycling, and more relaxing ones. Among the latter, the pair loved sketching local scenes and walking in the countryside, where they observed the wildlife and collected wild flowers.

After boarding school, Charles went to Pembroke College Oxford, where he was captain of the boat club and graduated in 1892 with a degree in Greek, Latin and Science. He had already decided that he wanted to be a priest in the Church of England. He also wanted a life full of interest, perhaps even adventure. In his last year at Oxford he speculated about his future in his diary: "What course have the fates mapped out for me? Shall I rise to the top pinnacle of fame? Shall I fall to the lowest depths of disgrace? Or shall I become a country parson and lead a humdrum existence in which one day is the same as another, and nothing happens from year's end to year's end to break the monotony of daily life?"[1] He answered himself by saying that he was not ambitious. He would be content if he got plenty of exercise, had a jolly time in general, and everything continued to run smoothly. He acknowledged that he had not yet faced disappointments, or looked at the "serious side of life". In other words, he recognised that he was young and inexperienced. Nevertheless, his wish for "a jolly time" stayed with him throughout his life and was reflected in everything he did.

After Oxford, he spent a year at Leeds Clergy School. In addition to the academic studies, he learned about preaching and taking services, and pastoral work among the people, especially the sick. He was ordained in 1893 and posted to Sydenham in South London (at that time in Surrey) as a curate. He met his wife Marion there, and they were married by his vicar in 1897.

Before he married, he went on a six-month-long trip to South Africa on his own. This had

---

1   From the diary entry for 1 January 1892. Only two pages survive from the 1892 diary which was the fifth year in which he kept a diary. We know this from the opening lines: "My dear diary, you are growing old. You are now commencing the 5th year of your life." The diaries for the first four years have not survived.

a major impact on him and his future. The wide spaces of Africa, the closeness to nature and the opportunity for adventures attracted him. He and Marion were to spend twenty years or so in Southern Africa.

But first he had to get some experience in England. He was a curate in industrial towns in Yorkshire for nearly ten years. During most of that time, he and Marion went every summer on adventurous holidays around England and the Continent. Emma joined them until she herself married in 1902. Some of their trips involved boats, with rowing or punting, and they cycled on others. They often camped. Charles wrote humorous accounts of each trip, illustrated with his sketches and Marion's photographs.

He and Marion first went to South Africa in 1908. They lived in Zululand until 1917. During that time, Charles painted a remarkable series of about 300 watercolours of wild flowers. He also painted some landscape pictures. He served in France as an army chaplain in 1918. After the war they went to Cape Town, where Charles was appointed editor of the newspaper of the Anglican church of South Africa. In 1922 he and Marion moved to South West Africa, where they lived for six years.

When in Africa they read widely, both books and magazines. Charles had wide interests and read not only about theology and church affairs but also about science and nature. He was especially interested in debates about science and religion, and new developments in physics. He wrote summaries of works that interested him in what he called 'the Book of Knowledge'. He also wrote notes on nature and the weather. The Book of Knowledge and the notes on nature provide much of the material for our biography of Charles during his African years, as he was no longer keeping a diary.

While based in Africa, Charles and Marion went to England on leave for a few months every two years or so. They returned to England for good in 1928. For a year Charles was a public preacher in Essex. He hoped to work in Africa again, but his health deteriorated and he died in 1930, aged 60.

Charles had a full and varied life. He travelled widely. He had plenty of adventures, and was happily married to Marion, who shared his interests. He did indeed have a jolly time.

The story in the remaining chapters is mostly arranged chronologically. But there are two thematic chapters on nature in watercolour and words, and knowledge and beliefs, which topics do not fit neatly into the chronological scheme.

CHAPTER 1

FAMILY, GROWING UP AND STARTING WORK

Charles had a comfortable early life and a good education, thanks to his family's solid middle-class position. His father, Theophilus Sigismund Hahn (Theo), was an engineer who spent sixteen years managing iron works in Mexico with his older brother Fred. Theo's father had sent five of his six sons to Mexico, hoping that they would prosper in the mining business after it opened up to British companies in the 1820s following independence from Spain. Two of them died, one in Mexico and the other in a shipwreck on the way back, and a third returned to England, but Theo and Fred persevered and accumulated savings. Theo also inherited money from his father, who was in the sugar-refining business in London and had real estate in the City and Wandsworth. He did not have to work after returning from Mexico for good in 1866 at the age of 41. He married Charles' mother in 1869 and in 1872 bought the house in Headley in Hampshire where Charles grew up.

The German name, Hahn, came from Charles' great grandfather, Frederick Hahn, who came to England from Germany around the middle of the 18th century. In 1756 he married an English woman who may have had some German blood but also had English ancestors. (Family lore recorded that she was descended from Casimir the Great, but this should be taken with a pinch of salt.[2]) He became a permanent legal resident in the UK in 1769. All Charles' other ancestors were thoroughly English; the only connection he had with Germany was his name.

Frederick started in London making

---

2.   Letter to Charles Hahn from his cousin Louisa Brownrigg, 16 November 1917.

clothing. Later he had a sugar-refining business in Old Fish Street Hill in the City. Many of the sugar-refining companies at that time were run by Germans, reflecting the fact that the technology and expertise for sugar refining originally came from Germany.[3] Together with other sugar refiners, many of them German, in 1782 he formed the Phoenix Fire Assurance Company, of which he remained a director until he died. His son, George Henry Hahn, continued in the sugar business.

There were businessmen on Charles' mother's side as well as his father's. His mother's father, Charles Walters, after whom he was named, was an engineer and manager. His mother's brothers included two bankers, a stockbroker and an artist. His mother, Helen Maxfield Hahn (née Walters), had money of her own in a Trust.

Both the Hahn and Walters families were solidly middle class. They had servants and lived in good areas of London and the counties to the south of London. There was sufficient income for the men to be able to retire well before the ends of their lives, and for the women, when widowed or unmarried, to live on their savings.

Charles was born on 1 March 1870 in the house of his grandmother, Mary Sophia Hahn, in West Hill, Wandsworth, which was then in Surrey, although soon to be incorporated in London. The house had been built by his grandfather in the 1840s when he moved the family up the hill from Love Lane (later renamed Putney Bridge Road) in the centre of Wandsworth. The family's happiness at Charles' birth was offset later in the year when his grandmother died in the same house on 22 September. The house, having seen, in the same year, the birth of the latest Hahn and the death of the first one to live there, was sold soon afterwards.

After Charles was born, Theo moved his family to The Priory, Frensham, Surrey. In 1872, Charles' sister, Emma Mary Hahn, was born there and Theo bought Headley Grange in Headley, Hampshire, which was to be the family home for 35 years. It was a large house with a garden that included a tennis court. The house had an interesting history. It was originally built in 1795 as a workhouse, where the poor, sick, elderly and orphans were sheltered. It was sacked by rioters in 1830 in a protest over labourers' wages. A builder converted it to a private house in the early 1870s, renamed it Headley Grange and sold it to Charles' father. It remained a private house thereafter. For a few years in the 1960s it was a hostel for students and in the 1970s it housed pop groups, including Led Zeppelin.

Education and youthful thoughts

Like other boys of his class, Charles was educated at boarding schools. He first went to the school in Allen House in Guildford High Street run by the unmarried Moody sisters whose father had been a vicar in Hertfordshire,

---

3. *The Influence of German Refiners*, http://www.mawer.clara.net.html.

and whose clergyman brother lived with them and was curate at St Nicholas, Guildford.[4] In 1881 Charles was one of 13 boys aged 7-13 at the school. He kept in touch subsequently with the Moodies (as he called them), especially after 1888 when the brother, William Herbert Moody, became vicar of Frensham which was the next village to Headley.

He moved on to Charterhouse, near Godalming, Surrey, in the autumn of 1883, where he was in Robinsonites. He did not stand out academically and had only reached the Middle IVth Form by the Spring Term 1887, when he left. According to school regulations, a boy who had not passed out of the IVth form by the age of 16 (Charles was 17) was normally asked to leave.

Charles went up to Pembroke College, Oxford, in 1888 where he studied Greek, Latin and Science. He graduated with a pass degree in 1892, suggesting that his academic performance was not very good. He obtained a BA in 1892 and an MA in 1895.

He started keeping a diary when he first went to Oxford, and kept it up for many years. The diaries for 1888-91 have not survived. There are only two pages left from that for 1892, and from these we learn that it was the fifth year of the diary.[5] The last diaries we have that describe his regular life and thoughts relate to 1901. We also have humorous accounts of his summer holidays in 1898-1907. The diaries were not only a

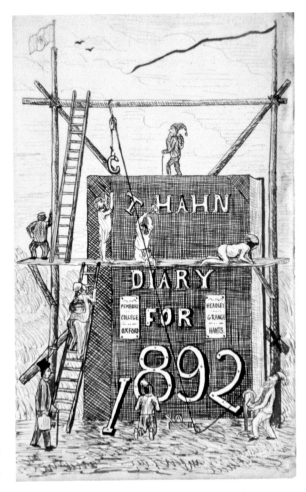

place for recording his activities and thoughts in words, but also for illustrating them with sketches.

There were no sketches in the first five diaries, although the beautifully drawn cover page of the 1892 diary, in pen and ink, shows his talent. Starting in 1893, he wrote the diary on loose pages which he bound later. This enabled him to include sketches and watercolours which were sometimes squeezed

---

4. There were six sisters there in 1881: Elizabeth Adelaide Moody, aged 41, Sarah Jane Moody, 37, Mary Grace Moody, 35, Annie Bliss Moody, 31, Alice Edith Moody, 28, and Georgina Moody, 26.

5. "My dear diary, you are growing old. You are now commencing the 5th year of your life."

into the side of a page and other times took up a whole page.

At Pembroke, Charles was very active in college rowing crews. Every year he went to Oxford up to a week before the terms began in January and April in order to train for the coming rowing season. There were two main intercollege competitions a year, the Torpids in February and the Eights in May. Charles was in the Pembroke eight in the Torpids in 1889 and 1890, and in the Eights in 1890, 1891 and 1892. He was also in the Pembroke eight that competed in the Henley Royal Regatta in July 1891. He was captain of the Pembroke boat club in academic year 1890-91. This was a particularly successful year, when Pembroke moved up from 18th to 16th among the colleges in the Torpids, and from 13th to 8th in the Eights.

Charles was elected to the somewhat exclusive Junior Common Room in Pembroke. Some of the other members of the JCR were active in the boat club, suggesting that the rowers had some prestige in the college.

Charles' connection with rowing at Pembroke continued after he left Oxford. He noted in his diary Pembroke's progress in the Torpids in February 1893. When in Oxford for a long weekend at the end of April 1893, he took the opportunity to watch the current Pembroke eight in action. He noted in his diary that he "gave them a fair ragging to wake them up" although he thought that they were good enough for a place or two in the forthcoming Eights. But this was not to be. On the contrary, they dropped two places, from 7th to 9th. When he later read in *The Times* that Pembroke had been bumped by Queen's, he noted that Pembroke's bow rowers were "too weak to be any good".[6]

Like many undergraduates, he devoted more time and energy to extracurricular activities, especially rowing, and to growing up, than to academic work. Looking back less than six months after graduating, he expressed some regret for such a way of life when he confided to his journal: "Those days when we rowed and drank and flirted and ragged and were ploughed in the Schools... We looked on athleticism as the proper end at which everyone ought to aim, and in our hearts despised all those whose tendencies were towards any other goal; and I think this is a very common failing at the 'Varsities." He was able to recognise that enjoyment of sport should not be at the expense of other aspects of life: "Athleticism does keep one pretty straight, and it is very good training morally, as well as physically, for after life. But it is not till one begins to see the true ideal, to realise that there is a God in the world, that one sees how beastly narrow-minded one has been, and what a very poor substitute anything else must be."

Four months later when he visited Oxford, he felt even more the distance between his current (and future) life and his undergraduate years. While recognising that the latter were the "four jolliest years in my life", he also noted

---

6. *The Times*, 22 May 1893.

that they seemed "too idle and empty". "The pleasures, which seem so round and satisfying at first, have had all their bloom rubbed off, and their sweet juice sucked away." Now, he wanted to press on, not relive his Oxford days. His commitment to the ministry was strong: "I want to live for God and to work for Him. That is the deepest pleasure a man can have. The more one thinks of Him, the greater and more overwhelming is one's happiness."

Leeds Clergy School

Charles had decided on a life as a clergyman before he left Oxford. It is not clear what lay behind this decision. He was not noticeably religious at Charterhouse or Pembroke. He was friendly with the rector of Headley and, as we have seen, the vicar of Frensham.[7] He also knew the vicars of the nearby villages of Churt and Thursley.[8] One or more of them might have encouraged him to enter the ministry, or he might have been influenced by a relative. An older cousin, John Key, was a clergyman, first in Kidderminster and from 1882 as a missionary in East Africa.[9] So were numerous second and third cousins,

although we do not know whether Charles knew them or even knew of them. As we shall see, he was soon to meet a second cousin of whose existence he had previously not known. Whatever prompted his decision, he derived great comfort and inspiration from his faith.

He trained for the ministry at Leeds Clergy School (LCS) in 1892-93. It was a Church of England theological college, founded in 1876 and closed in 1925. The Principal when Charles was there was the Reverend Winfrid Oldfield Burrows, who later became the Bishop of Truro and then Chichester. The school was on a hill overlooking the city centre from the north.

The training had three elements: academic study, preaching and taking services, and visiting houses, especially those with sick people. There were usually two hours of lectures a day and much reading. Charles was fairly conscientious about the reading. After he learned in early February 1893 that the exams for the priesthood would be as soon as late April, he increased his work rate and kept a score of the number of hours he worked. He promised himself that he would "read as hard as I can, trust in God, and then if I am ploughed,

---

7   Reverend Wallis Hay Laverty (1847-1928) was rector of Headley from 1872 to 1928. Reverend William Herbert Moody (c1848-1916) was vicar of Frensham from 1888 to 1908.

8   Reverend Augustus William Watson (1845-1917) was vicar of Churt. Reverend Francis Harcourt Gooch (1842-1931) was vicar of Thursley from 1886 to 1901.

9   The mother of Reverend Sir John Kingsmill Causton Key (1853-1926), the former Mary Sophia Hahn (1818-55), was an older sister of Charles' father, Theophilus Sigismund Hahn. John Key was a baronet, having inherited the baronetcy when his father died in 1899. As he died without issue, the baronetcy passed to his half-brother, Kingsmill James Key (1864-1932), his father's son by his third wife, after which it lapsed. John Key was a missionary with the Universities Mission to Central Africa from 1882 to 1904, and Canon of Zanzibar Cathedral. There was an obituary of him in *The Times*, 29 April 1926.

what does it matter? I shall have done my best." In fact, he averaged 6-7 hours a day, including the lectures, most weeks after that. He worried that he did not know very much and that he would not pass the exams. But he was well into the top half of the 21 students in an internal LCS exam at the end of March, and he passed the final exams held in London on 26-28 April. He did not do brilliantly (his own words), coming 5th in the third class, but this was much as he expected. His best papers were Latin and Old Testament; his worst was the viva voce in Greek Testament.

The priest who helped to run the exam, George William Daniell, was a relative of Charles', although neither knew it at the time. George said that he once had relatives called Hahn, and Charles commented later in his diary that he had heard "the Governor say that he once had relations" called Daniell.[10] Charles was actually the second cousin of George's father, who was over 50 years older than Charles.[11] George was very nice to Charles, although he warned him, after vivaing him in Greek testament, that his vicar would be grieved if he did not know his testament better.

He took services in various places around Leeds, including the Ida Hospital. He also conducted children's services and Sunday Schools. He served at communion and acted as a sacristan, which involved keeping the LCS oratory tidy and similar duties. He often preached, but found sermons difficult. When working on a sermon on nature, he admitted that he was writing to try to improve himself and was not thinking of the capacity of the congregation to take it in. As the draft moved on to issues of evolution, he worried that it was not possible to talk about it "without getting a little bit out of the depth of a perspiring old lady who has never been outside the town in which she was born". The Principal of LCS picked the draft to pieces, but then said that it was "very nice". When he eventually delivered the sermon at St Mark's Mission, in a service conducted by a fellow LCS student, he felt that his sermon and his colleague's intoning the whole service on the note of B were a little above the congregation of two men, a few old women, some children and babies.

Towards the end of his time at LCS he still felt that he could not write a decent sermon. He could only stick down a congealed mass of facts and doctrine; he could not expand and spread them out. It was "bad luck having to give people stodge which sticks in their throats." The Principal was not very encouraging. His comment on a draft sermon on the Holy Spirit that Charles was preparing

---

10   "The Governor" was Charles' name for his father.

11   Later that year, the Reverend George William Daniell (1853-1931), who was chaplain of Dulwich College at the time, was made an honorary canon in Rochester Cathedral (The Times, 11 September 1893). He was subsequently Archdeacon of Kingston-upon-Thames and Chancellor of Southwark Cathedral. His father, George Frederic Daniell (1818-88), was a clergyman in Sussex. His great grandfather, George Daniell, was a barrister who married Louisa Hahn, the sister of Charles' grandfather, George Henry Hahn.

for his future parish was that, while it was nice and orthodox, it was an essay, not a sermon. He added that he was sorry for the future congregation as it was very dry.

The students at LCS had to visit houses and, if necessary, say prayers with the infirm and others who could not go to church. This practice was called "keeping a dicker". The people Charles visited were poor, working class people who lived in simple accommodation. Leeds had many streets of back-to-backs, and it is possible that Charles was in some of them.[12] He did most of his dickers in Kirkstall, an area of Leeds he could easily walk to from LCS. He was struck by the foul smells in the streets, houses and even the people. Coming from rustic Headley to industrial Leeds, in which the pollution from the factories and domestic coal fires was ever present, was quite a shock to him. Although he had seen rural poverty, urban poverty was worse. While incomes were just as low, if not lower, in rural areas, access to open spaces and clean air made life a little more tolerable than in industrial cities. The economic insecurity of the urban working class was brought home to Charles when a strike at the forges left the affected families in a bad way.

Despite the smells and the dirt, he conscientiously kept his dicker. He became accustomed to the squalor, the people's living arrangements and their Yorkshire accents, which he tried to reproduce in his diary. He admitted "it is very interesting, "dickering", once one is there". It was a learning experience for him in many ways. Not only did he see how poor people lived and viewed life, he also learned about the stages of man, from birth to death. He commented to one woman with a baby that she always seemed to be washing. "Ay yes", she said, as recorded by Charles in his diary, "there is a lot of washing to be done when there are babies about. You see they are so mucky, and if you leaves them for a time they gets so strong." At the other end of the life span, he visited a man who was "frightfully ill" with consumption and dropsy. He refused to go to hospital, although he lived in a horrible place with his wife, a "beastly dirty woman". A month later he looked "most awfully bad" and was "going fast". Charles returned two days later to learn from the neighbour, in the most colourful terms, that he had died the night before.[13] In between the young and the old, Mrs Perrigo, who had a stomach disorder, was most upset that she had wasted the eggs that Charles brought her because she was not able to keep them down. On one visit she startled, and no doubt entertained, Charles by suddenly exclaiming "Ay 'ow I do sweat. 'Ow are you?"

He sometimes made broader sociological observations, for example that women tried

---

12   Back-to-back houses were terraces in which the backs of the houses in one street were built onto the backs of the houses in the next street. In earlier years there were no front gardens and therefore no outdoor spaces except the streets.

13   Among other things, the neighbour noted that he had gone blue and yellow, had busted legs and was covered in bed sores. Charles quoted her verbatim in the diary.

to make out that they were superior to their neighbours by wearing coats even if they had holes in them. (Presumably this contrasted them with women who did not have coats.) He was unsure whether they were earnest in feeling superior, or just sanctimonious. He noted that working class people were coarse and used obscene language; they lacked the modesty of the upper and middle classes. He attributed this to their living in squalid conditions and thought that it would take generations before their living conditions improved to those of other classes.

Apart from the formal training at LCS, Charles learned much from his experiences in Leeds about underprivileged people. They brought out the humane and sympathetic side of his personality, and so helped him later in his career as a priest in industrial towns in Yorkshire and a missionary in Southern Africa.

Judging from the frequency of entries in his diary, among the things he found most difficult adjusting to in Leeds were the environmental pollution and human stench. He rejoiced in getting out of "stinking old Leeds" on a visit to Harrogate and used the same expression on returning to Leeds after a few days in Headley. "As we drew near the land of chimneys, the sun became more and more obscured, and at last when we arrived at the city of dirt it had disappeared altogether and a beautiful drab coloured mist pervaded the place... You don't see God all around you half as clearly in a grimy old city as you do in the country". The human stench upset him even in City Hall, where he attended an address by the Bishop of Ripon (William Boyd Carpenter) to 3000 working men: "the hot smell of the profanum vulgus is not calculated to put one in a favourable mood, not even to listen to the most eloquent of orators".

As a bachelor in his early 20s, he naturally had an eye open for the young women. He was disappointed at the dearth of female beauty in Leeds. The women he saw in the street were under average height and he did not see one "worth turning round to have another look at". However, in the café he and his fellow students frequented, there were "not a few girls who are not averse to being winked at and liked being sketched". But he restrained himself that day because "an embryo parson" should not travel down that road during Lent.

Charles' year at LCS was not all work. Indeed, it is surprising how much time he was able to devote to relaxation and sport. He played soccer on the LCS team which had matches against area schools and colleges most weeks, sometimes twice a week. He recorded the scores of most matches in his diary, and sometimes included a brief report of the match highlights. On one occasion LCS played rugby against a team from St Peter's School, York. The LCS men did not know the game, and "were always scrumming up energetically among ourselves while St Peter's were scoring a try". Needless to say, LCS lost by a wide margin. Not that Charles had no interest in rugby. He enjoyed the England-Scotland rugby international which he attended when it was played in Leeds. He was impressed by the size of the attendance, nearly 30,000 people, and the resulting crush at the exit.

He and one or two other students bought bicycles and took rides out of town, including longer trips of forty miles or so to York and Giggleswick. He loved the open country, the varied scenery and the exhilaration of flying down the hills. He walked all over Leeds, his diary recording walks to Armley, Far

Headingley, Meanwood, Moortown and Beckett's Park, as well as the city centre and Kirkstall where he went frequently. He loved sketching, and often took his sketch book with him. He and other students sketched many different scenes, including the people in cafés, the pictures in galleries, the ruins of Kirkstall Abbey and wharves on the river. They went to the Leeds spring picture exhibition where Charles bought a season ticket and was a frequent visitor. He described one visit when they sat on a sofa and sketched all the time as exciting although he did not explain why. They went to the theatre a few times. The Principal objected to one such visit because it

was only two or so weeks before Charles was due to be ordained. This prompted Charles to complain to his diary that "I cannot really see where the wrong has come in. Perhaps I ought to be in that state where the theatre has no attraction for me, but I am afraid I am not yet. I want to be natural as far as I can without doing anything wrong. If I pretended not to enjoy the theatre I should be unnatural." Here, as elsewhere in his diary, he was seeking to establish his personal moral code.

Charles and his student friends usually managed to fit in stops for tea, and perhaps ices, on their shopping and leisure trips to the city. Chatting in cafés and "messing around" the town were relaxing activities. He also enjoyed smoking and suffered when he gave it up for Lent, except for Sundays. He noted on Easter Sunday that it was "jolly being able to smoke again".

The culmination of Charles' training at Leeds Clergy School was his ordination as a deacon in May 1893. He had been proposed for a job as Curate at St Bartholomew's in Sydenham in Kent, in the Diocese of Rochester, and went there for an interview in January. It is likely that this was arranged by the Principal of LCS, whose sister was married to the vicar of St Bartholomew's, Rev Moberly.[14] Charles was accepted, and Moberly pressed for him to come as soon as possible. That was why he took the exams in April rather than the following term, and why he started in Sydenham immediately after his

---

14   Reverend William Allan Moberly was vicar of St Bartholomew's from 1892 until he died in 1905. He was an honorary canon of Rochester Cathedral

ordination. The Principal was concerned that he was rushing it, but Charles was prepared for the challenge.

However, he first had to be ordained and even he admitted to some nervousness about the days in Rochester before the ordination service on Sunday 28 May: "How I shall hate it at first, walking about in black clothes and a topper, and always having my best manner on. I am afraid it will take me a long time to settle down in that direction." He did not feel comfortable in the topper, which he had purchased in London in January. At that time he called it "one of those relics of barbarism" which "that most flighty, inane and most shadowy of all tyrants, Fashion, insists on still inflicting on men". Wearing it then, together with the ulster he bought with it, he had "sallied forth a regular toff".

He arrived in Rochester on 24 May and had three days of instruction before the ordination. Much of it was led by Bishop John Richardson Selwyn, who was in between jobs as Bishop of Melanesia and Master of Selwyn College, Cambridge. Charles had to write a sermon on the theme of "Not everyone that saith unto me, Lord, Lord, shall enter into the kingdom of heaven". His cousin, George William Daniell, assessed it and said it was all right but not quite up to Sydenham form. He "advised a course of Edna Lyall", a contemporary novelist and feminist. At lunch on 26 May Charles sat next to Mrs Davidson, the wife of the Bishop of Rochester, who was to conduct the ordination on 28 May.[15] She impressed him with the homework she had done on him.

Charles' mother and sister arrived in Rochester on 26 May, and he saw them in the evening. Next day, he was surprised at evensong to meet his uncle John Hahn and Aunts Decima Hahn and Charlotte Hahn, his father's youngest siblings. Not only did the family turn out in force, but three family friends from Headley also came for the ordination.

The ordination took place in Rochester Cathedral on Sunday 28 May 1893. Unfortunately, we cannot say anything about it because the diary that might have contained Charles' notes has not survived.

St Bartholomew's, Sydenham

Sydenham is about seven miles south east of Charing Cross. Sydenham Hill, at 112 metres, is one of the highest points in London. The parish of St Bartholomew's had a population of about 4000 when Charles arrived in 1893. The area was moderately prosperous, having become fashionable after the Crystal Palace was rebuilt there in 1854. Charles was told that 3000 of the 4000 were rich suburban people and the rest were artisans. The church of St Bartholomew's was built in 1832 and expanded and extensively repaired in subsequent years. It appears in Camille Pisarro's painting "The Avenue, Sydenham", which is in the National Gallery.

---

15 Right Reverend Randall Thomas Davidson was Bishop of Rochester from 1891 to 1895 and later Archbishop of Canterbury (1903-28).

In addition to the vicar, there were two curates in the parish and two schoolmasters who were also clergymen. Charles was the replacement for one of the curates, Rev Crawfurd.[16] The clergy team conducted services at St Bartholomew's and a chapel of ease, St Matthew's, in the parish. Charles was told that his work would include plenty of mothers' meetings and men's bible classes, but he would not have to do much preaching. His stipend began at £110 per annum, rising to £150 by £10 each year. When he was offered the position, he was uneasy because he felt that the work would not be "practical enough", meaning that he would not spend much time helping the poor. He noted that the vicar had more funds for the poor than he knew what to do with: "There are not enough poor in the parish for the rich to support". He expected the poor to "seem comparatively wealthy after those at Leeds". He was not attracted by the prospect of preaching to "tremendously fashionable congregations" which would require "beautifully polished sermons without the sharp points which go home and do good". When he wrote this, he was still at the Leeds Clergy School, where he learned that ministering to the poor was most rewarding. His concern for the disadvantaged stayed with him the rest of his life and steered his career choices.

There were other considerations too. His widowed cousin, Louisa Brownrigg, who was 24 years older than Charles, lived nearby in Dulwich.[17] Her children were younger than Charles. However, this proximity detracted from rather than added to the charm of the idea of living in Sydenham. On the other hand, Charles was clearly excited by the prospect of being near Wallington "where someone lives". His diary does not reveal who the someone was, but she or he was sufficiently attractive to compensate Charles for having to live near the Brownriggs.

For someone as keen on sport as Charles, it is not surprising that he looked into sporting possibilities at Sydenham before he moved there. He noted that there was no football club, and the vicar could not tell him whether there was a cricket club. Charles concluded that there was a need for "a bit of stirring up in that direction".

On balance, despite his feeling that the position of curate in Sydenham was not quite right for him, he took the job, supposing it to be the best thing he could do. His father was sure it was. He remained curate of St Bartholomew's Sydenham for four years, apart from a six-month absence near the end of this time when he undertook a trip to South Africa. No diaries from his Sydenham period

---

16 Reverend Charles Hubert Payne Crawfurd was curate from 1888 to 1893, after which he moved to Dorset. From 1894 the other curate was Reverend Arthur William Dorman, who was ordained deacon in 1890 in Ripon and had previously been a curate in Knaresborough and Bath.

17 Louisa Brownrigg (1846-1931) was born Louisa Marian Key. Her mother was Mary Sophia Hahn, the sister of Charles' father, and her father was Sir Kingsmill Grove Key. Her brother was Rev Sir John Kingsmill Causton Key. Louisa married Dr John Annesley Brownrigg (1832-91) in 1872 and had eight children.

have survived, so we do not know what he was doing or thinking then.

Holidays at Headley

Charles liked to travel, and took many trips with his sister, Emma. After he married in 1897, Emma continued to travel with him and his wife on excursions to other parts of the UK and the Continent. This section looks at some of his holidays in Headley in 1893 and 1895. Chapter 4 covers his trips further afield.

Charles spent most of January 1893 in Headley during the holidays between the first two terms at Leeds Clergy School. He was also there in April for the Easter holidays, and for two weeks in June 1895. (Presumably he was there for holidays between 1893 and 1895, but we have no record of that period.) His diaries covering those periods provide a picture of the family and social life of upper middle-class families at the end of the 19th century.

His constant companion was his dog Jack, who went with him on many walks around the village and to neighbouring villages. When he moved to Sydenham, Jack went with him, and returned to Headley when Charles went there on holiday. Charles described their journey

together by bicycle from Sydenham to Headley in June 1895 in his diary. They set out before 5 am after Charles had cooked and eaten his breakfast. Jack ran alongside the bicycle for much of the way, but when he got tired, he sat in the basket attached to the front handlebars. He was nervous about this at first, but soon got used to it, although he did fall out once, a "nasty crack, when we were travelling at a good pace". People were surprised to see Jack in the basket, although whether a lad whom Charles sketched in his diary actually said "look at 'im; 'e 'as 'is brother up along with 'im" might be doubted.

Charles "chummed up" with another cyclist who was going the same way. A bricklayer by trade, his recreation was street preaching. He was earnest and ready to give up everything for Christ and had had some rough experiences among his mates. Charles enjoyed talking to him and observed that the world would be a better place if there were a few more like him. After a few stops, including calling at Moodies School in Guildford, Charles and Jack arrived in Headley at 1:30 pm. They spent the afternoon resting, not surprisingly after a fifty-mile journey including some hills and bad roads, and hot sun towards the end.

In Headley in winter Charles and Jack went rabbiting on the common where Jack put up the rabbits and sometimes caught them, and Charles tried to shoot them, with mixed success. On other occasions he helped Jack catch rats. He also shot pheasants with local friends. As in Oxford and Leeds, Charles

Listening at the 'pop-holes' to the ferret 'scrabbing' at the rabbit.

enjoyed sports and took every opportunity to play. He skated on the frozen pond at the Smithes of Everly House, who had a farm. He played hockey with other locals, including the family of the vicar of Churt, which was three miles away. On one occasion he was unhappy because some of the other players did not abide by the rules, and another time the game was unsatisfactory because of the muddy ground.

In April 1893 and June 1895 he played tennis almost every other day. Many of the houses in Headley and nearby villages had their own tennis courts, including Everly House, the Langdales', the rectory at Headley, the vicarage at Churt, Hilland House (home of Walter Phillips) and the Hahns' own house. Not all were in good shape. The one at the Churt vicarage was full of holes; nevertheless

Charles and his partner won two love sets. Nor were all the players in good shape. Mr Langdale "was irresistibly comic. He spent the time gyrating gracefully round the balls, and filled up the odd minutes with sitting down hard in front, and he bounded beautifully."[18] Charles was very competitive and recorded the

score of each match in his diary, while also noting the quality of the match and his own performance.

Emma usually joined Charles for the tennis games. She was often with him when he strolled round the village, including on his visits to people. Sometimes they would go out together to sketch local scenes. They loved nature and the outdoors. Charles was especially attentive to flowers, noting the primroses, violets, fruit tree blossoms, ladies' smock, kingcups, flowering dead nettles, stitchwort and germander speedwell in the spring and the cotton grass and ragged robin in the summer. He also delighted in the cut flowers in the house, including white hyacinths, daffodils and sweet briars. His close observation of flowers was the basis of the beautiful botanical paintings that came later, as we shall see. Walking through the woods with Emma in June he marvelled at the beautiful foliage of the trees and recalled Coleridge's "leafy month of June". A few days later, when he and Emma were sketching by a stream, he waxed poetic about the "water lapping deliciously round the wooden supports of the bridge", the moorhen "dabbling on the bank" and the "sun and shadow playing on the surface of the stream". In his diary he recorded a quote from Tennyson to express his feelings. Throughout his life he illustrated his thoughts and feelings with quotations from the poets. Sometimes he quoted from memory, not always accurately, and at other times he must have taken the quotations from books.

Charles rarely referred to his parents in his diaries, although he saw them every day. His mother was active with other church ladies. About the only mention of his father, whom Charles always called "the Governor" in his diaries, was when they and some male visitors were sitting round the fire after dinner. Charles recorded that "the Gov. got onto his Mexican experiences and told about a bag of jiggers which he had once picked out from under his big toe nail".[19] The tone of this entry suggests that Charles had heard his father's Mexican

---

18 This was probably Arthur Noel Langdale, who was 33 in 1893 and was living with his widowed mother in Beacon Hill House, Frensham, in 1891. But it might have been his older brother Alfred Augustus Langdale, a retired marine insurance broker, who was 46 in 1893; in 1891 he was living with his wife in Richmond.

19 Webster's Dictionary gives two definitions of a jigger: a tropical flea which burrows under the skin, or a mite larva which sucks blood and causes discomfort.

stories too many times, or that he thought at least some of them were tall tales.

Charles and Emma had an active social life in Headley. The village had a population of about 1800 in the 1890s. Much of the employment was in agriculture and related rural trades, building and domestic service, although some people were employed in the paper mill in the nearby village of Bramshott. A small middle-class population of wealthier farmers, clergy, retirees from the military, government or business, and others on rentier incomes made up the main social world of Charles and Emma. These families all had at least one, and sometimes many, domestic servants. Partly as a result, most of them had time for social and leisure activities. While some of Charles' tennis and other sporting partners were young people dependent on their parents, others were older people living on rentier incomes.

Their closest friend was Muriel Laverty, the rector's oldest daughter, who was a year younger than Emma.[20] They often called on her at the rectory and took her out with them or stayed for tea. Charles always referred to her in his diary as "the Dormouse", with Emma being "the March Hare" and Charles himself "the Mad Hatter". In his diary entry for 14 January 1893, he sketched the three of them sitting at a table laid for tea. There are similarities between this sketch and Tenniel's drawing of the same scene in *Alice in Wonderland*. In both of them, the Dormouse is sleeping but in Charles' sketch the Mad Hatter has his hat on the table whereas in Tenniel's drawing it is on his head. (We are guessing that the Dormouse was in fact Muriel Laverty. Charles nowhere states this, but it is highly likely given the context.) Muriel lived to 87 and never married.

Some of Charles' and Emma's socialising was with older people such as the vicar of Frensham and his wife and the Langdales. But mostly it was with people of their own age. Games, especially tennis, brought them together with other young people. However, the major social events were the dances that were organised at people's houses. The Hahns themselves organised an important dance in their house on 6 January 1893. Charles, Emma, their parents and the servants spent all morning preparing the house. Among other

---

20 The Reverend Laverty and his wife, the former Bessie Geraldine Delamotte, had three children: Muriel Delamotte Laverty (1873-1960), Cecil Hay Delamotte Laverty (1877-1955) and Gladys Fitzgerald Delamotte Laverty (1884-1962). Muriel and her sister Gladys, who also did not marry, lived their whole lives in Headley, first in the rectory and later together in a house called Abbeydore.

things, they had to stretch and wax a drugget (a coarse, durable cloth) that covered the dance floor. Guests started arriving at 4pm and were offered tea. The dancing started at 8pm, with Mr Edwards providing the music. About 58 people were there. Nearly 40 of them danced so that the room was comfortably filled.

Charles loved dancing and had a "grand time", with only one bad partner the whole evening. A partner who especially intrigued him was Miss Pilsbury who had been invited, with her brother, by Charles' mother on spec. He found her "awfully pretty" and "a very quiet sort of girl". He "did not quite get to the bottom of her, but she was awfully nice as far as I got". On the dance floor she was "very jolly and the best dancer in the room". Meanwhile, Emma amused herself by trying to elude Jack Overton, a local Headley suitor and tennis player.[21]

Two weeks later Charles walked across the Downs from Guildford, where he had spent the night, to Shere, a distance of about five miles, to visit the Pilsbury family. Mrs Laverty, the wife of the rector of Headley, was excited because she concluded that Charles went because of his interest in Miss Pilsbury. We do not know how the meeting went, or whether there were any further contacts with Miss Pilsbury. Her father was an artist and Charles, who liked to paint himself, admired his watercolours.

Should auld acquaintance be forgot.

---

21   John James Rudall Overton was the same age as Emma. He later became an electrical engineer and worked for the Indian Telegraph Department in Calcutta.

The dance at the Hahns went on until almost 3 am, after which those still around sang Auld Lang Syne and God Save the Queen. They had some more supper and then Charles and a few of the men sat with pipes and whisky, talking about the past, present and future until nearly 5 am. The next morning people rose late, but a few of them managed to dance a little more before lunch and to play ice hockey on a frozen pond in the afternoon. Other participants in the previous night's dance arrived in the evening and there was yet more dancing. "We had a very lively set of lancers, one or two polkas, a few waltzes and a pas de quadrille. And then subsided utterly exhausted." Thus did young people entertain themselves, and meet members of the opposite sex, in those days.

Less than two weeks after the dance at the Hahns, Charles went to Guildford for another dance in the Parish Hall. First there was an entertainment given by some performers whom Charles had seen some nine years earlier when he had been a pupil at Moodies' school. (He stayed the night with the Moody sisters on this occasion.) Two of the performers were the Miss Fixsen sisters. They recognised Charles from before and introduced him to many dance partners, one of whom he had met previously at a ball in Oxford. There were about 150 people at the dance, and Charles had "a jolly good time altogether, and not one bad partner." The only disappointment was that the vicar of St Nicholas Guildford insisted on having a theological discussion at a moment when Charles was anxious about losing his dance partner. However, "the supper was splendid: fizz and ices ad lib." He stayed until the party ended at nearly 3 am.

In April 1893 Charles and Emma went to a dance at Thursley vicarage, which was about six miles from Headley. Again, he "had a very jolly time and a long drive". He met some young women he knew, one of whom arranged for him and Emma to play tennis the next day. This necessitated another six-mile drive, this time in a dog cart. As Charles also managed to fit in three hours' study for his clergy exams, it is not surprising that he went to bed early, "beastly tired".

Dances were not the only entertainment during Charles' holidays in Headley. On the final day of his holiday in January 1893, Charles and the family went to see the dress rehearsal of a farce "Found in a Hansom". He was unable to attend the main performance the following day, at which the string band of the 20th Hussars also played. On another occasion, Charles and Emma went to a party at the Bewshers. Mr Bewsher was the Bursar of St Paul's School in London, but he also ran a small boarding school for boys in his house, Crab Tree House, in Headley. The party was for the masters of the school, their wives and some of the pupils. One of the masters was someone Charles had known slightly at Pembroke.

Charles interrupted his holiday in Headley in June 1895 for a couple of days to visit his aunt and uncle in Bognor. The trip started badly. He decided to go to Bognor by bicycle, a distance of nearly thirty-five miles. He was making good time when, about a third of the way there, the pressure he was placing on the pedals communicated itself through the chain to the frame of the bicycle, which bent and jammed the back wheel. A kindly passer-by picked him up in his dog cart and conveyed him to Midhurst from where he sent

the bicycle back to its maker and continued to Bognor by train. Charles was especially annoyed because the bicycle was only two weeks old – its inaugural outing had been the trip with Jack from Sydenham to Headley. Moreover, he had told the maker to build him one for hard work, and instead he had made one fit only for a cinder track. The maker of the bicycle wrote the following week to say that this was the first out of 150 machines they had made that had broken down in this way. Charles was not impressed by this excuse.

Thomas and Anna Walters were the two unmarried siblings of Charles' mother, who was born Helen Maxfield Walters. Thomas was in his early 60s and Anna was in her late 50s. They continued to live in the house just off the sea front where they had lived with their parents when the latter were still alive. Thomas was an artist who had exhibited at the Royal Academy and elsewhere. He had to go to London for some of the time that Charles was there, and in his absence, Charles had long conversations with Anna, both in the house and while walking by the sea. Among other things, they talked about love. Anna maintained that people should have sufficient self-control to prevent themselves from falling in love, in the same way that they resisted the temptation to steal. Charles was inclined to think that one could be overcome by passion, sometimes with adverse consequences. He had fallen in love several times and had recovered, so he felt he could view the subject philosophically. One way to avoid being swept off one's feet prematurely was to listen to the advice of friends, who could be more objective. It was important also to consider whether any prospective partner would make excessive financial demands because she had been used to a large house and much luxury. One should look ahead and think how the relationship might be after ten or fifteen years. "When the first heat is over, it is but a poor prospect if there is no respect and affection, a love which is the image of the Divine love, to take its place."

Charles expressed conventional male views about the ability of women to handle love affairs. He thought that many girls had a false idea about the workings of passion, derived from "indulging too freely in such insipid literature" represented by the "ordinary run of novels". Girls were also jealous of each other and could not be relied on to give their girlfriends unbiased advice about their current boyfriends. Men were different. No man would talk to his men friends about his love affairs, but if he did, he "would get, as a rule, a much too knock-me-down, sensible bit of advice".

Charles was not against reading novels, some of which might have qualified for the "insipid" characterisation. The day after he returned from Bognor he read a book by Rosa Carey whose stories he liked. They were "homely and quiet, with a beautiful soft tone about them", unlike modern novels which leave "one with the impression that the world is upside down, and that nothing short of an international revolution combined with an universal earthquake or collision with the sun will put things right". Ironically in view of Charles' critical views about the impact of novels on girls, Wikipedia notes that Rosa Carey's works "reflected the values of her times and were thought of as wholesome for girls".

Two years earlier, when on holiday in Headley in April 1893, he had felt that reading a sentimental novel from time to time was not a bad thing. It could act as a substitute for *micrococcus amoris*, which did not affect him at that time, even though he was of an age (23)

when he should have been affected.[22] His more critical attitude to sentimental novels when he went to Bognor might have been the result of experience and increasing maturity. Two years was a long time for someone in his early 20s, time enough to fall in love, as he had done. Or it might merely have been an instance of his trying out different ideas in his diary.

He did not reflect much on church affairs in his diary while on holiday in Headley, leaving aside the three or four hours a day he managed to study during the holiday in April 1893, when he was preparing for the clergy exams at the end of the month. It is a tribute to his energy that he also had time that month for many tennis games and other activities. He attended church in Headley every Sunday he was there, and sometimes preached the sermon, especially in June 1895 when he had accumulated two years' work experience in Sydenham. He was critical of both the rector and the congregation. He disapproved of the rector's practice of shortening the services whenever the weather was bad so that the congregation would not be wearied with spiritual burdens. On normal occasions the services dragged and were not elevated. The church in Headley was in a state of torpor and needed a good shaking up. Sydenham, by contrast, was full of life and energy. "Thank God one does not often come across such slack places as Headley, or there would not be much hope."

---

22   A literal translation of micrococcus amoris is the micrococcus of love, with micrococcus being a small bacterium. We might call it the love bug. The day he wrote this in his diary he finished reading Dear Lady Disdain by Justin McCarthy and began The Pleasures of Life by Sir John Lubbock.

After just over two weeks in Headley in June 1895, Charles and Emma left for a holiday on the Thames. Arriving in Oxford in the afternoon, they immediately borrowed a canoe (in those days called a Canadian) and went up the Cherwell river. It was a nostalgic trip for Charles who had memories of each bend. The second day Charles attended the ceremony in the Old Schools at which he was made an MA. This was the formal reason for their trip to Oxford. They were scheduled to leave Oxford in the afternoon to start a canoe trip down the Thames, but they were persuaded by George Odling to go up the Thames to Wytham in his canoe to eat strawberries. It is not clear how they knew George, but the latter remained a friend of the family to the extent that Emma married him in 1902, as we shall see.[23] The strawberries were good, but the unexpected excursion meant that they had to rush back to Oxford to pick up the canoe they had rented, and then work their way down to Abingdon where they had booked rooms for the night. It was nearly 10pm when they arrived, hungry and tired; Charles was "fairly done" and very stiff.

They spent ten days going down the river in the canoe. In addition to paddling, they sculled and sometimes pulled the boat from the towpath. Emma shared in the heavy work. On one occasion they took advantage of the fresh northwest wind to sail for five miles, using Charles' umbrella and Emma's parasol as sails. The longest daily trip was fifteen miles between Sonning and Marlow. The journey

ended at Richmond from where they took trains back to Liphook where their father and Jack met them with the chaise.

They stayed along the way at inns and hotels, which Charles rated in his diary for comfort, food, cleanliness and value for money.

23   In 1895 George Smee Odling (1873-1926) was an undergraduate at Magdalen College, reading natural science, specialising in physics.

He thought that the £1 12 shillings the Miller of Mansfield at Goring charged for dinner, bed and breakfast for the two of them was steep, while 18 shillings and 10 pence at the Swan Inn in Pangbourne was more reasonable.

They were in Pangbourne on a Sunday and went to church in the evening (they had taken communion in the morning at Goring). There were few others in the congregation and Charles was appalled at the sermon: "the old johnnie read in a sing song voice a discourse on the terrible earthquake at the end of the world". He and Emma went out on the river afterwards and thought how much more they could learn from the nature around them.

Most days they stopped in suitable places, both to sketch and to picnic. Charles sometimes swam in the river. The weather was good, starting out very hot and sunny, and raining only on the last full day. Charles' arms were sunburnt, and he had blisters on his hands for the first few days. But he recorded that the trip was a "gigantic success": perfect weather, no setbacks, "just enough exercise to make one feel at peace with all the world after a good square meal in the evening", plenty of sketching, and a variety of food, lodgings and scenery.

After this trip Charles spent the final week of his holiday in Headley before going back to work in Sydenham. Two of his father's sisters, Aunts Decima and Charlotte, were staying during the first few days.[24] Charles played as much tennis as he could, sketched with Emma and generally enjoyed being in the countryside. He reported in his diary a meeting of the Insane Society, which we will come across again in Chapter 4. The Insane Society was his name for the three people he called the Mad Hatter (himself), the March Hare (Emma) and the Dormouse (Muriel Laverty). He usually wrote about it in the third person, in a style with hints of Jerome K Jerome, but without the flair. Although he proposed a serious subject for discussion at the meeting, the two women talked about the next tennis party and what to wear at it.

On his last day in Headley, Charles reflected on how much he enjoyed being in the country and outside. While he was looking forward to returning to real work, he was unhappy at the

---

24   Emma Decima Hahn (1825-1905) and Charlotte Marian Hahn (1832-1902) did not marry. They often travelled on the Continent where they painted many scenes in watercolour. Decima died in Menton, France, and Charlotte died in Switzerland.

prospect of spending much of his time indoors reading and writing, and, when he was outside, looking at the asphalt pavements and rows of suburban houses in Sydenham. He was also not looking forward to having to change from light flannels to black cloth. He knew that Sydenham, although a nice place, was not for him. He was more at home taking plenty of physical as well as mental exercise. He even suggested that a parish in Australia that was as big as England might suit him best, giving him plenty of space to breathe and move about. He dismissed the thought at the time, recognising that he had had a "jolly good time all round", and thanking God for giving him so much happiness. But he was able to pursue the idea later in his life, as we shall see.

Marion Forrester

While Sydenham did not excite Charles as a place, it was where he met his future wife, Marion Forrester, who was two years younger than him. She came from a family of port merchants and shippers on both sides. Her father, Joseph James Forrester, was a port merchant in London. Her mother, Catherine Mary Fladgate, was the daughter of a partner in Taylor, Fladgate and Yeatman, a port shipper in Oporto. Both parents were British, although they were born in Oporto and baptised and married at the British Factory Chaplaincy in Oporto.

Marion's paternal grandfather, called Joseph James Forrester like her father, was born in Hull and went to Oporto in 1831 to join his uncle who was a partner in the house of Offley, Forrester and Webber. He made significant contributions to the mapping of the Douro river and port wine districts, and to debates about the regulation and taxation of the port business. He was created Baron de Forrester for life by King Ferdinand II of Portugal in 1855. He was drowned in 1861 when his boat was swamped in one of the rapids on the Douro. Marion's maternal grandfather was also a Portuguese baron: the Baron da Roeda, created by King Luis I in 1872. He was born in London and went to Oporto in 1837. He and his wife both died in London.

British families controlled most of the trade in port at that time and remained prominent for years afterwards. The Forrester and Fladgate names have continued to be connected with port into the 21st century. There is an Offley Forrester Reserve Port. Taylor, Fladgate & Yeatman (often simply Taylor Fladgate) is one of the largest port wine houses and owns the brands of Fonseca, Fonseca-Guimaraens, Taylor, Krohn and Croft.

Marion was born in Sydenham and baptised at St Bartholomew's where Charles later became a curate. She attended the church with her family and met Charles either there or in other gatherings in Sydenham. They became engaged to be married in 1895 or 1896 and planned to marry in 1897. But first there was a trip that Charles wanted to make that would take him away from Marion for nearly six months.

CHAPTER 2

SOUTH AFRICA

On 24 October 1896 Charles sailed to South Africa, where he spent four months, returning to England in April 1897. He said in his diary that he was hoping to broaden his mind by visiting a new country, coming on fresh scenes, meeting new people and having different experiences. Although he did not say this, it seems likely that he relished the opportunity to have time on his own without responsibilities before settling down to married life and his next job as a curate in Bradford.

He took the boat train from Waterloo to Southampton, where he joined his ship. Earlier in the day he had been taken to Liphook for the train to Waterloo by Emma, Marion and Jack the dog. Marion was already part of the family and she and Emma remained good friends.

The three-week journey to Cape Town provided many opportunities to meet new people. He shared a cabin with a young businessman who was very fond of pale ale and a "reverend gentleman from Aberdeen" of indeterminate (or possibly just unknown to Charles) sect. He felt that his fellow passengers lacked some refinement, although they were mostly good-natured. A man who sat next to him at mealtimes was fat, drank much beer, dined in his shirt sleeves and took salt with his knife. He was probably German but had lived in the US and went round with a group of Americans who chewed tobacco and did a lot of spitting. They did not know what they were going to do in South Africa but hoped to find something in the booming area around Johannesburg. So did a mining engineer who had once sung in the Leeds parish church choir. Indeed, there were many "gay young sparks going out to pick up a fortune if they can". One group of men was joining the Cape

Mounted Rifles; according to Charles it was probably a last resort for them as they did not consider thinking to be in their line. Another group played cards all the time, for money and even gold. There was a religious group, all called Brother something or other on the passenger list, who looked as if they had been taken "from the streets, gathered in from the byways and hedges". Many people were going out for their health. There were also men returning to work after leave, and women with children going to join their husbands. Some men were going to start businesses as commercial travellers, slot machine vendors or farmers, among others. While most of the passengers were British, there were also Frenchmen, Germans and Jews (whose nationality Charles did not mention).

Charles' haughty attitude towards many of the other passengers reflected his privileged upbringing, which encouraged educated Englishmen to believe that they were superior to others, especially to foreigners and people of a lower class. It came also from his lack of much exposure to people different from himself. He did, of course, meet poor people in Leeds and, as we have seen, deplored their coarseness, obscene language and lack of modesty, and thought that they would take generations to catch up. But, on the boat as in Leeds, he realised that he could learn from meeting a range of other people. It was good to have to interact with different types and not only those who have the same views. It "helps to knock the corners off". Moreover, he recognised that the English might be in most need of such experiences: "of all people, perhaps the real thorough-going Englishman is the one who requires to be put through this process more than anyone else".

In practice Charles spent most of his time with his own type. He had been given a letter of introduction to one man, Dr St Leger, by Mr Bewsher of Headley. St Leger, who was in 1st class (Charles was in 2nd), was travelling with his mother who was a Roman Catholic and thought that evolution was a heretical idea. Despite this, Charles had a long talk with her about Christianity in South Africa. He enjoyed conversations with some of the government officials who were returning to work in South Africa, and met other Oxford and Cambridge graduates, with whom he found things in common. There were two men, Bland and Crawford, whom he looked up in Johannesburg some weeks later. Bland was a photographer who was hoping to start a photography business. He had studied art and was fond of sketching, an interest he shared with Charles. Crawford was an actor.

Boats in those days could be uncomfortable. Charles experienced some rough seas, especially in the early part of the voyage, and some very hot weather later on. He was attacked by bed bugs which caused his face to swell up despite having sprinkled Keating's insect powder in his bunk. He tried sleeping on deck to avoid them. On one occasion rats ate the apples he had in the cabin. Charles took these setbacks in his stride, wearing his stiff upper lip as young Britons did in those days.

Three weeks on a boat, with only a few hours on land in the Canary Islands, can be boring as well as uncomfortable. Naturally, Charles took as much exercise as he could. He played deck quoits and cricket. He was also one of the main organisers of, and competitors in, the sports events. He played whist with Bland, two Miss Sheads, the government officials and others. And he read a number of books, including works by Charles Kingsley, Mrs Humphry Ward and Walter Scott.

He was inspired by Mrs Ward's book *Sir George Tressady* to write in his diary his thoughts about socialism and Christianity.[25] "I have been trying to get to the root of the social question, but it all seems so complicated and entangled." He seemed to be against the Poor Laws, which supported people who entered workhouses, and any public assistance that reduced the incentive to work. He opined that the law of Christianity was "If a man will not work, neither let him eat". This was harsh, but Christianity also said that we should love one another, which we could best do by improving the conditions of the poor through better health care and ensuring that work was available. "At the bottom of all social questions there is a moral one.....No system of government that is not based on Christian principles can achieve anything, and the more truly Christian it is, the less need there is of reforming." It would, however, take a long time to reach this goal.

The Captain usually took the services on Sunday, but he allowed Charles to take the service on the final Sunday.

Charles arrived in Cape Town on Sunday 15 November 1896. The boat sailed past Robben island on the left as Table Mountain rose up in front, covered with a blanket of white clouds. He found his way to his boarding house, Rouw Koop in Rondebosch, by the afternoon, and returned to Cape Town for the evening service in the cathedral.

Rondebosch was a pleasant residential area about six miles from the centre of Cape Town, to which there were frequent trains. The original Rouw Koop house was built in 1701 on an old estate. It had been expanded in the meantime and had once been the residence of a Dutch governor. It was of sufficient architectural interest that Sir Herbert Baker, an important architect in South Africa in 1892-1912, sketched it. It was demolished in the 1960s to make way for a block of flats.[26]

---

25   Mrs Humphry Ward, *Sir George Tressady* (Longman, Green and Co., London, 1896). A long summary and review appeared in the *Edinburgh Review*, January 1897, Volume CLXXXV, pp 84-109. Tressady was an MP whose opposition to legislation intended to improve the lives of outworkers was reversed under the influence of the wife of the politician promoting the legislation.

26   See www.andrewcusack.com/2010/rouwkoop for further details, including Baker's sketch.

1. A roadside flower, 2. *Heliophila*, 3. *Polygala hottentotta*, 4. *Solanum*, 5. *Prickly pear*, 6. *Lobelia*

Charles stayed in Cape Town for six weeks, after which he went to Johannesburg and Pretoria, where he was for 2-3 weeks. He followed this with six weeks in Natal, mainly in Durban, from where he returned to Cape Town. After 10 days in Cape Town he took the boat back to England on 19 March 1897. He had intended to spend time in Bloemfontein and Grahamstown, but instead stayed longer than originally planned in Cape Town and Durban, in the latter case because he was sick.

He was eager to get to know the country, both the nature and the people. He engaged with nature by walking around and looking, and by sketching. He was especially interested in the flowers, and many of his walks were aimed at finding them. On others he was looking for suitable views to sketch.

On one of his early walks he was surprised to see many butterflies that were the same as in England: painted ladies, meadow browns and black-veined whites were common. On the other hand, many of the flowers he had never seen before. Although he does not say so in the diary, he presumably knew that the Cape region is one of six plant "kingdoms" in the world and contains many plants that are unique to that region, as well as imported species. He learned about the plants he saw from books in libraries and conversations with South African residents, but he balked at buying the only good book on flora he could find because of the high price, £4 10 shillings. Among the local plants he was seeing for the first time was the silver tree. "The leaves, which are like a soft, smooth, glistening satin, grow in dense whorls round the branches, and are most beautiful when the wind catches them and they dance to and fro in the sun." One morning he saw a small species of dandelion, yellow petals with a dark eye in the centre, growing by the roadside in hundreds,

but, when he returned in the afternoon to paint it, he could not find one despite walking three miles. "It is very extraordinary that they should all have shed the blossom exactly at the same time."

He painted the flowers that he found most interesting, usually after taking them home. The paintings were 6¾ x 4½ inches, the same size as the pages of his diary. He stuck them into the diary when he bound it. There were five pages, each with 3-6 flowers (22 in all), which he painted as though they were standing

7. *Pelargonium cucullatum*, 8. *Aristea capitata*, 9. *Found on the slopes of Table Mountain*

10. *On the hills by Simonstown*, 11. *Bobartia spathacea*, 12. *Roella ciliata*, 13. *Lobelia*, 14. *Erica*

up, with some in front of others. Their names and the locations where he found them were listed on adjacent pages. He collected most of them during his first few weeks in Cape Town, many of them from the Cape Flats, the rather barren, sandy area to the east of Rondebosch.[27] One was in a bunch of flowers in a friend's house. It was a *Disa harveiana*, a rare form of *disa*, which is a South African orchid. "I made a sketch of it, as I may never have it in my hand again."

A dose of the Cape Doctor.

As well as painting flowers, Charles sketched landscapes. He took his sketching materials on many of his outings, and spent hours completing sketches at home, especially when rain or other inclement weather kept him in. As it was summer, the weather was sometimes very hot, and there were heavy rainfalls from time to time. In Cape Town, the wind, called the Cape Doctor, could be quite strong. There was not much shade on the sides of Table Mountain, and more than one expedition there had to be abandoned, sometimes because the sun dried up his paints, the umbrella he used for shade blew away or he got too hot and burned by the sun. His attempt to sketch an ostrich was interrupted when a "ferocious little gnu" charged down and frightened the ostrich away. The diary contains numerous pen and ink sketches and four watercolours of South African scenes. (There are also two watercolours of scenes on the boat journey from England, one of Madeira and the other of the Canaries.) The latter show the Devil's Peak and the mountains above Wynberg, with the white tents of the military camp in the mid-ground, both in the Cape Town area, and two scenes from the train to Johannesburg: the Great Karoo and the veldt in the Orange Free State.

One of his favourite places was a waterfall half way up Table Mountain on its east side. He first came across it a couple of weeks after arriving in Cape Town. He and Milne, an architect staying at Rouw Koop, set off for a climb, "and we did have a climb. The ascent of Snowdon is nothing to it. But we did not reach the top of the mountain for all that." The waterfall was in a shaded glen, filled with maidenhair and arum lilies. To go higher

---

27　The Flats were sparsely populated when Charles was there, and for half a century afterwards. Beginning in the 1950s, non-whites were moved out of Cape Town to townships and informal settlements in the Flats, which eventually contained a large part of the population of Greater Cape Town.

they had to climb 300-400 feet up an almost sheer precipice, and eventually reached an old signalling station where convicts were kept to build roads up the mountain. They enjoyed the fine views and sweet air, and the splendid flowers on the descent: pelargoniums, gladioli and ericas, among others.

A few weeks later, Charles returned to the waterfall. His companion this time was Houghton, a young man staying at Rouw Koop who had come out from England, where his father was a vicar in Devon, for his lungs. He and Houghton, with another

man from Rouw Koop, had been to a cricket match in Newlands a few days earlier to watch the Mother Country play the Colonial Born.[28] He disapproved of the behaviour of

28 The cricket ground at Newlands, the next suburb from Rondebosch and less than a mile from Rouw Koop, was the home of the Western Province Cricket Club. It is one of the grounds where South Africa plays international matches. According to Wikipedia, it is regarded as one of the most beautiful cricket grounds in the world, being overlooked by Table Mountain and Devil's Peak.

other spectators, many of whom appeared ignorant about cricket and spent the time talking to each other. "It is the place to go to if one wishes to see what the Cape can turn out in the way of beauty and fashion. The ladies here know how to dress if they do not know anything about cricket."

The first time he and Houghton went to the waterfall, the climb took them two hours and they had little time left before they had to return for lunch. The next day they went again, this time armed with sandwiches that Mrs Bobbins, the proprietress of Rouw Koop, had prepared for their lunch. The climb to the waterfall was strenuous, but the lunch was a treat.

Charles wrote expansively that evening about the scene. "The sandwiches and cake were washed down with the cool, clear water from the fall, and, by the time my pipe was going, I felt that I had reached the height of animal pleasure. The view was magnificent as it stretched away before us. At our feet, 2000 feet below, we could see Rondebosch, Claremont and Kenilworth, with their little white toy houses nestling among their little trees. Behind them extended the Flats, somewhat resembling a rather featureless map except for the large tracts of white sand, whilst on the horizon rose up the peaks of the Drakenstein range, little fleecy clouds hanging round their summits and floating down into their hollows; and as the eye swept round, far away on the right could be seen the blue waters of False Bay. Behind us the scenery was of quite a different type, crag rising up behind crag, with ledges on which grew trees and shrubs of various shades of green, until it made one's neck quite ache to gaze up to scan the topmost point. The gentle trickle of the water as it slid over from rock to rock appealed soothingly to the sense of hearing and helped to add to the harmony of the whole. Yes, there are moments in which one really and truly lives, and I think I live most fully when I am among beautiful scenery. There is something so inspiring about it, something that lifts one up. It is the same spirit that breathes through the 104th psalm, and culminates in the overflowing exclamation: 'O

Lord, how manifold are thy works; in wisdom hast thou made them all; the earth is full of thy riches'. So I felt as I sat there and drank in all the grandeur around."

He returned to his painting after this reverie, but not for long because the sun was beating down. He and Houghton started to climb again but found themselves in a gorge with steep sides from which they could not find a way out. They retreated and made their way to the old signalling station, where they enjoyed the view over Cape Town and Table Bay before dropping down into Rondebosch. They learned later that it was almost impossible to climb any higher on the route that they were taking.

Despite his enthusiasm for the beauty of the Cape Town region, Charles sometimes found it wanting compared with England. After an early sketching session in the glen at Groote Schuur. he wrote: "It is pretty but, with all its beauty, I don't think it can beat the scenery of the same type which is to be found at home, such as for instance many of the peeps in Arundel Park, or dream-like walks through Bolton Woods in the valley of the Wharfe. There is more of that misty cobalt in the shades in the middle distance, or the general soft harmonising of colour, which gives so great a charm to the scenery in England. Out here everything stands out clear-cut and well defined in the bright sunlight. Sometimes, however, there does happen to be more blue in the shadows and delicacy in the distance, but it is not often." His painter's eye is apparent

here, as well as less familiarity with South Africa, and perhaps a touch of chauvinism.

Ten days later, he went for an evening stroll through the same glen at Groote Schuur with Clarke, a friend from Rouw Koop, and one or two others. "It was very beautiful in the bright moonlight. The distant hills were almost as distinct as they are during the day. And the glow-worms were glittering beneath the shadows of the trees with their bluish-green light, like small stars which have fallen to the earth." No adverse comparison with England here, or in later diary entries.

While Charles had plenty of exercise walking and climbing, he also engaged in more active sports. He played tennis in Cape Town and Durban and was initially concerned that his game was not as good as it should be because he was unfamiliar with hard courts. He swam in the sea in Cape Town and Durban, and in swimming pools in Johannesburg and Pretoria. He even went horse riding one day, as a way of getting somewhere rather than for the fun of it. As we shall see, it was not much fun at all.

He met people in various ways. Some were other guests at the hotels and boarding houses where he stayed. Some were people he had met on the boat from England. Others were people he had known in England, or to whom he had been given letters of introduction by people in England. In addition, he introduced himself to the local clergy wherever he was and was warmly received.

One of his first contacts was with the

Tennant family, to whom he brought a parcel from England. They lived in Kenilworth, a suburb further away from central Cape Town than Rondebosch. Hercules Tennant was the registrar of the supreme court of Cape Colony. Mrs Tennant was very hospitable and invited Charles to stay with the family, which he did for one week. He met interesting people there, including Mrs Tennant's brother, Mr Graham, a barrister in the criminal court, and the military secretary of Cape Colony. The conversation was about local issues, such as the hospital and the new electric tram service, as well as big questions such as relations with the Boer republics. This was refreshing to Charles after the gossip and tennis talk among the residents at Rouw Koop.

He also had a letter of introduction to Mrs Wilshere. Her husband had been chaplain on Robben Island for 13 years, and her brother, Canon Baker, whom Charles also met, had worked there for 9 years.[29] Mrs Wilshere took Charles one day to the island. It was brown and barren because the strong winds prevented trees and most plants from growing. The population comprised 180 lunatics in an asylum, 550 lepers in an isolated settlement, convicts in a prison and a colony of attendants, warders, doctors and other officials. Charles was pleased to see that many of the lunatics recognised Mrs Wilshere and were happy to see her. By contrast, he was upset by the "simply terrible existence" of the lepers, who were confined to the island for the rest of their lives. Many came from the Orange Free State which paid Cape Colony to take them. These ones were used to the dry inland air, and many died from consumption in the moist air of Robben Island rather than from leprosy. Charles wondered whether it was morally right to force them to live in a climate that might kill them before their time. Added to the stress of the visit were the boat journeys to and from the island. The tug that took them, together with other visitors, 30-40 sheep and provisions for the island, could not reach the jetty and they had to transfer to small boats that were rowed by convicts, "and very evil looking fellows most of them were". The wind got up on the return journey and the sea was very rough. It took one hour and 20 minutes to cover the seven miles to Cape Town.

Dr St Leger, whom Charles met on the boat out to Cape Town, gave him an introduction to his married sister, Mrs Searle, who invited him to a tennis party. However, they did not play much tennis because rain intervened. The party retreated indoors where he met many people. They were kind and friendly and he realised that he could spend much time socialising with them. But he was torn, as he confided to his diary, between needing friends he could talk to ("one does get desperately tired of one's own company sometimes") and wanting to be free to do what he wanted, and to "tramp over the land and take in all the beautiful scenes in nature". Here he quoted Robert Louis Stevenson:

29   Reverend James Baker became a priest in Cape Town in 1850 and a canon of St George's Cathedral, Cape Town, in 1895. He was rector of Kalk Bay, Cape Colony, in 1880-96

Wealth I seek not, hope nor love,
Nor a friend to know me,
All I seek, the heaven above
And the road below me.[30]

He concluded this reverie with his oft-repeated phrase: "This is a jolly life, and suits me down to the ground".

He correctly anticipated that friendships could grow from the people at the tennis party. One of them, Mrs Horwood, invited him to tea the following Sunday. After tea, he joined her party for a walk round Groote Schuur, Cecil Rhodes' house on the slopes of Devil's Peak, with large gardens and open land on which African animals roamed.[31] On a subsequent Sunday he was invited to tea at the Horwoods, who were a cheerful family with a beautiful garden where it was a pleasure to sit. Another time he played tennis at their house. One day he went with the Horwoods and about twenty others to a picnic at Fish Hoek.[32] The men went swimming, ran along the beach and played rounders while the women made tea. (In this they were helped by "a black woman, who had made a fire and boiled some water".) After tea they wandered about among the rocks and enjoyed the cool of the evening.

Charles recorded that, "curiously enough, when the time came to return, it was only the chaperones who managed to catch the train". The young men and women were left to mix with each other without chaperones.

Charles and Houghton met a British naval officer, Duncan, at the picnic. He invited them to visit him on his ship, HMS *St George*, which was anchored at Simonstown naval base. They were shown all over the ship and its armaments, and "went away much impressed with the wonderful ingenuity that had been expended on such instruments of destruction". Charles did not like the idea of being on board during an action, "feeling that a torpedo may blow you to bits at any moment". He would have preferred to be in a cavalry regiment.

The clergyman in Cape Town with whom Charles spent most time was Rendle, who was one of the two curates at St Paul's, Rondebosch, the local church.[33] He was in his early 40s and had come to Rondebosch in 1894 after six years as a curate in England.[34] He told Charles that his work in Rondebosch was very similar to that in England, which is not surprising as nearly all his parishioners were of British origin. Rondebosch was one of the few places in South Africa where the members

---

30   *The Vagabond* by Robert Louis Stevenson. The second line should be "Not a friend to know me".

31   Groote Schuur had originally been a farm. Cecil Rhodes leased it in 1891 and bought it in 1893.

32   Now a suburb of Cape Town, at that time it was an undeveloped bay on the east (False Bay) side of the Cape peninsula. There was a train service from Cape Town.

33   There was another curate, Reverend Richard Dighton Machen, but Charles had little to do with him. He was at St Paul's from 1896 to 1901 and worked in England before and after those years.

34   Reverend Alfred James Rendle, BA (Cantab) 1876, Wells Theological College 1877-78, priest 1879 Bath and Wells, curate in English parishes 1878-94. He was curate at St Paul's from 1894 to 1902, and rector from 1902 to 1905, after which he returned to England.

of the English church exceeded those of the Dutch Reformed Church. Rendle said that the teaching of the Dutch Reformed Church was similar to that of the Scottish Presbyterians. Canon Baker, who was at the low end of the Anglican church and disapproved of high church Anglicans, felt that competition from the Dutch Reformed Church had the beneficial effect of holding the Anglican church back from ritualistic practices. (Three months later Charles met an Afrikaner on the boat from Durban to Cape Town who had switched from the Dutch Reformed to the Anglican church because a Dutch minister had falsely accused him of a serious deed. He said that the Dutch church in Cape Town was practically dead, with ministers sitting at home smoking their pipes.) At the very end of Charles' visit to South Africa, Rendle and Charles, together with two young ladies, climbed to the top of Table Mountain. We return to this memorable achievement later.

The rector of St Paul's, Canon Ogilvie, was very hospitable to Charles.[35] He was "a jolly old fellow", about 60 years old, who was always cheerful even when he was suffering from gout or a broken arm, as was the case on two separate occasions when Charles went to see him. He invited Charles to his house on many occasions, including to a large family party on Christmas Day. He enrolled him to take services at St Paul's, usually the early morning services on Sundays which were poorly attended and which he and the curates were happy to devolve to someone else. He also asked him to preach the sermon on at least one occasion. He had sufficient confidence in him that he proposed that Charles should look after the parish for a six-month period the following year when he was going to England on holiday. Charles liked the idea very much but was willing to do it only if Marion joined him in South Africa and his parents agreed. He immediately wrote to her and to his parents. Their replies came two months later. Marion was quite prepared to join him in South Africa, which greatly pleased him, but his parents were against the idea. He therefore had to decline Canon Ogilvie's offer, although he felt sorry to leave him without a replacement. Eleven years later, after Charles' parents had died, he and Marion arrived in South Africa where they stayed for most of the next twenty years.

Another clergyman in Cape Town was Bishop Gibson. He was the rector of St Saviour's, Claremont, an area of Cape Town near Rondebosch, and also the bishop coadjutor of Cape Town.[36] Charles was

---

35   Reverend George Ogilvie, BA (Oxon) 1855, teacher at Bradfield School and Buenos Aires 1852-58, head of St George's Grammar School, Cape Town 1858-62, Canon of St George's Cathedral, Cape Town from 1861, Principal of the Diocesan College, Rondebosch 1862-85, rector of St Paul's Rondebosch from 1885 to 1902, and Vice-Chancellor of the University of the Cape of Good Hope 1895-97.

36   Right Reverend Alan George Sumner Gibson, BA (Oxon) 1876, various parishes in Lincolnshire 1879-82, various positions in Umtata, South Africa, 1882-94. He was Rector of Claremont from 1894 to 1897, Bishop Adjutor of Cape Town from 1894 to 1906 and Canon of St George's Cathedral, Cape Town, from 1895 to 1906. He wrote books about the church in South Africa.

impressed by a sermon he preached at St Saviour's in which he assumed that it was the duty of Englishmen to convert the world to Christianity. This prompted him to record some thoughts on the subject in his diary. He thought that the English did not understand the obligation that Christianity and the British Empire imposed on them, and that the bishop's assumption that they accepted it was too optimistic. There were, however, signs that mission work was mentioned more frequently in England than it had been three or four years previously.

He was concerned by the criticism of missionaries he heard from Europeans in South Africa that they had taught Africans bad habits. (He first heard this from Mrs St Leger on the boat out to South Africa.) The Europeans would prefer to have African servants who were unconverted than so-called Christians "who have become acquainted with the tricks and crooked ways of civilization". Charles himself thought that the Africans picked up bad habits from European settlers, not from Christianity. "The native pure and simple, untouched by civilization, is more or less a straightforward man, but directly he begins to mix with those who come and settle in his land, he sees the way they drink (and men do drink out here) and all their selfishness and meanness, soon he learns all their bad habits, and seems to have the greatest facility in picking out all that is degrading and wretched and leaving the good."

A few weeks later Charles read an article in *The Johannesburg Critic* expounding racist views and ending: "The races are not equal. And never will be until 'the Caucasian is played out'". He thought it was too early to make judgments like this. The African "is generations behind-hand and it is not fair to judge him when his foot is only on the bottom rung of civilization". (He actually wrote "nigger", not African, using the word, as he also used "kaffir", in a descriptive, not demeaning, sense.) He was firmly convinced that "the words of our Lord's 'Love one another' must be preached to all peoples, nations and languages with the utmost vigour". Two days later he was delighted to hear a sermon in St Mary's, Johannesburg, in which the preacher defended missionaries and African converts, referred to the prejudice of colour, and asked where the English and their civilization would be "if St Augustine had not landed on the Isle of Thanet 1500 years ago".[37] A week later he was in Pretoria, where the bishop's wife addressed the "native question" from the point of view of an employer of domestic staff. She said that Africans had a strong sense of justice and could be treated with kindness if one was also very firm with them. They were a lazy race and needed to be taught how to work.

Two weeks later Charles took part in another discussion of missionary work when he joined the monthly meeting of the Durban Archdeaconry in the house of the vicar of

---

37 The preacher was Reverend Harrison Thompson, BA (Cantab), who was ordained priest in Carlisle in 1892 and went to South Africa in 1895 as a missionary with SPG (Society for the Propagation of the Gospel) in Boksburg, a mining town between Johannesburg and Pretoria.

Durban, Canon Johnson. There was agreement that Africans should become Christians. However, it was unreasonable to expect the missions to turn out converts who were morally perfect. Christianity had not achieved that among whites in 1900 years. It was also agreed that great harm was done by teaching that Africans and whites were social equals. Africans were behind in intellectual training and should instead be taught the dignity of labour and to "order themselves lowly and reverently to all their betters". (Here Charles was quoting the instruction to children in the Church Catechism.)

Charles was most impressed by a passionate statement by an African priest, Reverend Daniel Mzamo. He said that Zulus regarded Christian baptism as an oath that had to be obeyed. Converts therefore worked for Christ, including when they returned to their kraals (villages), where there were no missionaries, after working in the towns. Punishment under Zulu laws was extreme, including the death sentence for theft. The comparatively light punishment under laxer civil law had a bad effect on the Zulu, weakening his moral character and causing him to lose his sense of honour. This confirmed Charles' view that it was wrong to blame Christianity for the bad behaviour of Africans.

The widespread view among Europeans that civilization spoiled Africans was reiterated by a trader who had lived in Benin for some time, but had left just before the "Benin massacre" of January 1897, in which the Oba's forces had killed invading British officials and their supporters.[38] Charles met him on the boat from Durban to Cape Town. The trader thought that missionaries could do some good, especially if they taught the rudiments of Christian morality, namely that it was wrong to steal and lie, and that they should treat others as they would have done to themselves. But they should not be in too great a hurry and should be aware that Africans often adopted Christianity to improve their economic prospects. He said that the Roman Catholics were teaching the Africans how to work. A Natal colonist whom Charles met on

the same boat confirmed that the Trappists there ran the best schools and were teaching the people how to work, cultivate the land, bind books, make boots and other trades.

Apart from Reverend Mzamo and one or two other educated men, Charles' contacts with Africans were mostly limited to servants, rickshaw drivers and other workers. He was,

---

38   The Oba of Benin was the head of state and the traditional ruler of the Edo people in what is now Nigeria.

The Wash comes home.

however, interested in African culture and beliefs. A farmer from Natal, Mr Hutchinson, whom he met on the boat from Durban to Cape Town, told him about local superstitions, and how the history of tribes was entangled with legend. The son of the historian, George McCall Theal, whom he met at Rouw Koop, told him that the folklore of tribes on different sides of Africa was similar.[39] He had worked among the Basotho, among whom the missions

were making little headway. Nevertheless, he believed in the power of missions to lift Africans up, even though it would take many generations.

Later, on a train going through Natal, he did a quick sketch of an African kraal and summarised in his diary the simple life cycle of village men. When they were young, they worked hard to buy cattle. This enabled them to buy wives, who cost 10 cattle each. The wives then did all the hard work for him. He grew rich in proportion to the number of his daughters, whom he sold to admirers for the same sum. Each wife had a hut, and Charles counted as many as ten huts in a cluster in the kraals he saw from the train.

The political situation in South Africa was unsettled in 1896-97. There were two British colonies, Cape Colony and Natal, and two Boer republics, the Orange Free State and the South African Republic (also called the Transvaal). After gold was discovered in the Johannesburg area, in Transvaal, in 1884, there was an influx of miners and others, many of whom were British. By the mid-1890s foreigners, known as 'uitlanders', greatly outnumbered the Boers in Johannesburg, and were catching up in the whole of the Transvaal. The Transvaal government under President

---

39   George McCall Theal (1837-1919) was a prolific historian of South Africa and had been a missionary in 1875-80.

Paul Kruger passed tax and other legislation that discriminated against the uitlanders who were not allowed to vote. Cecil Rhodes, who was the prime minister of Cape Colony as well as an owner of gold mines, wanted to incorporate the Transvaal and the Orange Free State into a British federation alongside the British colonies. He encouraged the invasion from Rhodesia of a force led by Leander Starr Jameson in support of an insurrection by the uitlanders in Johannesburg. The so-called Jameson raid started in December 1895, but the uitlanders did not rise up, the British government did not support it (despite having secretly encouraged it earlier) and the Transvaal authorities stamped it out in January 1896. Cecil Rhodes was forced to resign, and the increased tensions led three years later to the Second Boer War, 1899-1902, between the British and the Boers.

By the time Charles arrived in South Africa in November 1896, it was clear that the Transvaal government was building up its army and some people were already predicting war. He wondered, along with others, how the tensions would be resolved, in particular whether and when the British would be able to take over the Boer republics. "Mr Kruger has scored one, and it may be some time before we can get level with him again." He deplored Britain's poor management of South Africa in the past, including the discrimination against the Boers. "There would be no Dutch republic now if her [England's] statesmen had not made so many blunders." Now the Boers were discriminating against the uitlanders in the

Transvaal, which Charles thought unfair as there was no discrimination between different European groups in Cape Colony. "The Boers simply despise the English and think that they can defy them. But Rhodes seems to be bent on procuring for the uitlanders their rights, and he is a man who knows what he is about." Charles quoted a translation of a vicious attack on the English in an Afrikaans newspaper. He then added that "it is sometimes good for an Englishman to see himself as others see him, and the above [ie the newspaper article] hardly coincides with our national ideas of our uprightness and our divine mission". He observed that the Boers thought God was on their side.

While Charles was in Cape Town, Cecil Rhodes left for England, where he was to appear before a committee of inquiry into the Jameson Raid. Many people wanted to have a major demonstration when he left, to send a signal to Britain that the future prosperity of the Colony depended on him, although they recognised that he had pursued a wrong course of action in a just cause. Others were worried that such a demonstration would stir up more ill feeling in the Transvaal. The barrister, Mr. Graham, whom Charles met at the Tennants, turned down an invitation to propose a resolution at a public meeting in favour of Rhodes because he did not want to compromise himself when the future was so uncertain.

Charles did not meet Cecil Rhodes but he saw both his brother and his sister. The brother, Colonel Frank Rhodes, was tried for treason in the Transvaal after the Jameson Raid because he had been campaigning in Johannesburg for the uitlanders. He was freed in June 1896 after paying a fine. Charles saw him outside Cecil Rhodes' house, Groote Schuur, the day it burnt down.[40] He was hurrying about giving orders, and Charles heard him say that they did not know how the fire started. Charles saw Rhodes' sister at St Paul's, Rondebosch, one Sunday when he was preaching. She sat in the front row and attracted his attention "by the free and easy manner by which she sported herself." She "generally behaved as if the whole place belonged to her." The Horwoods told him afterwards that she was always somewhat mannish in her movements but was very pleasant to talk to.

Although Charles did not meet Cecil Rhodes, he did see President Kruger, or Oom Paul (Uncle Paul, in English) as he called him in the diary, following local practice. He was walking past Government Buildings in Pretoria when Kruger came out and was driven off in his carriage with an escort of nine or ten policemen. He also saw a number of Randlords (the heads of gold and diamond companies) in Johannesburg. With the actor, Crawford, whom he met on the boat from England and who lived in Johannesburg, he went "between the chains", into that part of Simmonds Street that was chained off to prevent vehicles coming in and was the heart of the financial district. There they saw Barney Barnato, Soly Joe, Abe Bailey and other "bloated millionaires".[41] Charles thought they looked ordinary, despite being some of the richest men in the world. Soly Joe had his thumbs in the armholes of his waistcoat, a bunch of roses in the buttonhole of a light-coloured coat with a loud check, and a brown billycock on one side of his head, a striking contrast to "the regulation get up of the Stock Exchange man at home." At lunch in the Club in Pretoria, Charles saw "the great J.B. Robinson" and Samuel Marks.[42]

Charles did not take to Johannesburg. Having grown in only 11 years to embrace a population of nearly 200,000, as he was told, it was still a building site, with a few handsome new buildings alongside galvanised iron houses, in streets full of potholes. It was said to be the most immoral city in the world, which he could quite believe, as wickedness

---

40   Little of the house remained after the fire. It was rebuilt on the basis of a plan by Sir Herbert Baker. Cecil Rhodes lived there until he died in 1902, after which Frank Rhodes lived there. The house was the official Cape residence of the prime ministers of South Africa from 1910 to 1984. The historic agreement between Nelson Mandela and F W De Klerk was signed there in 1990.

41   Barney Barnato was born Barnet Isaacs in 1851and grew up in Whitechapel. He changed his name when he and his brother performed in music halls as the Barnato brothers. He controlled major diamond and gold companies and died in mysterious circumstances later in 1897 when he was lost overboard near Madeira. Solomon Joel, whose mother was Barney Barnato's sister, was born in the East End, and took over Barnato's business after his death. Charles called him Soly Joe in the diary. Abraham Bailey was born in South Africa, acquired land and mining rights in Rhodesia and was made a baronet in 1919.

42   Joseph Benjamin Robinson was born in South Africa, owned diamond and gold companies and was made a baronet in 1908. Samuel Marks was born in Lithuania and was an industrialist and financier.

could be seen on the street in broad daylight, including opposite the English church. (From the context, he seems to have been referring, delicately, to prostitution.) Betting took place in public, and there was much heavy drinking. In a billiard saloon with Bland, the photographer he met on the boat from England, there were "a few fellows who had been dining 'not wisely, but too well', and had just arrived at the pleasant stage, poor brutes, but it is rather a libel to call them brutes, for the beasts of the field do not know what giving way to excess is". This diary entry captures Charles' social snobbery and strong opinions, as well as his taste for biblical and poetic references. He was, however, seeing "plenty of the life of Johannesburg, and if it is not life in its highest form, it is the life which the majority of the population indulge in".

He was clearly uncomfortable with the money-grabbing ethos that gripped Johannesburg. The booming economy was such that "a good cook can save as much as a curate can earn in a year in England" and "a decent-looking barmaid is able to accumulate in that time as much as would go to form the incomes of four or five colonial bishops". (These were probably exaggerations, but aptly illuminate his dissatisfaction.) However, not everyone was successful. In Cape Town he had met one of the passengers on the boat from England who told him that a number of men who had come out on the same boat and gone to Johannesburg had returned because they could not find work. Some had returned to England on borrowed money. He was relieved to leave Johannesburg ("I don't think I am keen on ever entering the Golden City again"), a city "with a crooked eye, and where pure morality is not held of much account".

By 21st century standards, his views about Jews in Johannesburg were politically incorrect and anti-Semitic, though not unusual at the time. He observed that there were "a great many Jews, getting rich as they have a knack of doing". His landlady and four or five other men lodging there were Jewish, as were the millionaires Barnato, Joel and Marks ("who spoke with a decidedly Jewish accent"). He and Bland watched a billiards match between an Afrikaner doctor and a Jewish man, "a most repulsive looking little brute". They were delighted when the doctor won through steady play, while the Jewish man became overexcited and miscued critical strokes. He admired Kruger's behaviour at the opening ceremony of the Jewish schools, which he performed in the name of Jesus, and lectured the attendees "on their religious views, much to the consternation of the descendants of Israel".

As in Cape Town, Charles introduced himself to the local clergy in Johannesburg and Pretoria. The rector of St Mary's Johannesburg, Reverend Darragh, took him to lunch and persuaded him to preach the following Sunday.[43] He said that his work was very difficult. His bishop told Charles when they met later in Pretoria, that he

---

43   Reverend John Thomas Darragh, BD (Trinity College, Dublin), ordained priest in Bloemfontein 1881, curate Kimberly 1881-87, priest in charge Witwatersrand 1887-92, curate and, from 1895, rector, St Mary's, Johannesburg.

had made a mistake in appointing Darragh because he ignored the bishop's views and wanted everything his own way. The services at St Mary's, the church in the centre of the city, were crowded and the singing energetic, which cheered Charles. The following week, when Charles preached in the evening, there was standing room only, and it was extremely hot. There were plans to build a much bigger church to accommodate the rapidly growing population.[44] Charles was unsure he wanted to preach the following week because Darragh thought that everyone should preach without notes. In the event, it went quite well; at least Charles did not comment otherwise in the diary. He did, however, note that there were many passengers from the boat from England in the congregation. Among them was a man who had not been in a church for five years and claimed he caught a cold from sitting in a draught in the church. Crawford, who was probably responsible for leaking to the boat group that Charles was preaching, had brought him. After the service Charles went for refreshments with the curate, Reverend Kenyon.[45]

Johannesburg was in the diocese of Pretoria, and Charles called on the bishop when he moved to the latter city.[46] In a long talk he learned much about the woes of the church in that area. In particular, there was a shortage of good priests to work with the rapidly growing population. Many of the ones who came from England had left there because of poor health or some other reason. The colonial ones were better workers. The bishop was not too happy with the rector of Pretoria, Canon Fisher, although he was a colonial.[47] However, Fisher was much liked by the people, "being a very keen cricketer". The bishop said that priests had to have money of their own because they would otherwise have to depend on how much their parishioners were able to give. It was a hard, rough life, and was especially difficult for the wives. He was concerned about the influence of the low standard of morality in the cities on the clergy, among whom there had been many cases of drunkenness. He put Charles on to preach in his place the next Sunday as he was not very well. The cathedral was not as full as St Mary's in Johannesburg had been. Charles believed that "the sects here have a great deal more

---

44   The church was eventually replaced by St Mary's Cathedral, which was designed by Sir Herbert Baker's firm and consecrated in 1929. Desmond Tutu was appointed the first African dean of the cathedral in 1975.

45   Reverend Gerald Kenyon, MA (Oxon), ordained priest in Peterborough in 1892, curate in Orange Free State in 1894 before moving to Johannesburg.

46   The Right Reverend Hedley Brougham Bousfield was consecrated bishop of Pretoria in 1878 when the diocese was carved out of the diocese of Bloemfontein. It was his first job in South Africa, his previous twenty years having been spent in parishes in Hampshire. He was ordained priest in Winchester in 1856.

47   Canon Frank Hawkins Fisher was ordained in Cape Town in 1882. He was Rector and Canon and precentor of St Alban's Cathedral, Pretoria, from 1892.

influence than the church, and from what I hear the Presbyterians have a splendid choir".

Charles' main companions in Johannesburg were Bland and Crawford, his acquaintances from the boat. In Pretoria he spent much time with his future brother-in-law, Cecil Forrester, Marion's younger brother, who was working there. After dinner on the first day they sat out on the stoep smoking their pipes and "talking over family and Sydenham news by the light of a horned moon and the chirp of innumerable crickets. It is very jolly being with one of the family again and having all the familiar photographs ranged round the room". Charles was missing Marion, whom he had not seen for almost three months. He went with Cecil to the swimming baths and the theatre, among other places, and they played whist with Cecil's landlord and wife.

On Cecil's day off, they took a trip into the countryside. After beating their way through a thicket of blackjacks, a weed that left little black seed pods hooked onto their flannel trousers, they stopped for lunch on the summit of a rocky kopje which was strewn with empty cartridge cases left from when the Boers laid siege to Pretoria in the first Boer war of 1880-81.[48] They ate their lunch of bully beef and biscuits under a thorn tree, and then explored a large cave that was full of bats which managed to extinguish Cecil's candle. Deep inside the

cave they came across the spoor of a large wild animal. "After a brief consultation, [we] came to the conclusion that it might be awkward if he happened to be at home and we were to meet him at the end of the passage. He might take it as an insult if we were to call without an introduction, so we retired gracefully." On returning to Pretoria they got some tea, "and had more than one in spite of it being sixpence a cup", and then went swimming in the baths.

Charles found the physical appearance of Pretoria more agreeable than that of Johannesburg. There were grown trees, including willows and blue gums, and luxuriant foliage. In the cemetery on the

48   The first Boer war, which lasted less than three months in 1880-81, was started when the Boers in Transvaal rose up against the British rulers who had imposed a heavy tax. The Boers laid siege to all six of the British garrisons in Transvaal, including that at Pretoria, and defeated the British army that came from Natal to relieve them. The outcome was that the Boers obtained self-rule in the South African Republic and the Orange Free State while the British retained responsibility for foreign relations and some other matters.

outskirts of town he came across the graves of those who fell at the siege of Pretoria, and recorded one epitaph:

Billeted here by death,
Quartered to remain,
When the last trumpet sounds,
I will rise to march again.

Overall, he was reminded of a quiet English country town, albeit with Africans, Indians and galvanised iron shanties.[49]

He took the train from Transvaal to Natal, and was somewhat relieved when it crossed the border into British territory. He had felt a hostile spirit in Transvaal, although he thought the sensation might have disappeared if he had stayed long enough. Even though he encountered no personal animosity from Boers, he might have picked up some of the resentment towards the British stemming from the difficult relations at a political level that resulted in war only a couple of years later. On the other hand, he noted that British businessmen in Transvaal might prefer to remain under Boer rule, because a British government would introduce free trade, which would make business less profitable.

His first stop in Natal was Howick, where he wanted to see the Howick Falls on the Umgeni river. At 95 metres, they are among the highest falls in South Africa. The Castle Hotel where he was staying was close to the falls, but he needed to get further away for a view that would be good to sketch. With another hotel guest, Bangley, a Cambridge graduate who was taking a few days off from his job as a teacher at the Government High School in Durban, he set off to find the ideal sketching spot. They had to cross three kloofs (steep-sided ravines) to reach their destination, and unwisely decided to go down into the first one and up the other side. The sides of the kloof were much steeper than first appeared, and they had to grapple with sharp boulders hidden in scrub five or six feet tall on the way down, and a slippery, steep ascent on the other side. After that, they went round the ends of the next two kloofs, taking less time than they had taken to go up and down the first one.

While Charles was sketching the falls from the viewpoint they eventually reached, Bangley, who had developed "a kloof fascination", went to investigate another kloof. He reappeared later with his face scratched, his tongue hanging out and a hornet's bite on his ear. Charles operated on his ear and led him back by a footpath and a road, "as I saw the kloof madness coming over him again". Following this male bonding experience, they enjoyed each other's company the rest of the time in Howick and subsequently in Durban.

They had another encounter with a kloof the following day. Bangley's hat came off near the top of a very difficult climb up the side of the kloof and landed in the pool of

---

49 He wrote 'kaffirs' and 'coolies' rather than 'Africans' and 'Indians'. 'Coolies' was the name given to indentured workers brought from India. In other countries coolies might be Chinese, but in South Africa nearly all indentured workers were from India.

a waterfall below. Charles was so amused by the look on Bangley's face that he almost slipped from his unsteady position on a tree root on a steep bank. However, the walk as a whole was splendid, not least because they collected some plants, including sweet peas, pinks, maidenhairs, aloes and red-hot pokers. Bangley was especially keen on finding maidenhair roots, which he was planning to plant in his garden in Durban.

Their biggest expedition was to Karkloof Falls, which, at 98 metres, are slightly higher than Howick Falls. As they are about fifteen miles from Howick, Charles and Bangley hired some horses for the major part of the journey. Alas, the stirrup strap on one of the horses broke and the other horse had a most uncomfortable trot. They shared the burden by exchanging horses from time to time. They had to leave them at a farm near the falls and walk the final stretch, which was fine until the time came to collect them for the ride back to Howick. Then they had considerable trouble catching them, "to the great delight of all the Kaffirs on the farm". On the way back they ran into dense clouds of smoke from a veldt fire. They tried to ride round it, but the horses refused to cross a narrow spruit (small stream) and so they had to go back and ride as hard as they could through the smoke. Despite concluding that "riding was not the most exhilarating mode of progression in the world," it was a "glorious day". The falls "were grand, much more interesting and romantic than those at Howick".

After a week in Howick, Charles and Bangley took the train to Durban. It took six hours, including a stop for lunch, to cover sixty-five miles through hills and, near the coast, banana plantations. Bangley found Charles a room in a boarding-house, run by Miss Galloway on the Berea, the long low hill above the town. Charles could sit on the balcony outside his room and have a view over the town and bay to the lighthouse on the bluff beyond. The drawback was that it was infested with mosquitoes which produced blisters where they bit him. He also saw white ants and a gigantic cockroach on the wall.

He soon made friends with Reverend Walton, the curate of St Cyprian's.[50] They were contemporaries at Oxford, although they did

---

50   Reverend James William Walton, MA(Oxon), was ordained priest at Chichester in 1894 and was curate at St Cyprian's from 1896 to 1899, after which he returned to England.

not know each other there, and were ordained in the same year and had mutual friends. One evening after dinner, they sat on the stoep over their pipes and tea, with cicadas singing all around and fireflies sailing through the air. They "trotted out our Oxford experiences. 'Them was days.' Thoughtless days, but full of fun."

Walton did not have a very good rapport with his congregation, mainly because he was a "red hot ritualist" and they were more low church, or "half dissenters" as Charles called them, many being Wesleyans. He created a stir by telling his Sunday school children that they would go to hell if they did not fast on Fridays. His strong views were not good for him because the clergy relied on the congregation for income, and they could be starved out if the congregation did not like them. Charles thought that Walton did not have enough tact to lead the congregation without appearing to drive them in his direction.

Walton's views were not a problem for Charles, who enjoyed discussions with him. On one occasion, when Walton had been reading *The Sorrows of Satan,* a recent novel by Marie Corelli about the arrival of the devil in London in disguise, they jokingly agreed that the devil would be very good company. Later, Charles read the book himself on the boat back to England, with mixed feelings. "It is a wonderful book in places, but there is a good deal of spite in it. One can see it was written by a woman. But although it had great defects, it is a book worth reading. There is one thing about Marie Corelli: she always preaches reverence for the Deity, although she does talk a good deal of twaddle."

When the time came for Charles to leave Durban, he agreed with Walton not to try to keep up a correspondence. "Old friends drop out of sight; those one knew at school and college, and whose friendship at the time seemed everlasting, gradually fall away; our paths diverge." They are but *Ships that pass in the night, and signal each other in passing/ Only a voice and a light, then silence again and darkness".* (This was a slightly misquoted passage from Longfellow's *Tales of a Wayside Inn.*) "But one often hears of old friends through others, and the world is small, and communication rapid, so one often knocks up against them again in after days."

Walton's boss, the vicar of St Cyprian's, was Canon Johnson.[51] He had studied at Leeds Clergy School about ten years before Charles and had kept his dicker in the same district of Kirkstall as Charles. He was friendly to Charles and arranged for him to preach most Sundays at either St Cyprian's or St Augustine's, for which he was also responsible. He invited him to the monthly meeting of the Durban Archdeaconry that Charles found so interesting, as we have seen. Charles met other clergymen at Canon Johnson's house. Reverend Fernsby, who was about Charles' age, had just come out to Durban after a spell as curate in the Holbeck

51   Canon Herbert Johnson, MA (Cantab), was ordained priest at St Alban's in 1883. Curate in Essex, 1882-85, and Leeds, 1885-88. He was vicar of St Cyprian's, 1888-1902, and canon of Maritzburg, 1894-1902. He was vicar of All Soul's, Leeds, 1902-14.

district of Leeds.[52] He knew a few of Charles' contemporaries at Leeds Clergy School. At lunch at Canon Johnson's, Charles sat next to the Right Reverend Baynes, the Bishop of Natal, who was based in Maritzburg, the capital of Natal.[53] The archdeacon of Durban, the Venerable Baines, was present at the same lunch.[54] He had been the vicar of Hunslet, Leeds, before he went to South Africa, and had also studied at Leeds Clergy School. As Charles observed, "there seem to be a perfect nest of Leeds men out here." This was not an accident: Johnson no doubt knew Baines in Leeds and was probably instrumental in bringing him to Durban, and Fernsby might have been recommended to him by Leeds friends.

Fernsby went with Charles to visit Reverend Bromelow, the vicar of Pinetown, a town about fifteen miles inland from Durban.[55] Despite the short distance, the train took one and a quarter hours, but there was some compensation in that the Natal government allowed clergymen to travel half-price. Bromelow took them on a walk to the top of Cowie Hill, from which there was a splendid view of the countryside "undulating away until it reached the sea".

Until a few years earlier, there had been two churches in Pinetown, each with its own clergyman, and the two were at daggers drawn. The Anglican church in Natal had been split into two camps as a result of the rivalry between Bishop Colenso of Natal and Bishop Gray of Cape Town. John Colenso (1814-83) was recruited in 1853 by Robert Gray, the Bishop of Cape Town, to be the first Bishop of Natal. In the following years Colenso offended many people in both England and South Africa. He challenged the historical accuracy of the bible, and he was critical of the unjust treatment of Africans by the colonial government of Natal. Gray responded by deposing him in 1863. But Colenso refused to leave his post, and appealed to the Privy Council, which held that Gray had no authority to remove him. Gray instead excommunicated Colenso and consecrated a rival Bishop of Maritzburg. There were then two Anglican bishops in the same city, and in due course there were two cathedrals. The Colenso faction called themselves the Church of England party, and the others, who were

---

52 Reverend Arthur Robert Fernsby, BA (Oxon), ordained at Ripon in 1894, curate of Christ Church, Leeds, 1893-96, curate of St Cyprian's, Durban, 1896-98, after which he was a curate in England.

53 Maritzburg was the common abbreviation of Pietermaritzburg, which was the proper name for the city. Right Reverend Arthur Hamilton Baynes, was ordained in 1883 in Lincoln. He worked in England, including a spell as chaplain to the Archbishop of Canterbury, 1888-91, until he was consecrated Bishop of Natal in 1893.

54 Venerable Frederick Samuel Baines, MA (Oxon), ordained in 1884 in Ripon, curate and vicar in Leeds, 1882-93, canon of Maritzburg and archdeacon of Durban from 1893, and incumbent of St Peter's, Maritzburg, from 1894.

55 Reverend William Bromelow, ordained in 1879 in Gloucester and Bath, principal and chaplain of the Home and Colonial Training College. London.1881-91, curate St Cyprian's Durban, 1892-94, and incumbent of Pinetown from 1894.

more ritualistic, were the Church of South Africa party. By the time Charles arrived, the two sides had come together under the jurisdiction of the South African church in some places, such as Pinetown, but in others the warfare continued. Bishop Baynes had to exercise considerable tact in reconciling the Colenso faction to the new reality, not least because he had no legal authority over them. The clergy of the Church of England party could defy him without consequence, whereas the Church of South Africa clergy were subject to his rulings. Archdeacon Baines had been brought out from England in part to help the reunion move forward. Charles' sympathy was with the South Africa party, mainly because he disagreed with Colenso's view that "our Lord was only human, not divine". He did not express a view in his diary about Colenso's criticisms of the colonial regime's treatment of Africans.

In general, Charles' theological views were middle-of-the-road Church of England ones. He was neither low nor high church; the rituals of the latter group did not attract him. He was, however, tolerant of the extremes of the broad church. He was less so of other Christians, whether dissenters (non-conformists) or Roman Catholics. He could not bring himself to attend the service held by a Baptist minister one Sunday on the boat out from England and feared that the minister would think him bigoted if he had to explain why he was absent. He also had a fairly intolerant attitude towards engaging in secular activities on Sundays. He was disappointed that music halls and theatres in Johannesburg were open on Sundays, which were marked by drinks being available only at the bar instead of being served at tables as on weekdays. "Johannesburg is certainly very much wanting in the religious sense." He thought that there should be "some little difference between our amusements" on Sundays and weekdays. He was against reading novels that were written only to amuse, but a good novel that made one think "can often do more good than a hundred sermons". He persuaded himself that it was all right to sketch outside (which he often did on Sundays) because he usually sketched beautiful scenes of nature which inspired him so that he felt "raised right up into the very gates of heaven". He was not upset by the severe rebuke he received from a Scotsman on the boat from England for collecting names on the Sabbath of participants in the sports to take place the next day.

As we have seen, Charles was asked to preach at most of the churches he attended, including St Paul's, Rondebosch, St Mary's, Johannesburg, St Alban's cathedral, Pretoria, St Cyprian's, Durban, and St Augustine's, Durban. The vicars and curates in each case were only too happy to have someone else deliver the sermon. He also preached at the service he took on the boat returning from South Africa to England. He was always happy to preach as well as to take some services. Unfortunately, we have no record of what he said in his sermons.

One Saturday in Durban he received a communication from Mahatma Gandhi asking him to mention the Indian Famine Fund at the service the following day.[56] Gandhi was living in South Africa, where he developed his views about colonialism, political action and ethics. He experienced racism and humiliation at the hands of the Europeans in South Africa. He made himself especially unpopular among them by speaking about the bad treatment of Indians in South Africa when on a recent visit to India, and they tried to stop him disembarking at Durban in January 1897 on his return. He told Charles that only one European in South Africa had subscribed to the Indian Famine Fund, a fact Charles thought was attributable to Gandhi's unpopularity and to the arrival of large numbers of Indian indentured workers.

He enjoyed religious conversations with both clergy and laymen. He discussed the bible with two men in the train going from Cape Town to Johannesburg. They believed in God but could not accept that the bible was literally true. Among other things, they were much bothered by the origins of Cain's wife. As Cain was the surviving son of Adam and Eve, his brother being dead, his wife was either a daughter of Adam and Eve, in which case his marriage was immoral, or she was the daughter of someone else, in which case Adam and Eve were not the only people in the world, contrary to the bible story. Charles explained that the theory of evolution swept away all such questions, and that the theory was "pretty well agreed by now to be in harmony with theology". This might be disputed by many people in the 21st century, especially in the US, and even more so at the end of the 19th century. It is, however, interesting that Charles was a firm believer in evolution, although he doubted that he had persuaded his fellow travellers.

On another train, this time from Johannesburg to Pretoria, there was another religious conversation. His interlocutor this time was a man in clerical attire who had been running a school in Durban and was looking for a place to start one in the Rand.[57] (Also present was "a typical old Boer with a rough, frizzy beard, brown weather-beaten face and a merry little twinkle in his eye, the whole surmounted by a well-worn canvas helmet. He seemed quite delighted to find me smoking Boer tobacco in a Boer pipe and offered to teach me Dutch if I would teach him English.") Charles' travel companion believed that Christianity had proved that it was the truest religion because gigantic strides in civilization had been made in countries that professed it compared with countries that professed Confucianism, Buddhism, Islam or other religions. Unlike other religions, Christianity touched every point of life, and allowed the whole of human nature, body, soul and spirit to develop to the fullest extent. He did not think that everyone who had not been baptised or confirmed was in danger of being

---

56   Mahatma Gandhi (1869-1948) lived in South Africa from 1893 to 1914. He returned to India in 1914 and campaigned for independence, emphasising non-violent means. He was assassinated in 1948.

57   The Rand refers to Witwatersrand, a region that includes Johannesburg and the main gold mines of South Africa.

lost. As long as they were honestly searching for the truth, even if not baptised, they would be all right. But they would be in danger if they had become acquainted with the truth but had then turned away. Charles thought that such views were out of line with Church doctrine, and, reflecting on the conversation later, he wished he could "have another innings with him". Charles had a very long conversation with another traveller, on the boat returning to England from South Africa. He had first met Matthews in his boarding-house in Durban. He joined up with him again on the boat to England. Matthews was "in a very unsettled state, verging on the brink of agnosticism". He accepted that God existed but doubted the divinity of Jesus, whom he thought might have been a perfectly sincere man under a terrible delusion. Charles tried to persuade him that he should have faith, or at least "a grain of faith to make the first effort", accompanied by persistent prayer. Privately, in his diary, he recognised that faith came more easily to some than to others, as "constitutions differ". The conversation continued late into the night, after everyone else had gone to bed and the lights had been turned out. His sympathy for Matthews caused Charles to write that night in his diary: "I believe that all who have sincerely searched for the truth, although they may not have come very near it, and who have lived sincerely, are all right". This view was similar to that of the traveller he met on the train to Pretoria a month or so earlier, at which time Charles had noted that it was contrary to church doctrine. He was evidently not doctrinaire about theological and church matters.

Charles found Durban a beautifully clean and tidy place after the Transvaal towns, especially Johannesburg, with a more finished appearance even than Cape Town. The woodland scenery, with tall cactus trees and bamboos with feathery stems, was not like England. Brick-red and magenta zinnias, bright blue convolvuli and shrubs with large yellow flowers and a deep purple eye grew by the wayside. He enjoyed sketching the beautiful view from the veranda of the boarding house: the sea sometimes a delicate turquoise blue and sometimes emerald green, depending on where the sun shone and how close to shore one looked. The dark tree-clad bluff formed a contrast to the sea. He grew quite fond of the Berea, and the view of the bay and the bluff.

His stay in Durban was prolonged by illness. The symptoms were high temperatures, headaches and lack of energy. The doctor said he had dengue fever and prescribed quinine and analgesics for the headaches. He was in bed with a temperature for nearly a week, and stayed in the house, mostly on the veranda, for a few more days. Even when he was able to go out again, he was weak (or "slack" as he put it) and sometimes felt dizzy. He found it difficult to write in the diary; the entries were unusually untidy and brief. Reading was impossible at the height of the fever, but he managed to read a number of novels as he was recovering. He preferred the books of Edna Lyall, who was "human and refreshing", to those of Marie Corelli, the most widely read writer at that time, who had "a tendency to morbidness". As we have seen, he wrote later that Corelli talked "a good deal of twaddle". (He probably did not remember that his cousin, Reverend Daniell, had recommended, four years before, that he read Edna Lyall to improve his sermons.) The whole episode took about two weeks, so that he ended up staying a month in Durban instead of the planned two weeks or so.

Miss Galloway looked after him "like a trained nurse", "trotting in with beef tea, milk and other delicacies"; she was "a regular brick". His friends Bangley and Walton were frequent visitors, as were other guests in Miss Galloway's boarding-house. Canon Johnson and Reverend Brimelow also called in.

After he recovered, he felt that he had joined an exclusive club. "I have always rather envied the man who has experienced the fever in Africa or India. It always sounded so superior to hear such a one say off-hand like 'Oh, it's only a touch of fever, old man'. I shall now be able to sympathise with them instead. It's very gratifying to feel that I have managed to catch a complaint that cannot be caught at home. It is worth travelling to do that."

He was sorry to leave Durban when the time came, and to say goodbye to people there, not least Miss Galloway. "There are not many like her in South Africa." The heat had sometimes been tremendous, and "the sense of slackness that pervaded everything is very pleasant and soothing for a time".[58] He wondered how many days could be described by Tennyson's words:

All round the coast the languid air did swoon,
Breathing like one that hath a weary dream.[59]

Bangley came to see him off. They took a rickshaw down to the water, following the rickshaw containing Charles' luggage and that of another passenger. The man pulling their rickshaw was light and had difficulty preventing it from running away with him. The luggage rickshaw collided with a bicycle, and Charles and Bangley almost did a somersault out of the back of theirs. They embarked on a tug that took them over the bar of the harbour to the ship that was to take Charles to Cape Town. They had to jump from the tug onto a rope ladder hanging from the ship. This caused some excitement as the tug was bobbing up and down and moving towards and away from the ship. But it was preferable to the uninteresting alternative "of being fastened into a large basket and hoisted up by means of the donkey engine". When the bell rang for all ashore, Charles and Bangley parted with their watchword "Remember Karkloof".

The boat's departure from Durban had been delayed for a day to enable a theatrical company, who had performed the night before, to join it. The star of the company was Miss Fanny Moody, a famous opera singer

---

58   Charles often used the word "slackness" to describe laziness or tiredness.

59   Alfred, Lord Tennyson, *The Lotos Eaters*.

in the UK.[60] The journey to Cape Town was slow, mainly because of the lengthy stops at East London and Port Elizabeth to enable cargo, including hides and wool, to be taken on board. Mists and rough seas also slowed them down. Charles went ashore in Port Elizabeth which he found less untidy than most towns in South Africa. He sketched a couple of wrecked sailing ships that had run ashore when they had dragged their anchors in strong sou'easters. Being at sea made him feel poetic, and pleasantly removed from little cares and worries. "The gentle motion, the lapping of the waters, and the distance one seems from all the stern realities of life, tend to lift one up and lead one to look at things through a dreamy haze."

He checked into Rouw Koop on arriving in Cape Town. A letter from Marion was waiting for him. It reminded him how much he missed her, and, still in a poetic mood from the boat, he quoted Kipling:

I have heard the call of the offshore wind
And the voice of the deep sea rain;
I have heard the song – how long? how long?
Pull out on the trail again.[61]

He immediately booked his passage back to England the following week. Quoting from Reginald Heber's hymn (From Greenland's Icy Mountains), he wrote that "the land where 'Afric's sunny fountains roll down their golden sand' will soon be as a dream in the past".

His final week in South Africa was taken up with seeing friends and saying goodbye, punctuated by two memorable events. First, a fire broke out near the kitchen chimney of Rouw Koop, and black smoke billowed through the thatch. Charles, who was sketching nearby, was alerted by an old African ("baas, fire!") and rushed to the scene. He climbed onto the roof with two or three Africans, and they managed to put out the fire after half an hour by hauling up buckets of water handed to them by people on the ground. They were just in time because the house had old beams and dry thatch and would have burned quickly if the fire had got a hold.

The second event was the ascent of Table Mountain. Having failed to find a way up the mountain when in Rondebosch earlier, Charles was keen to conquer it before leaving South Africa. He had to abort a plan to go with Leary because of heavy rain and strong winds. The next day, a Sunday, he was at tea at the house of Mrs Horwood's father, Mr Ebden, when the possibility of climbing Table Mountain came up. Miss Horwood and Miss Ebden wanted to go, and Charles and Rendle, at whose house Charles had supper, agreed to take them the following day, when Rendle

---

60   Frances Moody (1866-1945), a soprano, was born in Cornwall and died in Dublin. She married Charles Manners, a bass, in 1890 in London. She and Manners performed together in London and on tour. After their successful tour of South Africa in 1896-97, they formed the Moody-Manners opera company in 1898. It was active until it closed in 1916 due to financial difficulties, and never became the national opera company presenting operas in English that Manners had envisaged.

61   From Rudyard Kipling, *The Long Trail*, slightly misquoted.

was not working and Leary was not free. They were well aware that steering the "two girls up and down that mountain would be a tremendous responsibility".

Charles and Rendle took the 7:35 am train from Rondebosch to Wynberg, where they met the girls with their packages of sandwiches. They took a Cape cart to Constantia Nek to the south of the mountain, from where they began the ascent. The route they took was one of the easiest, although long, because it was a steady rise all the way without major steep sections. As they gained height the views of the Drakenstein range to the north and the Cape peninsula to the south were glorious. They could see the white specks of tents in the army camp at Wynberg, from which the sounds of bugles and a military band drifted up. After 2½ hours they reached the forester's cottage, where they ate some sandwiches and enjoyed tea prepared by the forester's wife. Beyond that they passed the construction sites of the dams that were being built for Cape Town's reservoirs. At one point after that, the path skirted the edge of a ravine 70-80 feet deep where extra care was required not to slip. The girls caused Charles and Rendle some anxiety, because they were so excited that they did not exercise enough caution. Rendle had to catch Miss Horwood once as she was rolling down into the pool of a running spruit. They reached the edge of the mountain overlooking Cape Town 1½ hours after leaving the forester's cottage. The view from there was simply magnificent: Cape Town was below, with Table Bay and Robben Island beyond it, and

to the left and right were the Lion's Head and Devil's Peak respectively.

They returned to the forester's cottage 1200 feet below, where they had more tea and sandwiches. From there they took a different route from the one in the morning, and descended on the western side of the mountain, by Kasteelsport. The path was steep and rugged, and the sun was dropping towards the horizon. "Miss Ebden lost the sole of her shoe, and Miss Horwood thought she had ricked her ankle, and they both sat down to argue. We got them along somehow, but it was hard work, as they were both getting tired and one of them perverse."

They managed to navigate the most dangerous part before the sun set, but they still had to follow an isolated path in the moonlight, in and out of the gullies at the foot of the mountain, where gangs of Africans had "been known to waylay unwary travellers". Nothing untoward occurred, and eventually the path dropped down into Cape Town, where they caught a train to Rondebosch, arriving there at 9:30 pm. "In spite of such a grand day, we had had quite enough of it."

The next day both the girls were stiff, and Miss Ebden's foot was somewhat raw. Although they were young and fit, climbing a mountain in their long dresses cannot have been easy. They still had "the mountain on the brain" the day after, when they were gradually recovering from their efforts. Charles and Rendle both felt "as if we have done something".

Charles' boat left Cape Town on 19 March. He watched as Table Mountain gradually faded into the distance and wondered whether he would ever see it again. Two days before, busy with travel arrangements, he was reminded of Kipling:

We're going 'ome, we're going 'ome.
Our ship is at the shore,
An' you must pack your 'aversack
For we won't come back no more.[62]

He added that he did not know about not coming back. "One never knows what line life is going to strike out in next." Although he was looking forward to going home, he was reluctant to leave South Africa, where he felt that the life suited him well. The idea of returning stayed with him for the next ten years. As we shall see, he later moved to Southern Africa and spent the best part of twenty years there.

He had a positive attitude to the three-week journey home. "We are going to have a jolly time, as we have some really decent fellow passengers." Prominent among these were three men he had met at Miss Galloway's boarding-house in Durban: Legitt, Matthews and Seymour. They called themselves the Galloway Club and often played whist together. Legitt and Matthews were not always available, sometimes because they gave higher priority to talking to the ladies. On such occasions, Charles and Seymour played with the Miss Logies, "two nice old maids

who hailed from Edinburgh" who "could play a very decent game of whist".

Charles took the lead in trying to organise sports and entertainments. It was difficult to get people to participate, partly because it was very hot in the first two weeks or so.

One evening the temperature in the saloon was 87° Fahrenheit. The ladies were in short supply at an early dance, and Charles had to dance lady with the chief engineer. With the captain's encouragement, he took the services and preached on Sundays.

---

62   Rudyard Kipling, *Troopin' (Our Army in the East)*.

The heat was such that the bathrooms became unbearable, with the walls too hot to touch. The 1st officer rigged up a canvas bath on the forward hatch with a hose playing into it. As the men bathed naked, they had to go early in the morning before the ladies appeared.

Charles passed the time in various ways. He kept a daily record of the weather, the sailing conditions and the distance travelled. In addition to whist, sports and entertainments, he read books (as we have seen, Marie Corelli was one of the authors), sketched and talked to many other passengers and ship's officers. The 1st officer was a "very jolly fellow" who lived in Perry Vale, next door to Sydenham. The 2nd officer "thought that happiness consisted in being content with what one had, yet he was an awful grumbler". The chief engineer always made it a rule to leave all children alone on a voyage. The head steward thought that immorality was a necessity in the present state of civilization.

Charles visited two invalids in third class. One, an old Scotsman, had consumption. The ship's doctor thought he would not last out the voyage, but he did. He spoke optimistically about what he was going to do when he got better. He had been an engineer in a mine in Johannesburg, and told dubious stories about how he and a few other uitlanders rode into a camp of Transvaal troops and spiked their guns after plying them with whisky. He was in prison for six months after the Jameson raid for concealing arms. Alice Hill, a nurse from Johannesburg, also had consumption. It had affected her limbs to the extent that she might have to have an arm amputated. She had no friends and no money. The passengers raised money for her, and Miss Coleman, who had lived at Carshalton, near Sydenham, and worked with the rector, Lord Victor Seymour, said she would keep an eye on her and handle the money.[63]

Charles observed the social strains among the passengers. Within a week, two of the ladies were not on speaking terms. Some of the first-class passengers thought themselves too important to mix with the second-class passengers. And some of the second-class passengers resisted the overtures of the more friendly among the first-class passengers, because they thought they were being patronised. Charles was in second class, despite his mother having urged him to take first class, and even paying for it. He wanted to stay with the Galloway Club, who were in second class. He also thought that the company would be superior in second class. One would not be "so likely to meet Johannesburg Jews and barmaids and others who are made by money and not by manners." The only drawback was that second-class passengers did not have the run of the whole ship.

Charles and Seymour went ashore in Las Palmas. They hired a carriage for a beautiful drive into the hills, which were bare and brown, with valleys where bananas, potatoes,

---

63   Reverend Lord Victor Alexander Seymour was the rector of Carshalton from 1884 to 1901. He was the son of the 5th Marquess of Hertford and the younger brother of the 6th Marquess.

sugar cane and vines grew. There were hedges of double geranium and sweet-scented broom. They sampled a bottle of Canary wine at the Bella Vista hotel from which the view was indeed beautiful. They each purchased a bunch of bananas to take home, and had many difficulties getting them back to the boat. That evening, with the bananas standing in a corner of his cabin, Charles wondered why they had been so keen to buy them.

As the weather got colder, the South Africans complained about the English climate. The boat rolled considerably going up the English Channel, and Charles' cocoa spilled onto Miss Coleman's lap at breakfast. The passage up the Thames to Tilbury Docks, where they arrived on 8 April 1897, was smooth. Marion, Emma and Uncle George were there to meet Charles.[64] They took the train together to Fenchurch Street, from where Marion went to her family in Sydenham and Charles and Emma went to Headley where he found their parents well. The fields and hedges of England seemed strange to him after the great rolling expanse of Africa.

---

64   Uncle George was George Ranking Walters, the youngest sibling of Charles' and Emma's mother. He worked in the City and lived in South London.

CHAPTER 3

YORKSHIRE AND FAMILY

Only two months after he returned to England, Charles married Marion at St Bartholomew's in Sydenham on 16 June 1897. The wedding was conducted by the vicar, Charles' boss, Reverend Moberly. Charles' parents, Emma and Uncle Thomas were there, among other relatives, as was Marion's mother, but not her father, who had died nearly 13 years earlier. Charles and Marion did not have any children.

Parish work in Yorkshire

Their first home as a married couple was in Bradford, where Charles took up the position of curate at St Jude's later in the year. They were to remain in industrial towns in Yorkshire for the next eleven years. The vicar of St Jude's, John Eddowes, was over 70. In addition to Charles, he was assisted by another young curate, John Watson. Charles and Marion became good friends with the Watsons. After they moved to Almondbury, they returned to Bradford to see them, on one occasion for the christening of the youngest Watson child, of whom Charles was the godfather.

In 1900, Charles was appointed a curate in the parish of Almondbury, close to Huddersfield. His vicar was William Foxley Norris, and there were three other curates in the parish: Brocklebank, Cholmeley and Ellison.[65]

---

65 William Foxley Norris, like Charles, had been at Leeds Clergy School some twelve years before him. He went on to higher things after Barnsley, becoming Dean of York in 1917-25 and Dean of Westminster in 1925-29. John Wilfrid Royds Brocklebank had been curate since 1895. He had been at Leeds Clergy School the year after Charles. John Butler Cholmeley, who was a few years older than Charles, left St Mary's, Barnsley, in 1905 to take up the position of vicar of St Mark's in Hull. Henry Blomfield Ellison had been curate since 1897, his first job. He had been at Pembroke College a few years before Charles and they enjoyed gossiping about "old Pembroke men and times".

About a year after Charles started in Almondbury, Norris was moved to Barnsley as rector of St Mary's. He took Charles and Cholmeley with him. The other two Almondbury curates, Brocklebank and Ellison, left at the same time to allow the new vicar of Almondbury to appoint his own curates. They both went to South Africa, for which Charles prepared Ellison by lending him the diary of his 1896-97 trip to South Africa "to improve his mind".

Charles and Marion remained in Barnsley for five years, his longest term as a curate. In 1907, after apprenticeship in four curacies, he was appointed the vicar of Dewsbury Moor. He had one curate to assist him.

We do not know much about the eleven years that Charles and Marion spent in Yorkshire. If he kept diaries, they have not survived, with the single exception of the diary for 1901. Fortunately, this provides a good picture of Charles' work and their life as it related to the work. They were in Almondbury to the end of April, and Barnsley from May to the end of the year.

In Almondbury, in addition to parish duties, he had special responsibilities for the Longley area of the parish where he and Marion lived. Their home was in part of Longley Old Hall which had once been the home of the Ramsden family, which had owned much of Huddersfield and beyond.[66] They had two servants, a cook and a maid, and also Jack the dog and Mowk the cat.

To move around the parish and beyond, Charles usually went on his bicycle. This was not always easy as the terrain was hilly and the weather that winter was often wet and cold. One day he had business in central Huddersfield and then "had a rush up to Almondbury to take a funeral. I was on my machine, or I would not have been able to do it." When he had business in neighbouring towns he often went by bicycle. It was about fourteen miles to Wakefield, the diocesan centre, and about the same to Bradford. Barnsley, where he went to look for a house to move to, was about seventeen miles away. "It was one of the most trying rides I ever have had. It did not seem so bad when I started... However, when I got up to Lepton, a driving snow storm came on and then the sun came out and melted it, and the surface became awful; and right away on into Barnsley there were alternate sleet and snow storms. In some places the roads were unrideable." On this occasion, as on other occasions when Marion went with him, she took the train and met him at the other end. Charles joined her on the train back this time. Another time he rode both to and from Barnsley. "The distant moors were a grand sight with the sun shining on their snow-covered heads. Coming home was an awful grind – uphill most of the way, and a biting head wind."

He took a friend who stayed with them for a week on an outing to Barnsley. "Rode Arthur over to Barnsley and back, and about

---

66   Charles' diary clearly says that they lived at Longley Old Hall. However, they are recorded in the 1901 census as living at 187 Longley Road, which is not the same place.

did for him. He declared he is not going to ride in this country any more. However, he recovered after a good meal." Once he went at short notice to the House of the Resurrection at Mirfield, which was six miles away, to find a priest who could address a devotional meeting that day. He was successful but, "on coming home I got wet through. I went up to the church, but as I felt so damp I decided that discretion was the better part of valour, so came home and changed and thus missed an interesting service."[67] Charles rode his bicycle for pleasure and exercise, as well as to get to a destination for a practical purpose. "Being a dry day took a ride round. Met about three or four hundred people indulging in the same way. Went round by Bradley, Brighouse and Elland; then tried to make my way up on to the moors, but took the wrong road and before I knew where I was, I was slipping down into Huddersfield, so came home." Although his bicycle served him well, he decided to have a new one built for him, with BSA fittings throughout. It was the first bicycle he had had with a freewheel and a back-pedalling brake.[68] He was not sure that he was going to like them – the brake seemed to jam the wheel.

Charles' duties included taking services, preaching sermons, preparing candidates for confirmation and communion, running a bible class, teaching Sunday schools, contributing to the management of the church schools (including appointing and firing teachers), the parish magazine, visiting parishioners, and managing choir practices (with the organist), among many other things.

Marion assisted with many of the parish activities. She ran the Longley Girls' Friendly Society which put on entertainments. She prepared girls and boys for communion. She occasionally played the organ in church when the regular organist was not available. She operated the lantern for the slides that accompanied a talk that Charles gave on South Africa to the Longley Mission Association. And she helped to organise the teas, without which meetings would not have attracted many people.

Queen Victoria died on 22 January 1901. Charles wondered what to say in his sermon the following Sunday. "Down here [in Longley] they would think any allusion [to the Queen] beautiful, but as I am up in the parish church in the morning, I shall have to be careful." There was a day of general mourning a week later, with the shops closed and traffic stopped, and a well-attended service in the parish church. "I was very much surprised to see the church so full. It shows what a hold the Queen has had over her people."

---

67 The House of the Resurrection was the home of an Anglican religious community for men. It was inspired partly by Christian Socialist ideals which is why the House was set up in Mirfield, a working class area, in 1898. George Longridge, whom Charles arranged to address the meeting in Almondbury, subsequently became the superior of the community from 1914 to 1917.

68 In earlier bicycles the pedals turned at the same speed as the wheels, which was difficult to manage when going downhill.

During Wednesdays in Lent Charles gave six weekly addresses at the Almondbury parish church, on the theme of Sin and Redemption. He worried after the third week that he had been "a bit dull as the congregation is not so good. I am trying to give them fairly solid food, and perhaps most of them find it is more than they can manage to get down." The fourth week, he "ground away at my address which I gave at the parish church in the evening. Felt in much better form than last Wednesday." He took a short bicycle ride before the address in the fifth week to clear his head. The weather was wintry, with a biting wind and snow on the ground. He was glad to finish the course with the sixth address. "I hardly feel that I have succeeded in bringing out with sufficient clearness the point I was aiming at – how, in spite of our human weakness, we have power through Jesus Christ, to lead a perfect life, and yet lead that life of our own free will."

The Longley men's bible class, which had been renamed St Mary's Men's Class in 1900, took up quite a bit of Charles' time. (They referred to the building in Longley where they had services as St Mary's, but it does not appear to have been a consecrated church.) About 15-20 men attended the weekly meetings. They also had business meetings, at one of which they discussed whether to give prizes for attendance (they agreed to do so), and social activities. The latter included dances and cricket matches. The St Jude's Bible Class, which Charles had led in Bradford, came on a visit one Saturday with their wives and enjoyed a game of cricket. It was an exciting game which Longley won by one run, and was followed by tea, games and dancing. A few weeks later Longley lost a game by four wickets to the Working Men's Club. There was a record turnout, with standing room only, at Charles' last meeting with the class. He was pleased with their efforts and enthusiasm of the men and was concerned that the class might fall apart after he left.

By contrast, Charles was frustrated by his work with the Sunday Schools in Longley, mainly because he thought that the teachers were not up to the job. After superintending the Sunday School one day, he wrote in his diary: "I don't think I had grasped how utterly rotten most of the teachers are, but I suppose we are no worse in that respect than other places." The turnout at a teachers' meeting a few days later was poor; as Charles noted: "They are getting very slack about turning up." A few weeks later: "If I wasn't going, I would have to have a good stir round in Sunday School once more… There is absolutely no one who has any control over the children." Later, he was not pleased when only two Sunday School teachers came to a parish meeting of Sunday and day school teachers. "They are a slack lot; but the weather was certainly not very encouraging." (It had snowed heavily the previous day, and, although the snow had cleared away, it remained rainy and windy.) Charles was also sometimes disappointed by the children: "Senior Sunday School behaved badly, and I shall have to dismiss one of the bright specimens."

Low attendances at church services in

Longley also upset Charles. As well as services on Sundays, he celebrated Holy Communion at 7 am and Evensong on Wednesdays. Often no one would come to the midweek Holy Communion services. "The most disappointing part of this place is the communicants. No one appeared at 7 am." Another Wednesday when there had been no one at Holy Communion in the morning, Charles addressed a meeting of the Communicants' Guild in the afternoon. "They seem to like being addressed on the subject of communion, but it does not apparently make them attend at Celebration [Holy Communion] any better."

He was inclined to blame the fact that it was known he would soon be leaving the parish to go to Barnsley. One Wednesday: "It has been a disappointing day as far as services are concerned. Only ourselves at 7 am Holy Communion and 10 am Matins… About 20 present all told at Evensong. I think our coming departure is probably the cause of it. People have got disheartened." And the following Sunday: "They are a wretched lot of people round here. Now that it is thoroughly known that we are leaving they have given up coming to church. Had miserable congregations." With just a couple of weeks left before his departure, he wrote: "I shall be very glad when once we are away now. Everything is apparently only just holding together and is ready to fall. They are a wretched lot. Only a few of the older ones are at all solid. I don't think I have ever come across quite such an unstable lot of young men and women. It would take 5 or 6 years' steady work to create

anything like a right feeling among them." Even allowing for some exaggeration, and for the fact that "wretched" was not a very critical word at the time in the vernacular of Charles' class, he was clearly unhappy with the lack of commitment to the church of many parishioners.

When Norris first asked him to move with him to Barnsley, Charles was unsettled. He had been in Almondbury for barely a year and knew that it would take more time to make a significant impact – even if not as much as five or six years. He also felt that he would be letting down the young men and others who had come to depend on him. He had long conversations with Norris whom he trusted and admired. He also consulted Burrows, who was Principal of Leeds Clergy School when Charles was there and was now vicar of Holy Trinity in Leeds. Both Norris and Burrows said that he should not place so much weight on the problems of individuals. Norris also pointed out that his staying created the possibility that the Longley parishioners, who were his main responsibility, would not develop the attachment to the wider parish of Almondbury that was desirable. Charles therefore decided to go with Norris to Barnsley.

On Charles' last Sunday in Longley, there was standing room only in the Bible Class. They presented him with a photo, and Charles "urged them to give the next man the same chance as they had given me. I am sorry for them being left without a leader, as they are so thoroughly keen". The evening service at Longley was also packed, with some people having to sit in the vestry. "They had all come to be moved to tears by my farewell words. I preached an ordinary sermon in which all my teaching was more or less summed up, although I did not actually tell them so; so in as far as having their emotions stirred, they were thoroughly sold."

The outgoing rector of St Mary's in Barnsley, William Walter Kirby, had been there since 1878 and was in his late 70s. Charles met his two curates who "both seem to have had a thoroughly bad time with old Kirby, and the parish apparently is in a thoroughly rotten state". Charles was to have special responsibility for the St Barnabas mission as well as wider parish duties. The two curates told him that the mission was "the only place that any work has been done at" but that it "has been crushed and hampered by old Kirby bagging all the money they produced. I don't know how the people have stood it." Kirby lived for only six months after retiring. His remains came by train from Bournemouth, where he had been living. Charles was part of the procession from the station to the church and had a three-hour spell during the all-night vigil. The church was packed for the funeral service next day.

Charles, Marion, their two servants, Jack and Mowk moved to Barnsley on 3 May, Charles on his bicycle and the others on the train. Their house was smaller than Longley Old Hall, but not "nearly so bad as we thought it would be, although both Bradford and Longley have spoilt us for room. There is one great feature about the house – it is clean."

Charles emphasised cleanliness because the same could not be said about the rectory, which was "in a disgraceful state... paper coming off the walls, ceilings coming down, floors rotten". It would be months before the Norris family could hope to move in, and meanwhile they had to live in the Clergy House. St Barnabas Mission church also "looks as if it would do with a good clean down... It looks as if all round the parish things have been allowed to run to seed." The parish church itself was causing Norris to despair. "Among other things, he has discovered a drawer containing a rotting hairbrush and a half-burnt candle." While still in Almondbury, Charles had noted that Barnsley "is known under the salubrious title of 'mucky Barnsley'", but this was because it was the centre of a coal-mining area and not because of the state of the church buildings.

The clergy team at St Mary's consisted of Norris, the rector, and three curates: Charles, with responsibility for the St Barnabas mission, John Butler Cholmeley who, like Charles, had come with Norris from Almondbury, and Basil Mather, for whom this was his first curacy.[69] They met frequently in Synod to manage the affairs of the parish. One of their first decisions was to cap the amount that St Barnabas would transfer to central funds, allowing it to retain any funds above the cap that they had

---

69   Basil Mather was younger than Charles. He was ordained deacon in May 1901 and priest in 1902, and left St Mary's in 1906 to go to China as a missionary. He was the first dean of the Central Theological School in Nanking from 1922 to 1927.

collected. The Synod and the Church Council, which included lay members, had to deal with two other tricky issues: the debts left behind by the previous rector and curates (including a bill of £23 for cigars!), and the development plans for the next 15-20 years. Among the suggestions for the development plans were a parish room near the parish church for general purposes, a new church for St Barnabas, new schools for St Barnabas and decoration of the chancel of the parish church.

Charles placed priority on the new classrooms for St Barnabas rather than a new church, because there was serious overcrowding of the existing premises for the Sunday schools. He walked Norris round the St Barnabas catchment area and persuaded him to give his support. At the critical meeting in October of the committee of parishioners appointed to take the matter forward, Charles "made them sit up by telling them that because we are so on the verge of overcrowding, I had not asked a single parent to send their children to our Sunday school, nor did I ever look them up if they stayed away, yet our numbers were increasing every Sunday, and that I believed that, with visiting with Sunday school definitely in view, we could double our numbers." He explained that there were 700-800 children at the Board of Education schools for that area of Barnsley, of whom about 230 went to the St Barnabas Sunday schools and perhaps half that number to the Wesleyan Sunday school, leaving a large number who could be recruited by St Barnabas if they had the space to take them. It was agreed to develop plans for a new building for the Sunday schools. Various sites were considered before they decided to build it on land the church already owned that had been donated many years before by Sir Hickman Bacon. This happened in the following years, the building later being called St Barnabas Hall. In the meantime, they were planning in December to see whether they could hire the Board schools until their new building was up.

Charles was heartened by his first Sunday service at St Barnabas, two days after moving to Barnsley. "At evensong, there was a good congregation – room nearly full – but very few men. The choir are somewhat rough, but then they have had no practices, poor things. Everyone, so far, seems very keen and willing. They are full of hope for the new era which is now dawning for them, and we must try not to disappoint their hope."

One of the first things Charles did in the St Barnabas community was to set up a General Purposes Committee of laymen. The occupations of the members, who were all men, were linen draper, ironmonger's shopman, collier (two of them), gas-meter mechanic, hairdresser, debt collector and bootmaker. The linen draper was "a hard-headed business man… and the most well-to-do man we have at the mission". He was elected secretary. Charles valued their knowledge of the area and its people but noted that the committee found it difficult to come to conclusions. "I find this is usually the case unless I take some decided line on a particular subject, then they all follow like lambs."

The mission church needed serious cleaning. Charles and Marion set about cleaning the vestry in their first few weeks there. "The place is in an appalling state of dirt. ..... One hardly knows where to begin to get it straight." A local told them that it had probably not been cleaned since it was built nineteen years before. The General Purposes Committee decided that they should clean the Mission Room themselves, and so they did. When Charles and Marion returned in July from holiday they found that the Church Committee "had had the whole place, including roof beams and vestry, thoroughly cleaned. The chancel has been painted white and all the iron work blue. They have all subscribed together to get it done and are very proud of what they have accomplished."

As at Almondbury, the Sunday schools took up much time and effort. Soon after arriving, Charles and Cholmeley had to help organise the annual Whit Tuesday treat. That year it was decided to take the children from the whole parish to Stainborough, a village about three miles south-west of Barnsley. Transport, finance and teas had to be arranged, and parents persuaded not to come. The children were packed into nineteen horse-drawn wagons which "were quite an imposing sight as we paraded through the town" at the beginning of the one-hour journey. When they reached Stainborough, Cholmeley conducted races and Charles played football and cricket. Charles had to leave early on his bicycle as it was his turn to conduct evensong at the parish church. "Soon after 8pm the shouting

van loads arrived, having thoroughly enjoyed themselves. Although there were well over 400 children, there was not one accident!" Children under six were not allowed to go on the outing, so a special tea was arranged for them the next day.

Charles found that the St Barnabas Sunday schools were disorganised. Children of different ages were mixed up together, and even the teachers did not always know who should be in which class. He tried to organise things but "in spite of all one's efforts, there is not much cosmos evolved out of chaos yet. I am gradually gleaning names which have not appeared on any register. Among other things, the children sit in whatever class they fancy until they are tired, and then try another!"

As better order was imposed over the first few months, Charles turned his attention to the teachers. "One would be thankful for better teachers. They come to the meetings fairly well, but most of them make their classes read the bible without offering note or comment! I suppose it is the next best thing to teaching them wrong."

After the summer, he made some changes: "The best stroke of business I have done is eliminating the irregular teachers and degrading the bible readers. I now have only two hardened bible readers left, and I am giving them young classes, some who can hardly read, so they will have to talk to them in some way." One more reform he instituted was a system of prizes for attendance and lessons learnt, the details of which he had professionally printed and sent to every parent. The teachers did not like it, but Norris approved and wanted to copy it for the Sunday schools at the parish church. Later Charles wrote: "As a whole, they [the teachers] have taken the high-handed way in which I have treated both them and their classes extremely well." He managed to placate the two teachers who continued to object, in one case by working through her father who was also a teacher, and in the other case by giving "him supper, a good talking to, and cigarettes".

The choir of St Barnabas usually had an annual outing, but it had not taken place the year before. There was some residual ill feeling about the omission, which added to Charles' difficulty in persuading the men in the choir to make contributions towards the cost of the outing. He therefore hit on the plan of sending two choirboys round the parish asking for donations, in return for which each would receive 1s 6d. This worked out well: there was competition among the boys for the job, and the successful ones raised £6 5s 0d. While it was not enough for a trip to Llandudno, which was the choir's most favoured destination, it was enough for Scarborough, their second choice. Due to confusion about their seat reservations on the train, some of them "scored considerably" by ending up in first-class compartments. After dinner and tea at the Grand Hotel refreshment rooms in Scarborough, the choir looked after themselves, and Charles had time to do some sketching.

Marion supported Charles in his activities wherever she could. In addition, she supervised the sewing group which produced goods to sell for the benefit of church funds. She and others priced articles that had been donated for a rummage sale. She presented the prizes at the Day School annual prize giving, something that the rector's wife would usually do, but she was away. She led confirmation classes for some of the girls. Charles brought her in to teach at Sunday school, when he was reorganising the teachers. More generally, she interacted with the parishioners, especially the women and children, and helped with teas.

Most of the parishioners in Barnsley were working class, and socialising with them took place mainly at church or community events. There was a middle class that kept itself somewhat separate in the English way. Their socialising included friendly parties at people's homes, which was quite a change for Charles and Marion. "We did not know such a thing at Bradford or Almondbury. One notices pretty clearly the extra-parochial class tone among the better-to-do people here, as at Headley. They live at a different level (NB I do not say higher level) to the profanum vulgus." The doctor's wife, for example, would be "hurt if one suggests her name along with" the grocer's wife. Another lady wanted to become a district visitor, "but it is clear that there will be no doing anything with her unless she is allowed to boss the show and play the Lady Bountiful all round". Despite having to face such class snobbery, Charles admitted that "it is a pleasant change every now and then to get out of the parochial groove", that is, not to have to play the role of curate all the time.

For example, it allowed him and Marion to enjoy some tennis one September day at the home of "some nice and friendly people with a comfortable house and a pretty garden". As in the past, Charles had to comment on the game: "…not of a very high standard, but we had some good sets". He was impressed by Norris, who was also playing: "He is a very keen player, and a hard and violent hitter."

It was expected in those days, when the British Empire was believed to be a civilising influence in poor countries, that churches in England would support missionary activity both financially and in other ways. Consequently, most parishes staged events – talks or fund-raising activities. Charles was keen on supporting missions, and was disappointed, in both Almondbury and Barnsley, that there was not more interest. The churches in the Huddersfield area had set up the Huddersfield Joint Churches Missionary Association. He found one meeting he went to in 1901 a waste of time: "Icely is a rotten chairman; and a lot of time goes in exposing his foolish views".[70] Brocklebank spoke on the call to missionary service which made Charles wonder whether he intended to become a missionary – he did in fact go to South Africa later in the year as an assistant chaplain in the railway mission in Grahamstown.

After moving to Barnsley, Charles was disappointed that few communicants in the parish seemed to know or care much about missions and "so we shall have something to do to educate them". Norris started a Missionary Association, but was too busy with other things to give it much attention and it had few members. Charles noted that "hardly a person knows the obligation of helping missions, and even Clarke said the other day we had plenty to do at home without bothering about those outside." (Clarke was a member of the St Barnabas General Purposes Committee and a Sunday school teacher. He worked as a debt collector.) Norris arranged for the Mayor of Barnsley to chair a public meeting which was addressed by Isabella Bird, the famous explorer and writer. "There were a lot of people there, and a real good start was made in the way of stirring up the missionary zeal of the place. [Isabella Bird] spoke very well, and her remark that she would once ride three days round to avoid a mission station but what she had seen had converted her, went home." Charles himself read a paper on missions at the meeting in December of the Rural Deanery.[71] Arising from the discussion, it was agreed to form a Joint Churches Missionary Association for their area.

The Church of England was only one of the Christian churches in Almondbury and Barnsley in 1901. The non-conformists, as Charles called them, the Wesleyans, Methodists and Presbyterians, probably together attracted a similar number of adherents. Charles was disappointed at the

---

70   Albert William Icely was the vicar of Mold Green, Huddersfield, from 1894 to 1907. He had been in Tasmania in 1887-92 but otherwise had no overseas experience.

71   St Mary's belonged to the Silkstone Rural Deanery, of which Norris was the Rural Dean.

attitudes of some of his Anglican flock to dissenters (as he also called them). "It is rather surprising however sometimes to find how thoroughly trained Church people (or who ought to be) altogether miss the point of the relations of Church and Dissent.[72] They are either altogether hard and hostile, or else they go to the other extreme and compromise their principles." He was willing to have friendly relations with the nonconformists but, at a Nigger Entertainment Committee meeting in Longley, opposed a suggestion that St Mary's Class Niggers (a minstrel group) should perform in chapels if, by doing so, they helped "to increase the funds of nonconforming sects". "No true Churchman ought to be able to conscientiously go to help the spiritual work of nonconformists." The Church of England in Wakefield diocese worked with the nonconformists on temperance issues. Charles' bias showed when he recorded in his diary that "the non-cons displayed a tendency to rant" at a conference to discuss a government report on temperance, and the Bishop [of Wakefield, who was chairman] made some very apt remarks that the overstatement of a case was detrimental to it."

Charles was almost as suspicious of high church Anglicans as he was of nonconformists. St Peter's in Barnsley had a high church tradition. The priest there, John Lloyd Brereton, proposed to other clergy in the area that they should form a South West Yorkshire Clerical Society (SWYCS).[73] After an address at St Peter's given by the Bishop of Lebombo, the visiting clergy were surprised "to find ourselves ushered into church, and after a wait of 20 minutes or more, Brereton appeared clothed in gorgeous vestments, followed by a man clothed in a greasy tailcoat bearing a book". They celebrated "mass" (Charles used the inverted commas to signal his disapproval of the term), at which no one communicated, and then sprung on the assembled group the idea of the SWYCS. Norris tactfully offered to host the next meeting. It turned out that Brereton and others wanted the Litany to be said in Latin if there was no "mass". The discussion at the next meeting, which followed a "splendid address" by Walter Frere of the Community of the Resurrection on "Nationality in Religion", was disputatious.[74] Charles noted that "this must be one of those societies which the pen of Walter Walsh delights to attack".[75] He and his colleagues at St Mary's called the SWYCS the Sou' West Wind.

72   Church people refers here to members of the Church of England. Nonconformists were often referred to as Chapel people, because their meeting places were called chapels, not churches.

73   John Lloyd Brereton was the priest in charge of St Peter's, Barnsley, from 1881 to 1905. He had been a curate at St Mary's from 1867 to 1881.

74   Walter Howard Frere (1863-1938) was a cofounder of the Community of the Resurrection and its first superior. He later became Bishop of Truro from 1923 to 1935.

75   Walter Walsh (1847-1912) was a writer and journalist. He wrote a critique of the Oxford Movement, *The Secret History of the Oxford Movement* (1897).

When they went away for a day together, Charles had an interesting conversation with Norris about the big decline in the number of men seeking to be ordained. Charles suggested that recruits should be drawn from a wider field. Norris disagreed because "working-men parsons were not as a rule satisfactory". He thought that standards had been too low in the past, and so men "had come to think little of the life". He also said that the opening up of careers in social work enabled men who wanted to help others to do so without being ordained. He was working on the issues, and had been in correspondence with the Wesleyans and Congregationalists who were having similar experiences. He was to give an address on the supply of clergy at a conference in York a few weeks later.

As we have seen, Charles was concerned, especially at Almondbury, about the lack of interest in the church among the population. He therefore grabbed the opportunity to express his views when the Bishop asked the clergy what they thought were the main barriers to the influence of the church in the current social and economic conditions. At the time Charles was in Almondbury where he had a low opinion of the teachers at the Longley Sunday Schools, but felt that his men's Bible Class was a success.

With this in mind, he wrote a letter to the Bishop along the following lines. What children were taught in Sunday school was too dogmatic and did not relate to their lives. (His actual words were "did not reach [their] true feelings" and gave them "no firm ground on which to stand".) Once a lad went to work in the mills and workshops, where religion was not taken seriously, he gave up the church and everything connected with it, as his father had done before, "because there is nothing in it that appeals to him". The remedy was to focus on Bible classes whose teachers have "the power of leading rather than driving". There should be classes for both lads and men, with incentives to attend provided by prizes and various clubs. He concluded: "The working man is quite ready to be friendly, but his recollections of Sunday School have left a wrong impression in his mind as to what the church really is. My experience of socialists and even agnostics is that in most cases they are ready to take a clergyman as their leader if once they are satisfied that he is a rational animal."

Charles went to Wakefield two days before the move to Barnsley to hear the Bishop talk about what he had learned from the replies to his questions to the clergy. He was disappointed that he chose to avoid controversial subjects but pleased that he "quoted my remark about lads and mills and discipline, among other things".

Charles enjoyed conferences and other meetings of clergy especially when there was time for informal conversations. He went to the triennial festival at Leeds Clergy School in June, arriving in time for breakfast but having missed the early Holy Communion because "there was such a vicious head wind to cycle against". Even to arrive by breakfast he must have set off very early, as the distance to Leeds was well over twenty miles. The day consisted of services, lunch, speeches and talks. The

Bishop of Bath and Wells preached a "homely sermon" at Mattins. Charles thought that Burrows, the Principal of LCS when Charles was there, with whom he had supper, felt rather out of the festivities.

The first LCS man to be made Bishop, Frederick Baines, whom Charles had met in Durban in 1897, was there. He formally became the Bishop of Natal later in the year when he was consecrated in Cape Town Cathedral. Others from his year at LCS, one of whom was Norris, presented him with a ring and cross to honour his appointment. In the evening Norris opened a discussion on the reform of Convocation, "and found the junior clergy very revolutionary". Charles did not stay for it as he had a long ride back to Barnsley.

Later in the year, he attended the Diocesan conference at Wakefield with Cholmeley. They had intended to go by bicycle, but Charles had a boil on his rear end so they took the train. The conference was a good one, as far as Charles was concerned, and very crowded. "The Bishop hit the ritualists [clergy, usually high churchmen, who emphasised rituals in their services] hard when he spoke of the whimsical ideas at the present day." Other speakers "pleaded for the return to the good old-fashioned English Sunday" and discussed ways of promoting unity among Christians. Charles was active socially: "It was very jolly meeting old friends once again and have a thorough good talk with them."

Charles always liked to read, and he also liked to record what reading he had done.

This was but one example of his passion to write down everything that happened. He kept a record of his reading in the last five months of 1901. It amounted to about eight hours a week. Most of the books he read were on theological topics, bible studies or the work of the church.

Charles' diary for 1901 is our only source for insights into his life and work in Yorkshire parishes between 1897 and 1908. (We return later in the next chapter to the journals about the holidays he and Marion took during those years.) As we have seen, it reveals a serious young man who was prepared to work hard and learn the job. He was well organised and liked to impose structure on his life and the church activities for which he was responsible. He managed his relations with the many volunteers and helpers in the parish reasonably well. The diary contains reflections on how best to do this in particular cases, but we should allow for the possibility that he underreported cases that did not go too well. His faith was strong, and his views about liturgy and theology were fairly middle-of-the-road Church of England ones. He was disappointed that too few other people shared his commitment to the faith and the church but believed that he could help to bring some of them round to what he called "a right feeling".

Although he worked hard, he also played hard. He liked to get as much exercise as possible, which in practice – given his busy schedule – was mostly achieved by cycling. He was not put off by inclement weather, of which there was much in the winter months in Almondbury. He also played football, cricket and tennis when the opportunity arose. He enjoyed the company of friends, who were mainly other clergy. Altogether, he could reasonably claim that he had a jolly time in Almondbury and Barnsley in 1901.

Family

Soon after Charles and Marion moved to Bradford in 1897, his mother died at home in Headley. She was 63 and had been married to Charles' father, Theo, for 28 years. She left half of her not insignificant estate to Charles and half in a Trust to Emma.

Although older than his wife, Theo was still in good health at 73. He continued to live in Headley where Emma took over housekeeping duties, which included managing two young domestic servants, one of whom was the cook. As the only son, Charles felt some responsibility for ensuring that his father and sister were all right, although they were quite capable of looking after themselves. Theo was naturally concerned about Emma's future. In a private conversation with Charles in January 1901, he "was evidently keen on getting her settled with some decent fellow, but she will persist on distributing her favours broadcast, and especially on those nine or ten years younger than herself."

Both Theo and Emma came to stay with Charles and Marion in Yorkshire on a number of occasions, and Charles and Marion visited them in Headley when they could. Emma joined Charles and Marion for their summer holidays, which are described in detail in the next chapter.

Emma's visits to Yorkshire often took place when Theo went on a trip of his own. Thus, she went to Almondbury in May of 1900 when Theo was visiting his younger brother John in Dorset. The following year she was there again in February when Theo went to Brighton where his older sister, Henrietta, was ill. Soon afterwards, Henrietta moved to Upper Norwood, and Theo spent time with her there too. On 31 March 1901, the day of the census, while Theo was with Henrietta, Emma was visiting her cousins in Dulwich nearby. Three cousins, Louisa Brownrigg, her sister Laura Key and Mary Woodthorpe were there, together with Louisa's two unmarried daughters Kathleen and Hilda Brownrigg. (Henrietta died in May, aged 80.)

There was a major crisis in the family later in the year. Charles recorded each stage in his diary as it unfolded, under headlines in capital letters. The first entry on 28 August 1901 was A CRISIS AT HEADLEY. "Emma has been letting herself well in for it at last, and one can hardly say what the end of it will be. After a space of just three weeks of tennis and picnic acquaintance she has got engaged to a fellow without money, profession or even prospects as far as we can gather. It was sprung suddenly on Father, and without having had time to think the matter over he has evidently given an unconditional consent!" Theo later had second thoughts and wanted to back out.

The wife of the rector of Headley, Mrs

Laverty, was pushing for a wedding at Easter. Charles therefore wrote to her suggesting that any wedding should wait until Girling, the man in question, was making an income of his own. "I should not think any man worthy of Emma who would be mean enough to settle down on what money Emma has without any effort on his part... I believe this is the only way in which I can get round Father and put him in a more comfortable frame of mind. If he felt he was opposed altogether, I am afraid the worry might shorten his life, and I am sure it would be an ever-present sorrow to Emma if she felt she had acted against his will." He also wrote to Girling "with the idea of gleaning from him his intention to work and his prospects. As far as we have at present heard, he makes his money by singing, and had the magnificent income of £1 per week when in full work!!!"

Mrs Laverty and the rector were in full agreement not to push for an Easter wedding. But Theo was still very upset and was not helped by his brother John who was staying there and had "old fashioned ideas of propriety". Theo thought that nothing further could be done at the moment, and things should take their course. He wrote to Emma's (and Charles') Uncle Thomas, her mother's brother, who responded by writing an insulting letter to Emma. "In a disgustingly caddish way", he said that Girling may only be a beach singer.

In the meantime, Charles had received a reply from Girling which was "not altogether satisfactory. He does not seem to realise the income business at all and speaks of being married at Easter." Although Charles had heard that he was a "thoroughly decent fellow", he suspected that Girling was more attracted to Emma's secure financial circumstances than to Emma herself. Theo's concerns were similar. In a letter to Charles, he said that he did not see why he should leave his money for Girling to spend. Charles broke this gently to Emma, expecting that she would pass it on to Girling. Emma's response in a letter to Charles was that she and Girling had given up the idea of a wedding in the spring and were ready to wait for years. Charles reflected "it will be that wait which will show of what sort Girling really is".

Theo wanted Charles to go to Headley to talk to Emma and Girling, to try to discover what Girling had been doing. For various reasons a trip was difficult to arrange. Then, to Charles' surprise, he heard that they were all coming to Barnsley. "Father evidently does not approve of them travelling alone, so he is coming as chaperone! Emma is very keen on bringing Girling up. I am afraid the situation will be somewhat strained."

About five weeks after Charles first heard about Girling, he started a new page in his diary with the headline: THE HEADLEY CRISIS ARRIVES AT BARNSLEY. He went for a walk with Girling and "had a thorough good talk with him. He is a pleasant and harmless sort of individual as far as actual vice is concerned. But all his worldly possessions consist of £20 a year and a powerful voice. His weak spot is want of energy, and I believe he would settle down on Emma's money if he got the chance without a murmur." He told Girling that he should earn at least £100 a year before he should think of marrying. Girling floated some idea about his sister starting him in the music profession, but Charles was unimpressed. "Altogether I do not think things are looking very rosy as far as Emma is concerned. Our main line certainly is to prevent things hurrying on too fast."

Girling and Emma went to Lincolnshire for a few days to stay with his sister. Theo remained in Barnsley until Emma returned. He seemed to enjoy his visit. He went for walks and got to know the neighbourhood and nearby country quite well. He liked Barnsley better than Bradford where he had visited Charles in a prior year. He was eating better than Charles had ever seen him before and was more careful of himself. He was resigned about Emma, expecting her to get married. He and Charles had "been doing our best to let her see clearly what it will be like keeping house on £250 or £300 a year. The worst of it will be that, unless she has introductions, she will be thrown onto a lower grade of society than that to which she is accustomed."

Girling stayed in Lincolnshire when Emma returned to Barnsley. "She said he was rather depressed when she left and was talking about not marrying on under £500 a year! I think he is beginning to feel that it is a bit off now that he has woken up to the meaning of getting engaged. He is not so keen on work." He did not reply to the letters Emma wrote to him after she left him. This prompted more capital letters in Charles' diary: "The Headley Crisis has now become THE HEADLEY MYSTERY. Girling has disappeared!!! Leaving no trace!!!

... What has happened? Has he bolted abroad? If so, where has he found the money to do so?"

Two weeks after Theo and Emma went back to Headley, and two months after the crisis was first declared, the final headline was penned: THE HEADLEY MYSTERY SOLVED, AND THE CRISIS CONCLUDED. There was a lady, Mrs Hillyer, who had initially encouraged Girling to pursue Emma. She now found him and talked to him. She then "wrote to Emma telling her that her most dignified course would be to write and break the engagement off, which she has done. I am sorry for Emma. It is rather a hard smack in the eye. But it may do her good, in the way of teaching her not to make herself so cheap to every fool she meets. It was a providential thing we were able to test the young gentleman's motives for getting engaged. The remarkable part is how he collapsed so utterly, suddenly and completely, without making the least effort to show that he had any manhood in him. He is a poor (in more senses than one) specimen."

Mrs Hillyer also did not escape Charles' censure. She "must be a bit of a snark. It was she who put him up to it, evidently thinking Emma had a good deal more money than she really had. And now she has got him out of it, without any danger of breach of promise – not that it would ever have come to that. But evidently she has been running the show, and when it has not paid in the way she expected, she has adroitly closed it."

Having escaped one engagement, Emma did not lose time in entering another. Within a few months, she had become engaged to

George Odling. She had known him for many years, at least since 1895 when she and Charles went boating with him in Oxford. We do not know the reasons for the consolidation of their relationship. Had George had an interest in Emma for a long time, and struck when she was reeling from the Girling affair? Or was it Emma who sought a refuge after the Girling debacle? Or perhaps there was a growing realisation on both sides that they would be happy together. In any event, the relationship was sufficiently secure to take them through their marriage and parenthood, up till Emma's death.

At least there would be no financial problems. George, unlike Girling, was better off than Emma. He had just inherited a substantial amount of money and property from his uncle, Alfred Hutchison Smee, who died in November 1901. He was living in the house his uncle had built in the fine garden created by his grandfather, Alfred Smee, in Wallington, Surrey. Normally, weddings were held in the home town or village of the bride. But George and Emma were married on 10 July 1902, not at Headley, but at St Mary's Beddington, where George's parents had been married, and his grandparents, Alfred and Elizabeth Smee, and uncle Alfred Hutchison Smee, were buried. Charles officiated, assisted by the rector of St Mary's. The reception was held at George's house, The Grange, Wallington.[76]

George Smee Odling came from a family of distinguished scientists. His father, William Odling, was Waynflete Professor of Organic Chemistry at Oxford. His mother, Mary Odling, was the daughter of Alfred Smee, who invented a battery, was surgeon to the Bank of England, and wrote many scientific books and papers. His uncle, Alfred Hutchison Smee, was also a scientist, although less renowned than his own father, Alfred Smee.[77] George grew up in Oxford and went to Magdalen College. His degree was in Natural Science, with physics being his speciality. He worked as a civil engineer, mainly on water projects in Surrey. In 1900 he was appointed a magistrate in Surrey.

A condition of Alfred Hutchison Smee's will was that George should change his name from Odling to Odling-Smee. The intention was to preserve the name Smee in Alfred's branch of the family, as it would otherwise disappear on Alfred's death. George and Emma therefore changed their names by deed poll from Odling to Odling-Smee in October 1902. They lived in The Grange for the first few years of their marriage. After their first two children, Charles William (known as Bill) and Alfred John (known as Jack), were born they moved to Guildford. There they had a third child, Barbara (Barbie), and Marion was her godmother. A year later, in 1911, disaster struck: Emma died of food poisoning at the age of only 39. George, left with three small

---

76   At the time, the address was sometimes given as The Grange, Carshalton.

77   Further detail about George Odling's family is available under Histories at www.odlingfamily.com.

children, married again, to Amelia Casson, who had been one of Emma's bridesmaids.

Within days of Emma's wedding, Theo went to Switzerland where his youngest sister, Charlotte, was seriously ill. He may have travelled with either his brother John, his other remaining sister Decima, or both. Charlotte died at St Beatenberg, near Interlaken, on 27 July 1902.

Theo's life changed after Emma got married. He no longer had her company, and he had to engage a housekeeper to replace Emma in the domestic sphere. He was assisted in both respects by his family. Decima, who had been living with Charlotte in St Leonards now spent much time with Theo – we do not know how much, but she may have moved in fairly permanently. Three of their nieces (Charles' cousins) came for separate visits of a few weeks at a time: Louisa Brownrigg and Laura Key, both of them daughters of Theo's sister Mary Sophia, and Mary Woodthorpe, the daughter of Theo's sister Rosina Sarah.

Charles also visited Theo. He always went in the summer at the end of his holidays, which are described in Chapter 4. He usually went at least one other time during the year. He often had serious talks with Theo on those occasions. Theo would have liked Charles and Marion to move to southern England to be closer to him, but "from his point of view the North is far better than the colonies". Theo knew that, ever since his South African trip in 1896-97, Charles wanted to go and work in one of the British Empire countries with wide open spaces. Charles understood that he could not do this as long as Theo was alive. The North was as far away as he should go.

Charles and Theo sometimes spoke about religious matters. After one conversation in January 1901, Charles wrote: "His ideas are very interesting, in that he is entirely independent. He has a strong faith and takes a very broad view of the truth. He has a happy way of seeing the inherent good in things, and thoroughly realises that charity is the essence of religion. I don't know that he has a very clear idea of what the church is, but he evidently thinks there is a good deal in her position. He reads the bible carefully, and judges from that, unaided by any other help beyond his own reason." These remarks suggest that Charles, who was still only 30, was able to have an adult conversation with his father, whom he obviously respected. Theo, in turn, could open up to his son. Such a father/son connection was not too common in those days of cool and formal family relationships.

Decima, Theo's only surviving sister, died in Menton, France, on 20 February 1905 aged 78. His only surviving brother, John, died in his house in Tulse Hill, London, on 20 September 1907, also aged 78. Only three weeks later, Theo himself died in the same house on 10 October, aged 83. He was the last of the twelve siblings to die, and the longest lived.

Charles was the executor of both Theo's and his uncle John's estates. In addition, he was a trustee of the trust his mother had set up for Emma. There were many complications emanating from the property and other transactions that the Hahns had engaged in over the decades. Charles had quite a responsibility for managing it all, although much of the heavy work was done by his faithful solicitors, Foyer and Co., of Essex Street, off the Strand. His inheritance from Theo, added to what he had inherited from his mother, gave him a private income that enabled him to donate funds to church work in Africa, and to forgo a stipend in at least one case. He and Marion could also afford to travel abroad and to take longer holidays than would have been possible if he was wholly dependent on his salary as a clergyman.

Meanwhile Marion's mother, Catherine Forrester, had died on 27 July 1903, aged 61, in Marylebone, where she had been living for a few years with her unmarried, oldest daughter Jessie.

CHAPTER 4

SUMMER HOLIDAYS

From 1898 to 1907 Charles and Marion went away for a holiday for a few weeks every summer (winter in 1902). Before she married in 1902, Emma went with them. Charles kept a journal for each trip recording their adventures – and they did have some real adventures. They may also have had holidays in 1896 and 1897, but we have no record of such. However, the journal for the days in 1905 when they were in Llanfairfechan compares the town then with how it had been nine years earlier, suggesting that they were there in 1896. If they had a summer holiday in 1897, it would probably have been their honeymoon following their wedding in June. In 1895, Charles and Emma had a boating holiday on the Thames, as we have already seen.

Before describing the holidays, we need to acquaint ourselves with the style that Charles adopted in the journals. Most strikingly, they were all written in the third person. He continued the conceit he had used earlier when writing about life in Headley, according to which there was The Insane Society consisting of the Mad Hatter (himself), the March Hare (Emma) and the Dormouse (Muriel Laverty). When Marion arrived on the scene, she was given the unflattering title of the Dodo. As Muriel Laverty did not join them for the summer holidays, he sometimes referred to them collectively as the Touring Section of the Insane Society. Once he called them the "famed Society for the Cultivation of Hilarity among all Classes of the Community". They were also the Noble Three (the Noble Two after Emma married), and, more often, just the Expedition. Whatever the name of the group, Charles wrote in the third person throughout the ten-year period, and always called Marion, Emma and himself by their nicknames, the Dodo, the March Hare and the Mad Hatter respectively.

As noted earlier, Charles' style when writing about his activities in the third person had hints of Jerome K Jerome. He was humorous, especially when describing mishaps, of which there were quite a few. He liked to have adventures, and adventures do not always turn out as intended. But he could also be long-winded and contrived. He did not have the elegance and light touch of Jerome K Jerome. Nevertheless, the accounts in his journals are well worth reading, both as a record of his many interesting holidays, and as a picture of the times. The writings were illustrated with Charles' sketches and watercolours and, starting in 1900, Marion's photographs. On occasions, rather than write a continuous text he drew a series of cartoons with brief captions to describe what was happening. The illustrations in the journals are so vivid and apt that they are a vital part of the stories.

Seven of the holidays between 1898 and 1907 were in England and Wales, and three were on the Continent (Italy, Normandy and Norway). With the exception of the Italian holiday, they were planned to provide plenty of exercise – something which Charles saw as an essential component of a jolly time. Two of the holidays were cycling trips, and there was a considerable amount of cycling, by Charles at least, on some of the others. They camped in fields on three of the trips. They lived on sailing boats on the Norfolk Broads, and another year spent every day travelling down the River Wye in a small boat. On many of the other holidays Charles found opportunities to take out small boats for a punt or a row. When near the sea, they bathed regularly.

All of the holidays began in Yorkshire: in Bradford in 1898 and 1899, Almondbury in 1900, Barnsley in 1901 to 1906, and Dewsbury Moor in 1907. And they all ended in Headley, where Charles spent time with Theo, Emma (until she married) and friends before returning to work in Yorkshire. The usual form was for Charles to leave Yorkshire on his bicycle while Marion took the train and the bulk of the luggage.

They went to North Devon for their holiday in 1898. Their base was Lynton where they took rooms on the North Cliff with fine views across the Bristol Channel to the South Wales hills. Their main activities were walking

and sketching, with breaks for picnics and tea, brewed with water heated on a small stove. After walking to Woody Bay one day, Charles thought he had spotted a short cut back to Lynton round the base of the cliff, thereby avoiding a zigzag path to the top of the cliff and a descent the other side. However, they encountered a series of obstacles: huge rocks which they had to climb over on their hands and knees, a path up the side of a cliff about

150 feet high, with rough steps cut into the side of the precipice, and a locked gate marked "Private", which they climbed over. Despite these hazards, "the three were undaunted. There was no idea of turning back! Besides the tide was on the turn!! Would there be no time to retrace their steps? No, they would 'scorn the h'action'."[78]

The women were wearing, as they always did, long skirts below tight belted waists, hardly the most convenient clothing for such an adventurous walk. Charles sketched them scrambling over rocks, crawling up the cliff face and climbing over the gate. He himself enjoyed the challenge of the uncharted route and concluded that "never have the three done a short cut in more time. They arrived at North Cliff Cottage "fair clemmed" for want of nourishment."[79] On the way to Lynton, they had spent a night in Ilfracombe, which

---

78 "Scorn the h'action" is a line from *The Lancashire Lass*, a play by H J Byron. Uneducated people who dropped their h's were thought to insert h's in the wrong places when speaking to educated people.

79 "Fair clemmed" was a Yorkshire expression meaning very hungry.

was a popular holiday centre for less well-off people. Charles' disdain for such places, and also his pedantic writing style, are well illustrated by his comments: "After partaking of refreshment, they set out to explore the ancient town – ancient it must be, for it was able to send six ships to the siege of Calais to Liverpool's one – and after a general survey have come to the unanimous conclusion (and it must be remembered that the members of the Touring Section are by no means inexperienced judges of such matters) that if the flavour of the "profanum vulgus" were not so distinctly prominent, it would be a nice enough place, for the coast scenery is rugged and grand, and there are many pretty bits about. But think of the discord – a glorious sun, falling like a ball of fire into a golden sea, whilst near at hand there are a dozen Salvationists making good use of their lungs, a Punch and Judy show, and a brass band, to say nothing of half a hundred children yelling and moving rapidly about. No, the Insane Society is anti-social in its tendencies. It longs to be away from mankind, alone with nature, where it can listen to the charm of its own peculiar noises undisturbed."

There was class snobbery in these remarks, as well as irony. But it was certainly true that Charles, Marion and Emma really did love nature and enjoyed it best when other people were not around.

They spent 10 days in Headley after their holiday in North Devon. It was the first summer since Charles' mother had died, and therefore especially important for Charles to be with his father. One day Theo took them

for a picnic, "which he ran entirely on his own lines, and a very pleasant time we had of it". They went in his horse-drawn chaise to Selborne, where they visited the grave of Gilbert White, the naturalist. On the way back "Father then decided he would take the chaise up to the top of the Hanger [hill], but everyone we met told us such a thing would be impossible, and said the only way round was by Newton, three miles off. This only made Father more determined..." They soon found themselves in a farm lane with such deep ruts that the wheels of the chaise did not reach the bottom and could not turn. "Old Chuffles [the horse] was soon out of breath and required frequent intervals of rest; and what with father pulling at his head and me pushing at the back, we were both glad to reach the top."

Marion and Emma walked up, and the party grilled some chops on a piece of wire netting over a fire. They took a different route down but were blocked by a gate with chains nailed round it. They managed to force it open "and the triumphant procession moved through, congratulating themselves on being public benefactors in doing something to keep open a right of way." With both Charles and Theo leading their families into near-impassable routes in the same month, though in different parts of the country, it appears that the apple had not fallen far from the tree.

Charles and Marion concluded their summer holiday in 1898 with a week based in Southwold on the Suffolk coast. There they joined members of Marion's family, including her mother and two of her sisters and their husbands. Charles' main activities were cycling, bathing in the sea and visiting churches.

Charles' record of the summer holiday in 1899 is missing, except for the maps he drew of the route. The main part of the holiday was a trip in a rowing boat on the River Wye from Hereford to Chepstow, sixty-five miles away. They followed it with another boating trip on the upper reaches of the Thames just below Cricklade, but this was cut short by bad weather. They took a tent with them and set up six camps on the Wye and one on the Thames.

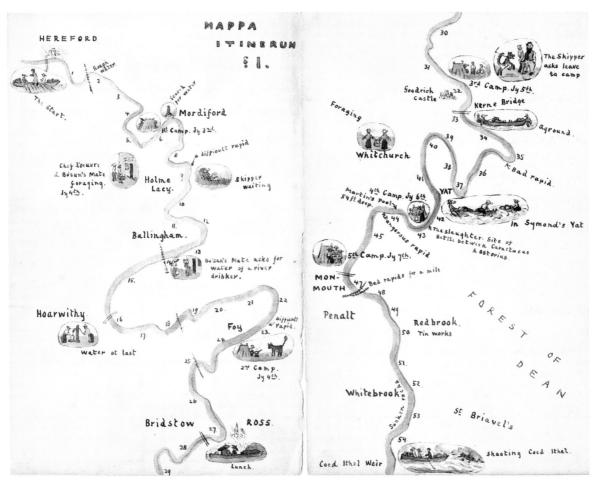

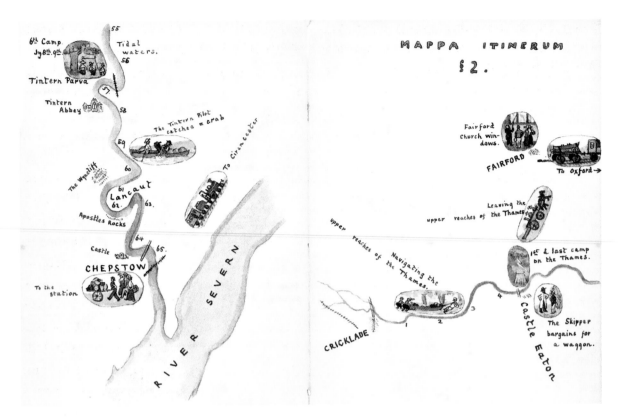

The maps were beautifully drawn and painted. The first one, entitled Mappa Itinerum §1, showed the Wye and the second, Mappa Itinerum §2, the Thames. The rivers were painted blue and drawn precisely to scale, with mileage markers and all the bends correctly located. Places of interest, such as Tintern Abbey and Goodrich Castle, and characteristics of the river, such as rapids and sunken rocks, were noted.

The most attractive features of the maps were the tiny watercolours of the holiday party. No more than one inch long and usually less, they were oval miniatures showing their tent at each camping spot, with its occupants cooking outside or doing other jobs, the party in the boat (including both rowing and pulling the boat, shooting rapids and running aground), encounters with locals (including a cow), and taking the train at the end of the trip on the Wye.

In 1900, Charles, Marion and Emma were joined by a fourth person for their holiday, a bicycle tour of North Wales. We know nothing about her except that she was a woman. As usual, Charles left home in Barnsley on his bicycle and met Marion, Emma and the new person in Chester, where they went for a scull on the River Dee. The next day, Marion and Emma took the train to Colwyn Bay, while Charles and the new person cycled together for thirty-five miles when the latter opted for the train for the last eleven miles and Charles boldly cycled on to Colwyn Bay. There was some concern about the stamina of the new person. "The three seasoned members, as they sat on the beach after supper at Colwyn Bay and watched the sun sink to rest over the hills above Llandudno in a blaze of golden light, came to the conclusion that the new member would soon have enough of it." As it turned out, they were wrong. She kept up well with the others all the way and was especially helpful in making practical arrangements. "She is now firmly installed as Courier of the Noble Society. She takes rooms, asks prices and does the general work of the Expedition in much more businesslike manner than any other member has been able to attain to."

The day they cycled from Colwyn Bay to Betws-y-Coed was very hot. The hotel where they were staying in Betws-y-Coed was hotter still, and the rooms not very attractive. They were therefore well disposed to follow the plan that Marion "produced out of her fertile brain" during supper. An hour after supper they left the hotel for a "midnight ride

through the heart of the mountainous district of Wales". The route to Barmouth, their next stop, involved "a long stiff climb" of almost 1200 feet over a pass. "As they mounted up, the dim outline of Moel Siabod towered up, standing out, mysterious in its indistinctness, against the waning light of sunset. The full moon, lightly veiled by a misty cloud, showed the forms of other peaks around." They passed through Blaenau Ffestiniog, a centre of slate quarrying, where "it was startling in the middle of the night, every now and then, to hear in the stillness the sudden slip of shale in the gigantic slate quarries". The road took them down to Harlech at sea level where looking back there "was a glorious sight. Hill and mountain rose up in rugged outline and, behind all, dawn was breaking. The clouds were suffused with a most delicate pink, and the white mists began to rise from out of the purple hills. The two would-be artists [Charles and Emma] drank it in."

They were exhausted when they finally arrived at Barmouth, thirty-nine miles from Betws-y-Coed. It was still early, and their hotel had not yet opened. Charles therefore "took the opportunity to have a wallow in the sea". The women were too tired, but they were proud of their achievement. To subsequent

generations, it appeared all the greater in that they were wearing long skirts and riding bicycles without sophisticated gears.

The cycling part of the holiday came to a premature end after Marion fell off and hurt her knee as they were approaching Worcester. With no more group cycling in prospect, the new person went home, and the others took the train to Oxford. After one night, they moved on to Shillingford for a few more nights. Charles and Emma rode their bicycles there, but they took a wrong turn and they "found themselves on a by-road which finally led into a field and there ended. Nothing daunted, they pressed on, lifting their machines over stiles

What
the bicycle tour
came to.

and other obstacles, until they emerged in the little village of Long Wittenham." Charles' leadership had taken them eight miles further than necessary. All three then "tumbled into a boat and had a thoroughly slack time on the river" [Thames], a favourite pastime of theirs.

From Shillingford they went to Headley, with Charles cycling the whole fifty-three miles, Emma part of the way, and Marion sticking to the train. Charles kept detailed records of weather, distances travelled and road surfaces. He had cycled 358 miles in 13 days, Emma 235 miles, Marion 166 miles and the new person 201 miles.

For their holiday in 1901, they decided to go sailing on the Norfolk Broads, having rejected the Lake District on the grounds that it rained too much there. They met up in Kings Lynn, Charles having cycled all the way there from Barnsley (125 miles), Marion having cycled only the last stretch from Sleaford where she had met Charles, and Emma having come by train from London. They took five days to cycle to Wroxham where they hired a lugsail yacht for a week and stowed their bicycles with the boat owner. The boat was called "The Mystery" which Charles thought was quite appropriate as it was "a mystery as to how they are all going to sleep on board, or as to where they are going, or as to how they are going to cook their food, or if they will be able to get the thing along at all, or whether it will buck up in a breeze and chuck them all overboard". In fact, things turned out quite well. The cabin of the yacht when the awning was up was a "luxury compared with living in

— Preparing Lunch —

a tent". They sat on seats and not camp stools which suddenly gave way. There was room to stow things away, and there was a good stove. Most importantly, they managed to sail the boat successfully.

Naturally, there were a few mishaps. Marion fell into the water as she was trying to step from the bank into the passing dinghy which they towed behind the yacht. They ran aground, on one occasion requiring Charles to

jump into the water to push the boat off the mud bank while the others pushed with poles. And they ran out of vital supplies when they misjudged how long it would take to find a shop that was open.

There were plenty of subjects to sketch, "what with wherries with their big brown-black sails, and the cattle dotted about the marshes". But they were so busy "managing the craft, and cooking the meals, and washing up that there is hardly a moment to spare". In the mornings they bathed in the river. While the evenings "are almost the best part of the day. Everything is so still and quiet. The wind has dropped to sleep and sounds from passing boats travel far across the water. One can sit and watch the brown sailed wherries gliding silently by, and listen to the grasshopper chirping on the bank, and feel the spell of the moment. This is the real antidote to work. At such moments as these one is far from the stir and worry of everyday life. There are moments when the life of a wherryman – drifting on by warp and reach, sailing through the sunshine and the twilight – seems specially blessed."

After returning the yacht and collecting their bicycles, they headed for Cambridge, with Charles cycling the whole way as usual and the others only part of the way. Charles was so attached to Oxford that he could not resist the notion that Cambridge was inferior. He found Midsummer Common disappointing compared with "the towpath at Oxford, … Christchurch Meadows, …the Broad walk and the Barges. Poor Cambridge!" He acknowledged that King's Chapel was "most inspiring" but the rain was so dispiriting that the party wanted to leave Cambridge as soon as possible. The next day they went to London where they stayed the night with Marion's mother in Marylebone. Charles and Emma then went on to Headley.

In 1902 they went to Italy. It was their first trip to the Continent together. It was also the only trip in ten years that was not in June or July. They left England (Charles and Marion from Barnsley, and Emma from Headley) on 14 February and returned on 26 March. The reason for the change of season was presumably because Emma was planning to get married in the summer, and this was their last opportunity to have a holiday together. The holiday fell into five sections, each about one week long. First, they took a boat from Tilbury to Naples. It called at Gibraltar and Marseille, but they did not go ashore. After that, they spent a week or so in each of Naples, Rome, Florence and Venice. It was their Grand Tour.

Unlike their other holidays, the emphasis was on visiting museums, galleries, churches and historical sites. There was no opportunity for the cycling and boating activities that they often enjoyed on holiday, although they did plenty of walking. Their plan to climb Vesuvius did not materialise because of bad weather. There was, however, time to sketch and take photographs. They were conscientious about visiting all the main sites. One day in Rome they went "down to the Vatican once more and did a hard morning's work". In Florence, Charles recorded that they put in "a solid morning's work in the way of frescoes". Most of the sites exceeded their expectations. Thus, the interest of Pompeii "was far more than we ever expected". The paintings in the Uffizi and the Pitti Palace, many of which they knew from reproductions, held their attention – at least in the case of Charles and Emma, the "would be artists". "It is difficult to say which contains the most beautiful – the Pitti or the Uffizi."

Charles had a traditional Church of England adverse reaction to the ornate decoration of many Catholic churches, and to the practices of their worshippers. He was disappointed on entering St Peter's. "The proportions of the building certainly are very grand, but then the general effect is altogether spoilt by decoration. The massiveness of the central columns is broken by niches for statues, and by slabs of marble which adorn them." The Church of the Gesù in Rome, which they visited just after seeing the Pantheon, "a splendidly stern building", was "the most gorgeous in Rome, which perhaps helped us appreciate the plain grandeur of the Pantheon all the more". In St Peter's, they watched the faithful kissing the toe of St Peter's statue. "The profanum vulgus performed the ceremony without any preparation. The more refined polished the toe with their handkerchief first, whilst the ultra-delicate covered it with their handkerchief and kissed through!" A room in the Vatican devoted to the Immaculate Conception displayed "a magnificent casquet containing the dogma written in languages from all parts of the world". On reporting this in his journal, Charles exclaimed: "Poor Rome! Will she ever find her way back to the straight paths of biblical truth?" On their Sundays in Rome, Florence and Venice, they escaped such heresies by going to services in the English church.

Like all tourists, they had to contend with people asking for money, or offering unwanted services. Their guidebook warned them that people in Naples were "very importunate". They adopted an English stiff upper lip. "By preserving a stoical indifference to all that was going on around them, they got along very well." Compared with Naples, it was quite a relief to be able to walk through the streets of Rome "without being pestered on all sides". However, they slipped up in Florence and "were nicely had". In the Duomo, a man offered to show them round. They agreed, thinking he was a verger, only to discover that he was self-employed. There followed "the inevitable row in the road" and they ended up giving him 3 francs instead of the 5 francs he asked for. This experience may have made them more careful because they decided not to linger outside St Marco's in Florence, despite Ruskin's advice that an hour's study of the reliefs of the campanile "would be an inspiration for a lifetime". Charles thought that "it would require the stolidness of a bull of Bashan to be able to stand there for that length of time, with all the beggars, guides, cab-drivers and all the other riff-raff which go to make up the variety to be found in the streets of an Italian city pressing around".

The weather in Italy was not favourable for sightseeing, being cold and wet much of the time. In addition, all three members of the party suffered minor ailments, including colds, sore throats, stomach upsets and a swollen face. They still managed a full programme of visits but decided to go home earlier than they might have otherwise done. The train journey "through the mountains has been most lovely – full moon shining on the snowy peaks towering up right over the railway line – the sound of running waters from the melting snows – the dark mysterious shadows in the deep recesses where the moonbeams failed to reach – all this went to make up a scene of fairy enchantment".

But the English countryside also had a strong pull on Charles. When cycling to Headley from the station at the very end of the trip, "the air was full of the fresh scent of damp earth, the yellow celandine was twinkling in the hedge rows, blackbirds were piping tunefully to one another across the fields, while a mellow south-west wind blew softly through the land. Yes, it is good to be in England."

For their summer holiday in 1903, the first since Emma had married, Charles and Marion

Resting.

Double reefed in a gale.

revisited the Norfolk Broads. This time we can let Charles' own words sum up the trip. "Well, the cruise is now practically over. It has been one of great variety – rain, cold, heat, wind – the only thing with which the crew has not been favoured has been a dead calm, and all the way through, even at the worst, they have

thoroughly enjoyed it. When the tempest has been at its height, the wind whistling through the rigging, and the rain beating down upon the awnings, they have felt with Katisha:

There is beauty in the bellow of the blast
There is grandeur in the growling of the gale.[80]

When the sun has been pouring from the heavens, they have lain in it until the skin has peeled off from their hands and arms, and their noses have shone like ruby lamps upon a summer's night, and exclaimed "this is to live". The more one sees of Broadland, the more one feels the fascination of it stealing over one and entwining itself into one's life. There is nothing exactly like it. If there is hard work wanted, it is there, and plenty of it at any time. If one is of a lazy turn of mind, there is nothing to do, beyond cooking the next meal.

---

80   From a song of Katisha's in *The Mikado* by Gilbert and Sullivan.

Hickling Broad.   June 22. 1903.

If you wish to stop, you stop. If you wish to progress, you progress. All there is to do is to furl or hoist your sail as the case may be; and wherever you are, you have your house and all your belongings with you. There is no seeking shelter for the night because you are always at home. Then there is the constantly changing scenery – the fascination of the water – the soft-eyed cattle in the meadows – the tangle of wild flowers in the marshes – the multitude of birds – the reeds and rushes of the river and broad – the arch of the sky and the rolling clouds – the white marsh mists and the golden sunsets – one is ever living in the spirit of the 104th psalm."[81]

After returning the boat and picking up their bicycles, they headed for Norwich where they spent two nights, followed by one night in each of Ely and Oxford on their way to Headley. Charles cycled some of the way on each day, while Marion took the train. As though they had not had enough time on the water, in Ely

81   Verse 24 of psalm 104 in the King James version is: "O Lord, how manifold are thy works! In wisdom hast thou made them all: the earth is full of thy riches."

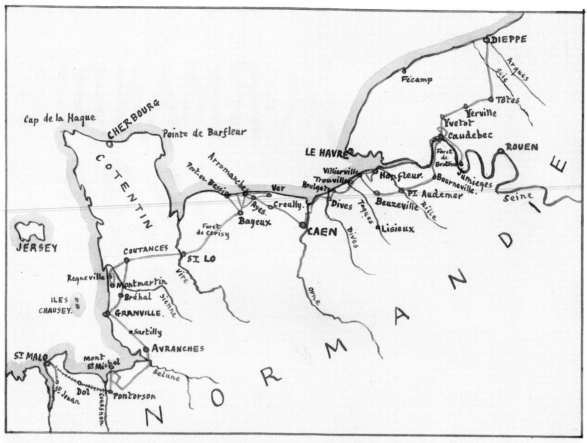

THE TRACK OF THE EXPEDITION. 1904.

they chartered a canoe "and went for a paddle on the Ouse – a somewhat cramped method of progress after the ease and comfort of the Jubilee [their boat on the Broads]".

Charles and Marion ventured to the Continent for their summer holiday in 1904. They took their bicycles on the ferry to St Malo in Brittany, and cycled through Normandy to Dieppe, from where they returned to England. They were in France for about three weeks. Although some days they cycled all day, they had many shorter rides, some legs on the train (on one such trip of twenty-eight miles, they had to pay a halfpenny for each bicycle!), and a few days when they stayed in the town where they were. They had plenty of time to look around and sketch, paint and take photographs.

There were a number of minor mishaps, beginning in England when they arrived at Marylebone station from Barnsley to find that their bicycles and luggage were not on the train. These arrived on a later train, giving them just enough time to cross London to Waterloo, and reach Southampton in time to catch the overnight boat to St Malo. In Mont

St Michel, Marion's sketch book "blew over the walls into the foaming waters below". She was never too keen on sketching, so it was probably not much of a loss for her. Between Coutances and St Lô, they were attacked by dogs. "The country people are all very friendly as we pass along, and often wish us bon voyage, but the dogs are far otherwise – they fly out suddenly from the cottage or shed where they are in hiding, barking fiercely, and come straight at the machine." The chickens on the road were another hazard as they "hurry nervously hither and thither, and then at the last moment decide to bolt for the farmyard. We have not killed one yet, although they have spoilt many a good coast." Motor cars were rare. They hardly met one in the first 12 days or so, but they became troublesome going along the coast road in the region around Deauville. Their bicycles suffered various punctures that Charles usually fixed on the road. As they were cycling towards Dieppe on their final day, both had punctures. While Charles was able to fix Marion's, he had to

1.-
July 2nd. Sat.
the Expedition set out from Caudebec-en-Caux. "Au revoir, Monsieur et Madame. Bon voyage."

2.- They ascend the hill behind the town.

3.- At 10 kilometres the Dodo bursts.

4.- They try a new tube in the valve, but with no success, so have to walk into Yvetot.

5.-
They find a repairing shop, & explain that the tyre is crev But the Mechanicien is at lunch, so they de cide to have some too.

6.- They return in 1½ hrs time & find the mechanicien stuck to the inner tube with Millenium puncture stop, & the fluid oosing from various holes. No patch will stick. They decide to have a new inner tube.

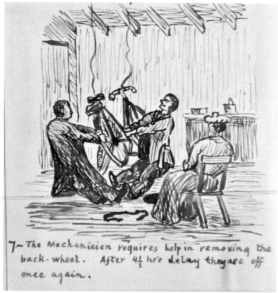

7.- The Mechanicien requires help in removing the back-wheel. After 4½ hrs delay they are off once again.

8.- But just through Yerville the Mad Hatter feels an omenous bump, & soon discovers that he also has crevé'd. He proceeds to locate the damage.

9.- Meanwhile the Dodo with commendable persistency searches the country for water, wherewith to locate the burst. A gentleman in attendance on cows understands that someone has fainted on the road.

get assistance from a mechanic who was not very skilled. This puncture and repair alone delayed them by 4½ hours. Charles told this part of the story in cartoon like sketches rather than the usual text.

Although the countryside was fairly flat, there were many small hills along the way. As the weather was mostly hot and sunny, some of the rides were exhausting. Near Arromanches one day when the sun was beating fiercely down, Marion made a comparison with cycling in the Swiss mountains. Charles explained in his diary that when she "talks about bicycling in the Swiss mountains, she means that, at that precise moment, bicycling anywhere is really the most inane and foolish performance that anyone could ever indulge in at any time".

The ride from Honfleur to Caudebec, a distance of forty-three miles, was the hardest one of the whole trip because of the headwind. On the steep climb up from the Risle valley, they felt the effects of the hill and the hot,

10.—
Once again on the road.
At Tôtes they turn into a Route Nationale & run to Dieppe.

windless day, and it was a relief to get into the breeze at the top of the hill. But they could really relax only when they reached the ferry across the Seine at Caudebec. A reward was that "the last part of the ride was very beautiful with the forest of Brotonne on one side and the river on the other".

They explored the towns and villages, especially the churches. "What a country this is for Norman churches. Iffleys and Adels are scattered in profusion up and down – Ryes, Ver, Asnelles, Vaux, and many others. It makes me long to settle down among them and study them bit by bit."[82] In

11.—On arriving at Dieppe, 11 p.m, they search diligently for Hotel d'Albion. At last they are compelled to ask. Their simple question produces much thought, but little else. A woman at last remembers that "it is feenished". And they had forwarded their baggage on there!

---

82 Iffley in Oxford and Adel in Leeds both have fine Norman churches.

The Seine from Caudebec. June 30. 04.

Caen, they "settled down to a study of the churches", many of which they visited, and "grand buildings they are". "The personality of the Conqueror of England still seems to dominate the place" although he has lost much of his "fearsomeness, since he is now known among the English community as Uncle Billy". This was the community that worshipped at the "little tin English church by the side of the canal", where Charles and Marion attended a Sunday service. By contrast, "St Etienne, William's church, is most impressive in its plain stern massiveness". They saw the spot where his body was buried, although "his bones have since been scattered to the winds by the Huguenots".

They enjoyed being near the sea on many of their rides and overnight stops. In Arromanches, they sat in their hotel room overlooking the sea "listening to the murmur of the outgoing tide, as a golden sunset melts gradually into the purple of the night." Two mornings later Charles was so overcome with "an inordinate desire to bathe" that "before he knew where he was, he found himself up to the neck in the briny with his pyjamas on! He did not stay there long, however, as the temperature did not altogether suit him."

Charles' summing up of the holiday was that they had had "a grand time and glorious weather. They have seen Normandy in the only really satisfactory way – on bicycles."

At Arromanches.   June 22. 1904.

In 1905, they decided to go back to North Wales for their summer holiday. This time they took a tent with them and camped near Abersoch rather than staying in hotels as in 1900. Although nearly all the journey was by train, they had to carry the tent and other camping equipment on their bicycles for the final stretch to the field where they camped. Charles' bicycle toppled over from the difficulty of balancing the load on it - he drew the scene in one of his humorous sketches. A more typical cycling misadventure occurred a few days later when Charles proposed to take a short cut home. After the first attempt ended at a cottage, they tried a route that came to a farm beyond which was a path that led steeply down into a valley. They followed it, "much to the surprise and interest of a herd of black cattle, who evidently had never seen bicycles before. But at the bottom there was no way through at all, and we had to retrace our steps once again." Another day they cycled along

On the way to the camping-ground.— transport difficulties.

the sands but had to cross about a mile of boulders to reach a path that climbed 200 feet to the road above.

Camp life was hard work – "there is but little time for lazing or moralising" as "they are either preparing the next meal or partaking

93

of it". Charles kicked over the kettle just as it was on the boil, and accidentally left the beef in the drinking water. He was disappointed to see that the Chapel had "a strong hold on the affections of the people" with the Church being "right out of it in these parts". He asked "whose fault is it?" but declined to answer his rhetorical question. They were in a Welsh-speaking area, which created some difficulties. Marion tried to buy a handkerchief and emerged from the shop without knowing whether she had bought one or many, or how much she had paid. Charles' attempt to buy some chops in a small butcher's shop ended up in his "being the happy possessor of a scrag-end of a neck of mutton for the sum of 7½d."

There were some very strong winds while they were there. The morning after the first windy night, they "bathed in a boisterous sea". In the evening they "went round to smoke a pipe in the next camp". On their way there, they noticed that the sea was higher than they had ever seen it before. While there, they heard that someone was struggling in the waves. It turned out not to be a person, but the wooden bathing machines that had been standing on the sand until undermined by the high sea and washed away. The men in the group plunged into the sea to save what they could. "They managed to tip two machines over onto their backs higher up the sand bank, but within five minutes one of them had careered out to sea and gone to pieces like a tinder box." The wind the following night was even stronger – "so violent that at times it seemed as if the tent would be torn from its moorings". But it weathered the storm "splendidly", and Charles and Marion managed to sleep "in spite of all". In the morning they found that the sea had created a four foot drop down to the shore where previously there had been a sandy slope.

They decided to break up the camp after nearly two weeks and spend their last five days in North Wales in rooms in Llanfairfechan. Charles had been there nine years before, and he did not like the changes that had taken place since then. "There are shelters along the front and niggers on the beach, and the place seems more than double the size."[83] He hoped that Abersoch would be protected from too many holiday makers coming by train: "May Abersoch be preserved for long from a railway and excursionists." He was also disparaging about the visitors to Llandudno, a larger seaside resort, "where everything is provided to interest and amuse all those who have never learnt the art of interesting and amusing themselves".

---

83   Charles used the word 'nigger' here to mean a member of either a minstrel group or a socially disadvantaged class rather than a dark-skinned person. In his usage, it was not a derogatory term.

Charles and Marion became friendly with the people staying nearby. In addition to a number of outings together, five of them (Charles and Marion, and another man and two women) went on a forty-eight-mile bicycle ride, "the event of the week". It involved a ride along the coast followed by a climb up into the mountains along the same route as the midnight ride five years earlier, before coming down to the coast again. Charles and the other man were hazy about the distance in order not to discourage the women. After a strenuous ride in the morning, "there was a question as to whether half the party would not return by train". They were ready for a meal when they stopped at the Royal Oak in Betws-y-Coed, "the whole party feeling that they would require a sheep each followed by a stone or two of really solid suet dumplings before their hunger could in any way be satisfied". After lunch, no one opted for the train; they were all ready to press on. But climbing up to the summit was arduous. Marion "did not actually call [Charles] a liar when he said they were not far from the top of the pass, but gave him to understand this was what she thought of him". One of the other women got off her machine and "declared she never wanted to see a bicycle again". However,

A Quiet Morning.   Cader Idris.

After Lunch at 'the Royal Oak'.

they all managed to complete the trip, fortified by tea at a wayside inn on the road down from the summit. Charles concluded that they all arrived back at Llanfairfechan "tired but satisfied with all that they had accomplished".

The next day they forwarded their tent to Barnsley and took the train to Headley.

They headed off to the Continent again for their holiday in 1906, this time to Norway. A pattern of every second year on the Continent and the intervening years in England had become established. After spending the night

The Hohenzollern in the Puddefjord.

at the vicarage in Hull, where Charles' former fellow curate in Barnsley, John Cholmeley, was now the vicar, they sailed to Bergen. The Kaiser was visiting Bergen at the same time. Although they did not see him, they saw his ship, the Hohenzollern, which Charles sketched. The next day they took a boat to Balestrand (at that time called Balholm) in Songefjord. They stayed at Kvikne's Hotel, now the Kviknes Hotel. It suited Charles and Marion "down to the ground" except that "the square meal of the day, as it is throughout Norway, is at 2 pm – an impossible time for an exploring party such as us". But the hotel did give them lunch packets to take with them on their outings.

Knut, one of the two Kvikne brothers who took over the hotel in 1877, had an English wife. After she died in 1894, he built an Anglican church, St Olaf's, in her memory. It was wooden, in stave church style. Marion attended the choir practice on the Saturday evening they were there, and they both went to the morning and evening services next day. Charles read the inscription on the brass tablet near the chancel, "with the telling words "The mountains shall bring peace". There was no need of a sermon, with the mighty hills all round and these words to think of. However, we were not spared – at least in the morning. The evening service was choral, but minus the discourse." Charles was always inclined to be critical of other clergymen's sermons, especially if they went on too long.

After Balestrand, they moved every few days to other small towns on fjords until they returned to Bergen, about two weeks

after setting out from there. Their days varied between the energetic, when they climbed mountains or rowed on the fjords, and the restful, when Charles sketched or they went on tours in horse-drawn carriages or boats - they also relaxed over leisurely teas and other meals. (In one hotel they were disappointed to be given ham and cheese sandwiches for tea when they had ordered cakes.) They were close to the Jostedalsbreen glacier, the largest glacier in mainland Europe. A number of their expeditions took them onto the glacier or one of its nearby arms. In areas where there might be hidden crevasses, they were roped together. They always had guides, one of whom "was ready to discuss the sagas (which were one too much for the expedition), the metric system and the roots of the European languages". The hikes were strenuous; one involved a climb of 6000 feet from sea level, through soft snow, which was heavy going, in an icy wind.

They went to the Lutheran church when staying in Fjaerland. It was "a bare little place" and they were surprised to see that "the Lutherans are much more ritualistic than one would suppose, going in for vestments and such like enormities in the eyes of the Church Association at home".[84]

The most dramatic hike was the "passage of the Jostedal glacier". They set off from their hotel at 7:45 am with two guides and four German tourists. It started to rain soon after they began the climb. The sun came out briefly when they stopped for their first meal after two hours. "But the pleasure did not last long, as when we had got a little higher, we got into a snowstorm." After zigzagging up the steep side of the glacier to the summit, at 4500 feet, conditions suddenly changed. "All landmarks disappeared as if by magic, and we found ourselves in the folds of a blizzard. The snow cut across our faces like small knives." The guides consulted their compasses and "we plunged forward into the great unknown". Although they were roped together, it was still "a matter of stumbling forward with half an eye open every now and then to see the person

The Passage of the Jostedalbræ.

---

84   The Church Association was an Anglican evangelical organisation that was actively opposed to Anglo-Catholicism and ritualism.

in front". The wind dropped a little, making it more endurable, although it was still snowing hard. In time they "came to land, looking like an expedition who had come out of the Arctic regions. All around lay the newly fallen snow." They started to descend, "and then sat down by a clear pool of snow water for our second meal. Once again we were favoured with a passing gleam of sunlight." The Germans "had brought all sorts of specialities in their knapsacks and finished up by solemnly handing round a small tin of acid drops for pudding".

The 3000-foot descent was steep. At first, they were on steps that the guides had cut with ice axes. Then the rain started coming down heavily. "Moreover, most of the stones were loose and there was a constant torrent of water running through them. Every step required the utmost care." Eventually they reached the valley where "not only was there the roar of the torrents to be heard, but also the crash and thunder of the avalanches breaking off from the great Lunde glacier above". A short walk brought them to Lunde farm where there was a wood fire blazing away. The farmer and his family lent them some dry clothes and brought home-brewed beer, coffee, bread and jam, buns, hot fish and new laid eggs, until they had to explain that they were full. The farmer and family then rowed them in two boats 12 kilometres down Jølstravatnet to their hotel at Skei. "It was a long plug, but they stuck to their work well... They looked a happy and contented lot, as anyone who had to spend their life at Lunde would have to be,

as a sterner, darker looking spot it would be hard to find, surrounded as it is on all sides with precipices of grey black rock, unbroken by any spot of green, rising up 3000 feet, and overhung with glaciers." They reached their hotel at 9:30 pm, ordered a fire in their room, got out of their wet clothes, and "ended up with hot coffee and cheese sandwiches in bed".

Up in the mountains there was little in the way of flora and fauna, although they did see some ptarmigans and the *Ranunculus glacialis*, or glacier buttercup, which flowers at very high altitudes. They also saw cloudberry, which Charles had not seen in England, and two or three small plants whose name he did not know. Down by the fjords "the Norwegian flowers are very similar to the British and appear to be of a deeper colour".

The journey on the fjord steamer back to Bergen was rough after they emerged from the fjord and were less "protected from the violence of the sea". Marion had to "hurriedly seek a haven of rest". The sea crossing from Bergen to Hull was also rough: only two ladies and twenty-six men out of about seventy passengers appeared for breakfast. They learned later that a gale of almost unprecedented severity and duration for the time of year had been raging over the North Sea, "so taking it all round, the Expedition have passed through something in the course of their travels". In Headley the evening after docking in Hull in the morning, Charles was "now sitting in his shirt and trousers, panting, after having been dressed for the last few days in his winter underclothing, a pair of knickerbockers under his trousers, stockings on as well as socks, a couple of flannel shirts, a woollen sweater, a coat, and a Burberry on the top of all, and yet having felt the cold".

In 1907 Charles and Marion were ready for another camping holiday in England. They chose South Devon this time, and were accompanied by a clergyman whom Charles called the Jabberwock, continuing the *Alice in Wonderland* nomenclature.[85] They set up their two tents in a hollow behind the sand dunes by the sea at Thurlstone, near the mouth of the river Ham. Their days were taken up with walking, bathing in the sea, rowing and sailing in the boats they hired, fishing, cooking and looking after the camp. The weather was mostly quite hot, but the sea had not warmed up much, so their dips were short. Their fishing efforts were remarkably unsuccessful, but they kept trying. On returning to camp one day after an afternoon of fishing, they discovered that their steak and bacon "had disappeared in the same mysterious way as their chops had done a few days back".

The evenings were a restful time. "Supper was partaken of in the glow of a glorious sunset, and the pipe of peace was smoked beneath the shining of the myriad stars." Another evening, "the tide was swelling gently in over the bar" and the crescent moon was reflected in the still waters. "The attraction proved too great" so they launched the boat and "paddled out into the night. It was very peaceful out at sea. Phosphorescent light shone in the ripples which broke from the bow of the boat and in the splash of the oars, and only an occasional seagull's squawk broke the silence which reigned around. All nature seemed at rest, including the bass and mackerel and pollack, because, although they spun diligently, they caught nothing."

Two weeks after arriving, they packed up the camp and went into Exeter. The Jabberwock went to the hotel "where he had left his bag and reappeared in a complete set of clericals". Charles and Marion explored Exeter and spent the night there. The following day they went to Headley.

7.30. Where are the chops?

What had probably happened to them earlier in the afternoon.

85   We do not know who he was, but he set out with Charles and Marion from Dewsbury Moor, and so it is possible that he was Charles' curate there, Arthur Talbot Godson. He was young, having only just been ordained, after graduating the year before.

Life on the Ocean wave.

One of the aspects of the times that stands out from Charles' accounts of their summer holidays was the relative ease of transport and communications. Trains in England and Wales may not have been especially comfortable or fast, but they were frequent and ubiquitous. You did not have to go far to a station, or to wait long for a train once you got there. The railway was the main means of transport between towns and villages as motor cars were fairly rare. In addition to carrying passengers, trains carried unaccompanied luggage. Charles was therefore able to send his bicycle home, or on to his destination, whenever it was convenient. He also sent unaccompanied tents, camping gear and heavy luggage when he was not going directly to the same destination. With few exceptions, the system worked well.

Messages could also travel quickly round the country. Letters were delivered next day, helped by there being two deliveries a day, or even more in some places. Letters could be sent to post offices for collection. This was a service that Charles used frequently during their summer holidays when he wanted to keep in touch with family and friends, or just to make reservations at their next port of call. It worked quite well in Italy and France when he and Marion were travelling there, as well as in England and Wales. (He did not mention visits to post offices in Norway.) It was also possible to send telegrams (wires) through the post office.

Charles sought to have a jolly time on their summer holidays. We can see that one of the most important components of this was exercise, as he had written in his diary in 1892. He also liked being outdoors, whether for exercise or to observe and commune with nature. He took in his stride the many difficulties that the vagaries of the weather posed for the outdoor life. After exercise, he liked to sketch and paint. His main cultural interest on holiday was visiting churches. In Italy, the museums and galleries also interested him, as they related to his knowledge of the classical period and painting.

A word about the Englishman Abroad – and indeed at home. He was travelling at the time when Englishmen often believed that their country was superior to others. Charles was not immune to such snobbish sentiments, which were reflected in some of the observations in his journals. We do not know whether he behaved in an arrogant way towards foreigners in real life, although it is comforting to think that his belief that all men are equal in the eyes of God would have prevented this. At holiday at home, he preferred to avoid what he called the 'profanum vulgus' or sometimes the 'οι πολοι'. In part, he was reacting against the kind of amusements that were provided for them in holiday resorts and which spoilt the natural environment for him. He worked with them all the time in his parishes in Yorkshire without looking down on them. But as we saw, he noted in his diary for 1901 about life in Barnsley: "it is a pleasant change every now and then to get out of the parochial groove".

CHAPTER 5

ZULULAND

Charles did not hesitate when the opportunity to work in South Africa arose, even though he had only been in Dewsbury Moor for a year or so. He had always yearned for the wide-open spaces of a country like South Africa or Australia. His visit to South Africa in 1896-97 had left an indelible mark, and a strong wish to return. However, he did not want to leave England as long as his father was alive. But after Theo died in October 1907, he was free to go. He had told his family by January 1908 that he would soon be going abroad.[86] It is not clear how long he had been actively planning this, or whether he had gone to South Africa to prepare the ground. His future boss, the Bishop of Zululand, met him in Barnsley while he was a curate there up until late in 1907.[87] A painting he did of a scene on the road to Pretoria was reportedly dated May 29-31 1906, but there is no other evidence that he visited South Africa then, and the date might have been incorrectly transcribed.[88]

Charles and Marion sailed from Southampton to Cape Town on the Union-

---

86   A letter from his cousin, Laura Key, on 21 January 1908 referred to his impending travel abroad.

87   The Bishop gave the date as 1908 in the obituary he wrote of Charles in 1930 (*The Net*, December 1930), but he must have remembered it incorrectly. *The Net* was published quarterly in London by the Zululand Missionary Association. It was started in 1897 as the successor to *The Net Cast in Many Waters: Sketches from the Life of Missionaries*.

88   The painting is reproduced in J P Rourke and J C Manning, "The Ven. Charles Theophilus Hahn, a hitherto unknown Edwardian botanical illustrator in Natal, 1908-1916", *Bothalia*, 1992. It is possible that the date on the painting was misread, as such dates were not always easy to read. We return to this article in *Bothalia* later.

The Battlefield in the neck, stone cairns marking the graves. Isandhlwana.

Castle ship *Tintagel Castle* on 26 September 1908. From Cape Town they went on to Durban where Charles was reacquainted with scenes and friends he knew from his visit nearly twelve years earlier. Their final destination was Zululand, further up the coast from Durban. Here he began a nine year stretch as a missionary.

Zululand was the home of the Zulu people, whose army the British had defeated in 1879. The Zulus had an early victory at Isandhlwana, but the British recovered some prestige at Rorke's Drift where 150 British and colonial troops held off over 3000 Zulu warriors. There were large numbers of casualties at both Isandhlwana and Rorke's Drift. Subsequently, the British brought in reinforcements and eventually defeated the Zulus, exiled their king, Cetshwayo, and ended the Zulu nation's dominance of the region. Zululand was incorporated into the British colony of Natal in 1897. It was bounded by Transvaal Colony and Swaziland in the north, the rest of Natal in the west, and the Indian Ocean in the south-east. Since 1994, Zululand has been one of the

eight regions of the South African province of Kwazulu-Natal.

Zululand is generally hilly, rising from the coastal plain to the foothills of the Drakensberg mountains which are to the north-west of Zululand. The climate varies from subtropical near the coast to temperate on higher ground. At the beginning of the 20th century the economy was based on subsistence farming. The few towns were small. The great majority of the population were Zulu, with some members of other African tribes. The white population of European, mostly British, origin was small. There were also people of Indian and Chinese descent who had been brought to Natal as indentured labourers, and some mixed race people, known to the Europeans as 'coloureds'. The Europeans

This is me, feeling very small, paying a visit to some miners, who are growing beards.

were farmers, small businessmen, miners, traders, government employees and a few professionals.

The Anglican Diocese of Zululand was less than 40 years old when Charles and Marion arrived. The first bishop "for the Zulus and the tribes towards the Zambezi" was consecrated in 1870. The fourth bishop,

Wilmot Vyvyan, was consecrated in 1903 and remained in that position until 1929.[89] There were two archdeacons who assisted the bishop in managing the diocese and the priests, the archdeacon of Eshowe in the south and the archdeacon of Vryheid in the north. There was no cathedral in the diocese, but St Peter's church in Vryheid was a pro-cathedral, which is a parish church that acts as a cathedral on a temporary basis.[90]

The area of the diocese in 1915 was 25,290 square miles and the estimated population was 418,000, of whom 408,000 were African, 5000 European and 5000 other, mostly Asian. There were 18,804 Anglicans, of whom 17,275 were Africans and 1,529 Europeans, with the equivalent numbers for communicants being 6,354 Africans and 613 Europeans. The income of the diocese in 1915 was about £10,000. Nearly half of this came from the

---

89 The Right Reverend Wilmot Lushington Vyvyan was ordained in 1888 and served as priest-in-charge of the Charterhouse Mission in Southwark from 1892 to 1901. He went to Zululand as a mission priest in 1901 and was elected to be bishop in 1903 by the clergy and laity of the diocese. His obituary was in *The Times,* 28 August 1937.

90 Sir Herbert Baker later designed a new St Peter's church, the foundation stone of which was laid by Bishop Vyvyan in 1911. A cathedral, St Michael and All Angels, was subsequently built in Eshowe. St Peter's in Vryheid continued as a parish church thereafter.

UK (mainly the Society for the Propagation of the Gospel and the Zululand Missionary Association), a third from local Europeans and Africans (mainly for school fees in the latter case) and the rest from the South African government as educational grants.

Charles started in Zululand as a curate at St Cyprian's, Etalaneni (sometimes written Ethalaneni). Etalaneni is in the Nkandla district in the south western part of Zululand, and is about 3600 feet above sea level.[91] From the house where Charles and Marion lived, they could see the 4800 feet high Itala mountain, and the monument on top in memory of the British soldiers who fell there in the Boer war in 1901.

an admiring crowd.

The posting to Etalaneni enabled Charles to learn something about being a missionary in Zululand, while giving his superiors a chance to assess his qualities. The most important superior was Fred Roach, who was the archdeacon of Eshowe as well as being a priest in the Etalaneni area.[92] He first went to Etalaneni in 1886, and knew the Zulu language. Among other activities in Charles' short time in Etalaneni was assisting the Bishop and Archdeacon Roach in dedicating the new church in Enkonjeni. In addition to the usual priestly functions he had to perform, he, together with the Archdeacon, did some last minute carpentry work the day before to ensure that the church was ready.

Charles impressed his superiors and was given his own parish after less than a year. From 1909 to 1916 he was priest-in-charge of the Inhlwati Mission station. (Inhlwati was sometimes written Inhlwathi or Nhlwati.) He was responsible for a large territory, including the town of Nongoma which had more population than Inhlwati. He therefore moved around from place to place, staying a few days, weeks or months in each place depending on what was needed. In practice he spent most time in Nongoma, followed by Inhlwathi. He also stayed sometimes in Ngome.

Nongoma is about ninety miles north-east of Nkandla and Inhlwathi is about twenty-five miles from Nongoma. At 2600 feet above sea level, Nongoma is lower than Etalaneni. It

---

91   Jacob Zuma, the president of South Africa from 2009 to 2018, had a private home near Nkandla. The scandal surrounding the financing of improvements to the property contributed to the pressures that led to his resignation.

92   The Venerable Frederick Roach was ordained deacon in 1886 and priest in 1888. He became archdeacon of Eshowe as well as a canon of St Peter's Vryheid in 1905. In 1913 he was appointed assistant Bishop of Natal, a position he held until he died in 1922, aged 66.

stands on a ridge which affords many hill-side views. There are steep drops to wide valleys below, "from which the broken country rises, hill beyond hill, and fold upon fold, right away to 50 or 60 miles off".[93] When Charles was there, the area was a mixture of forest and grassland.

Nongoma later became the home of the hereditary leader of the Zulus, who has a number of palaces there. The mission and district doctor in Nongoma, Frederick Walters, had a similar background to Charles'. He was ordained a priest in Rochester in 1888 and served as a curate in parishes in South London, including St Philip's in Sydenham, only a few years before Charles was at St Bartholomew's in Sydenham. He was taking medical training at the same time and went to Zululand as a medical missionary in 1893.[94] He and Charles were actually distant relatives. They were third cousins, both being descended from the same great-great-grandfather, Thomas

---

93 Charles wrote this in November 1919 on a later visit to Nongoma.

94 Reverend Frederick Wilford Walters (1863-1934) graduated from Exeter College, Oxford, in 1890, and became MRCS and LRCP in 1892. After curacies in South London in 1887-92, he joined the medical mission in Isandhlwala in 1893 and was mission and district surgeon in Nongoma from 1894 to 1924. He was rector of Nongoma from 1925 until he retired in 1930. He died on 18 August 1934 in Maseru, Basutoland. He married Helen Mansfield in 1888 in Worthing and their children grew up in Zululand. Full details of the many branches of the Walters family, including Charles' and Frederick's, are presented in Frederick Walters, *The Family of Walters of Dorset, Hants* (1907).

This house is in our garden. at present it is occupied by a member of the Royal Family. The Princess is one of those sitting in the foreground.

Walters (1726-66), in Charles' case through his mother, whose maiden name was Walters. We do not know whether they knew each other before Charles went to Zululand, and, if so, whether Frederick had encouraged Charles to come out. In any case, they and their families became good friends, and spent time together. Frederick was 30 years in Nongoma, where he was the rector for the last five years, 1925-30. His wife having died earlier, he retired to Basutoland (renamed Lesotho at independence) where his daughter lived, and where he died in 1934 aged 70.

When Charles started in 1909 as priest in charge at Inhlwati, he was assisted by Rev G Ncgobo. Frederick Walters looked after some of the outstations.

Mission work at that time was not easy. Traditional religions had a strong hold. The proud and independent Zulu people were not rushing to convert to a religion promoted by British rulers, especially as memories of British brutality in the Zulu-British war of 1879 and the more recent suppression of protests in 1906 over a new poll tax remained fresh. Other foreign Christian groups were competing in the same market place. Few Zulus spoke English, and the Zulu language was not easy to learn. Money was always a constraint. The missions were largely financed by donations from supporters in the UK who had to be reassured that the work they were supporting was bearing fruit. In addition to money, the supporters sent supplies. For example, Marion regularly distributed clothes for the native clergy and catechists and their families. The clothes arrived in what was called the Mission Box. The main vehicle for keeping supporters informed was *The Net*, the quarterly magazine of the Zululand Missionary Association, a UK-based charity that helped to collect funds for mission work in Zululand and Swaziland.

Working in favour of the missionaries was the perception among many Zulus that they could advance both economically and socially if they became Christians. The schools and medical facilities that the missions provided helped in this, as did the English language, for those who had opportunities to learn it. Some Zulus reasoned that the religion of the foreign rulers must be useful if it had enabled the British to rule half the world. More broadly, many Zulus were attracted to Christianity for the same spiritual and moral reasons as people were in other countries.

Charles' responsibilities as a priest and missionary included meeting and ministering to the Christians in his area, taking services, seeking new converts, conducting confirmation classes, training the catechists[95] and teachers in mission schools, and managing the affairs of his area. While there was a church in Nongoma,

---

95   According to Websters, a catechist is "a native in a missionary district who does Christian teaching".

Easter Day— Visitors from the out-stations camping out in our garden.

a service in an unfinished 'church'. The natives are building it themselves out of sods of earth.

A "Kraal" Service.

District visiting.

temporary and ad hoc arrangements had to be made elsewhere. A new "native church" was opened in Ngome in 1911, and the first celebration of Holy Communion in Zulu took place there at Christmas that year.[96]

Charles wrote in *The Net* about a visit he made to Dukumbane, a distant part of his area.[97] While noting that a mysterious fire was sometimes seen coming out of a rocky cliff, and that there was an abundance of wild animals, he focused on "the most interesting feature from a church point of view", namely the community of coloured (mixed race) people who lived there. Having both European and Zulu ancestors, they were caught between two societies, not being fully accepted by either. Their mother tongue was Zulu, but they wanted their children to know English and had built a school where the schoolmaster conducted services on Sundays. As the schoolroom was small, they started a fund to raise money to build a larger church. Charles noted that the native chief refused to give them permission to use the land but hoped that he would eventually agree.

Charles' main interactions with Zulus

---

96   *The Net*, March 1912.

97   *The Net*, September 1915.

Taking shelter during a thunderstorm in a hut. The family party are busy shelling mealies.

an Indaba.

The Zulu way of saluting.

Marion says this is very much like what my father now is.

In this country the ladies work in the fields, whilst the gentlemen discuss affairs at home.

Indaba enkulu.

were through his church and missionary work, as well as those with servants and other working people. However, there were many other opportunities for meeting people, ranging from chance encounters, as when he had to shelter from the rain in a hut where the family were shelling maize, to a casual chat – an indaba (a story, also a meeting) – over the garden gate. There were also bigger gatherings, such as those

The new year's party at Nongoma was very refined.

Clergy v Laity at Eshowe.

Going out to a lunch party.

"Northern Zululand Gymkhana Club meeting".

for an indaba enkulu (a great story, or a big meeting) or a celebration. He and Marion learned about Zulu customs and practices, such as the division of labour between women and men and sartorial standards, depicted here in a sketch. (Other sketches, such as those illustrating rather bizarre fashion tastes, are too patronising, when judged by 21st century sensibilities, to show here.)

The small European communities in Zululand settlements had a busy social life. They organised parties, such as one at the New Year and, of course, cricket matches. As everyone rode horses, there were equestrian events, such as gymkhanas, as well as races.

The ladies had their own exclusive social activities, and Marion sometimes dressed up to attend a ladies lunch.

Living arrangements were simple. The houses and furniture were basic. Kerosene lamps and candles provided light in the evenings. Food was normally adequate, although an outbreak of East Coast fever

Front view of our new house. Aug 1910.

The mealie cob season has now commenced.

In the lap of luxury.

The missionary at home.

The Pioneers at work.

Unexpected visitors enjoy the dough, which the inkosikazi has put out in the sun to rise, before baking it.

The Inkosikazi digging up her new potatoes.

Fixing iron sheeting when the wind is blowing.

in 1911 wiped out the cattle and there was no beef. Mealie (maize) was popular with Charles and Marion, as well as being the staple diet of the Zulus. Unfortunately, there were sometimes droughts and mealie crop failures that created severe shortages of food for the Zulus. Given the repetitiveness of their diet, it was a great luxury for them on the rare occasions when they were able to travel to Durban or further afield and dine in style (as in the picture in the Marine Hotel, Durban). The ready availability of servants made life much easier than it would otherwise have been. Even with servants, they were very busy with household tasks. They waxed and cleaned their saddles and shoes. Among other things, Marion baked bread and grew vegetables. (Inkosikazi means wife in Zulu.)

Charles worked hard to improve their living arrangements. He built, largely with his own hands, a brick cottage in Inhlwati, and a wood, iron and stone house in Nongoma. (He gave the latter to the diocese when he left.) He chopped firewood and carried out most of the necessary house maintenance.

Travelling around Charles' large area from Nongoma, including further afield to the diocesan centres of Eshowe and Vryheid, was quite challenging. The only means of transport for local journeys were horse-drawn carriages or carts, or horseback. (Bicycles were not practical because of the rough tracks.) Railway and sea transport were available at the coast. The nearest railway to Nongoma was about ninety miles away at Empangeni, which was on the line that ran down the coast to Durban. A trip to Cape Town from Nongoma, which Charles made occasionally for meetings or other reasons, took a week or more: two days on horseback or carriage to Empangeni, one day on the train to Durban, five or so days at sea from Durban to Cape Town, or a similar number of days on the train.

In the Wilds of Africa. The first appearance of a bicycle

Trekking up to nongoma.

Journeys were often eventful because of flooding, carriage breakdowns, adverse weather conditions or problems with horses. The impact this had on Charles is reflected in the fact that many more of his sketches depict travel adventures – something he obviously enjoyed – than any other subjects, as we shall see.

He wrote an article entitled 'The Vicissitudes of Trekking' in *The Net*. It is worth quoting in full because it captures very well both the realities of travelling in Zululand and the excitement Charles derived from it. He was truly having a "jolly time":

"One of the many attractions of this strange country is the uncertainty of getting about. Of course it is possible to do many journeys without anything untoward taking place, but then there is always the chance of something unforeseen turning up, and, as this may happen any moment, it gives quite a zest to what might otherwise become a somewhat monotonous undertaking. In the summer season the chances are sometimes sufficient to satisfy even the most adventurous. It is possible to be struck by lightning, or carried away when crossing a swollen river, or to take the wrong path on the veld when a mist has come suddenly down, or for one's horse to die through having been left at night in an unsafe place. In the parts of the country down towards the coast there may even be an opportunity of meeting a lion, or falling in with a crocodile, or coming across a python, or a black mamba, which is much worse, although, of course, such varieties are only reserved for those whose business takes them down that way." [Here he noted that 'Nhlwati' means the python's place.]

"A newcomer soon learns that it is hardly

good enough to try cross-country treks alone for the first time. Signposts are very few and far between and owing to their peculiar construction are apt to be a little perplexing, especially when there is no path visible across the veld in connection with them. Moreover, he finds that it often takes a shorter time to go a long way round than to go straight from place to place. Many dongas on a short cut look innocent enough from a little distance, but unless a passage is known they may involve the traveller in all sorts of difficulties. He also learns, sometimes by bitter experience, that it is well to be acquainted with the vagaries of the animal on which he is riding before letting him go when off-saddling on trek, also that it is good to inquire the character of a horse he is about to mount for the first time. The Bishop once lent a certain priest one of his carriage horses, on which to meet him at a place to which he was travelling round by another way. The animal displayed a most unfriendly feeling when he first felt the unusual weight in the small of his back. However, he was got under, and all went well for fifteen miles or so, when the priest in the kindness of his heart got off to give him a short rest. On remounting he found himself shot suddenly into the air, one of the reins broke, and before he had properly taken in what had happened, the beast was careering away alone across the veld. Anyone who has had the experience of pursuing a runaway horse through an uninhabited country will be able to picture the sensations of the pursuer. For six miles the fruitless chase continued; it came on to rain, and the horse finally vanished into a think bank of mist,

This is me.

nov 9th 1908.

In the Umhlatuze River.

We had nearly half an hour of this sort of work without getting the horses to move, when I had a happy thought. They had had some mealies & I suggested that the boy should carry the bag out in front of them. As soon as they saw it they walked out like lambs.

taking with him the priest's lunch and all the Bishop's letters! There was nothing left but a weary tramp home. However, all ended well, for the next day the horse was caught and brought back by a couple of natives, with the

Zaiko!
Gone away !!

20 miles from home, - raining hard, - & the horse vanishing into the cloud

The descent into the Suberi. a motor would soon get down this road.

lost in a mist, - consulting the compass.

saddle and everything intact. These are some of the vicissitudes of trekking."[98]

Walking was also a way to get around, and some treks were made on foot. Despite Africa's reputation as the home of wild and fierce animals, Charles' sketches showed nothing more dangerous than a springbok and a large iguana. One hazard were the holes that aardvarks, or ant bears, dug – Charles sketched Marion and, on another occasion, a horse stumbling into an ant bear hole. More serious were the snakes, which caused serious panic when they were found.

98   *The Net*, June 1912.

on trek

a little diversion on an
afternoon's walk.

Another method of crossing the White
Umfolosi. There is a pleasing uncertainty
as to what lies before the next step.

One of the little surprises of an afternoon
walk on the Veldt. The holes of the Ant Bear are
concealed in the grass.

Oct 13. 1909. 95° in the shade.   Oct 14. 1909.   49° in the shade.
Ups & downs at Etalaneni.

The weather was not always conducive to outdoor activities, as it could be very hot or, at other times, raining heavily. In a single 24-hour period in October 1909 in Etalaneni, Charles recorded a temperature range of 49°F to 95°F. They were often caught outside in the rain, as when Marion had to dress in Charles' cassock because she had no other dry clothes.

A few of Charles' many Zululand sketches found their way into *The Net*. The March 1912 issue, for example, included sketches of celebrations (dancing, fireworks and a tug-of-war) at Christmas in Ngome, and the September 1914 issue showed Zulus adopting modern ways (riding a bicycle, and carrying an umbrella), together with the splendid figure of a man in morning attire and top hat. Charles also illustrated some of Aesop's fables that had been translated into Zulu by Rowand, a Zulu scholar.[99]

Free wheeling.

A Visit to the old folks at home

THE OLD AND THE NEW.

arriving wet through at Nhlwati, where our wardrobe is limited. Marion has got into my cassock.

Charles took on a number of tasks and responsibilities outside his area. While on his first leave in England in 1910, he attended the annual meeting in April in Church House, London, of the Zululand Missionary Association. His remarks were reported in *The Net*, June 1910. He first talked about how different it was working in Zululand compared with England. The Zulu language presented "almost insuperable difficulties": for example, there were no words for God, eternal life or belief. Customs were different, for example what people found to be funny. He then went on to emphasise two things: the importance of training catechists and teachers who did so much of the work of the mission, and the problem of relations between blacks and whites. Charles was only one of the speakers

---

99 *Izinsumansumane Zika Aesop,* translated by Rev A Rowand and illustrated by Ven C T Hahn (1914).

and had time to sketch two of the nuns in the audience during one of the other speeches.

After returning to Nongoma that year, he and Frederick Walters took over editorial and financial responsibility for producing the Zululand Diocesan Magazine. In 1912 he was appointed a canon of St Peter's Cathedral, Vryheid, and in 1913 he was made Archdeacon of Eshowe. In both these positions he was succeeding Frederick Roach, who had moved to Natal diocese as assistant bishop. They involved his assisting the Bishop in the administration of the diocese. In 1912, when the Bishop went to England to raise more money for their work (£2000 to finish building a training college for native teachers, and £500 a year extra income), he left Charles to look after the diocese. Charles was given the title of Vicar-General and had to do his own work as well as diocesan work. In a letter to friends in Barnsley in December 1912, he wrote that it was "very difficult as I want to be in two places at the same time".

Charles and Marion went to England on leave twice while living at Nongoma. After the first trip in 1910, they went again in 1914. Each time they were away for four to five months, including travel time. They usually took the Union-Castle line ships that ran weekly from Cape Town to Southampton and back, the one-way journey taking three weeks. In 1910 they took the longer route from South Africa, going up the East Coast of Africa and through the Suez Canal, stopping at many ports on the way.

There were many things to do in England. Charles gave talks about the mission work in Zululand to encourage donations, and attended meetings such as the one in Church House in 1910. They bought clothes and supplies to be shipped to Zululand. They also

The opposite side of the road   May 20. 10.

had time to visit family and friends, and to relax in other ways. In 1910, they saw Charles' sister Emma and her family in Guildford, his uncle Martin in Bognor and Marion's siblings. They also saw Charles' cousin John Key, who had returned from East Africa in 1904 and was now vicar of Little Wittenham in Berkshire.

English Cup Final
Barnsley v Newcastle.
apr. 23. 1910.

They went to their old haunts in Barnsley in 1910, and later displayed their loyalty to the town by attending the FA cup final on 23 April at Crystal Palace in which Barnsley played Newcastle United. The match was drawn, and Barnsley lost in the replay. Charles sketched the scene at the ground, showing the crowd of 77,747 crammed into the stands, the players on the field in front, and the Crystal Palace itself looming in the background. While they were in England in 1910, King Edward VII died. Charles and Marion joined the crowds watching the funeral procession on 20 May, and Charles sketched them on rooftops and stands, as well as the police, sometimes mounted, holding people back, and St John Ambulance men rescuing the sick and injured.

Charles and Marion met the Governor General of South Africa, Lord Buxton, and Lady Buxton, when the latter visited Nongoma in July 1916.[100] Lord Buxton had many questions about the state of the natives, and Charles told him that the older ones were thoroughly loyal. He wrote in his notebook: "One after another at the indaba [a meeting of senior Zulu men] rose up and expressed sympathy with the King and Government." Their main complaints were about local problems, such as the increased fee for dipping their cattle. Lord Buxton was dressed in ordinary clothes rather than the full dress uniform he wore a couple of weeks later in Eshowe. Charles thought that this was a pity as the Africans were more impressed by sartorial splendour. One said

---

100   Sydney Buxton had been a Liberal MP and president of the Board of Trade until he was appointed Governor General and raised to the peerage in 1914. He retired as Governor General in 1920.

CTH 157 Leguminosae.
Found on the veld at Nongoma April 1912

of the diocese when a European priest was chosen to accompany 10,000 Africans who were sent as part of the 21,000 strong South African Native Labour Contingent in France. To fill the resulting gap, Charles was appointed priest-in-charge of Empangeni in 1916, while retaining his oversight of Nhlwati and Nhambane (the latter was a region of Mozambique). The Bishop noted that giving Charles dual responsibilities was unsatisfactory, but it was the best that could be done at the time.[101]

Empangeni was a town on the edge of the coastal plain, about 100 miles from Durban to which it was connected by railway. The climate was sub-tropical, and was usually hotter than Nongoma and Nhlwati, which were at higher altitudes. Eucalyptus and sugar plantations, and a sugar refinery, had been started during the previous decade or so. They had brought with them a small European population that made for a whiter shade of the church congregation than in Nhlwati and Nongoma.

to him when he learned that Buxton was the Governor General: "What, that little man who makes no shadow?"

The war in Europe affected the operations

Charles and Marion lived in a small rondavel, a round African-style hut, in Empangeni. They

---

101 The Bishop's letter in *The Net*, December 1916. In the same letter he commented that it was unfair to send African labourers to France because of the climate there in winter. Charles wrote in his notebook that the Zulus were reluctant to go to Europe, partly because they thought that the British were finished and they were being called out "as a last chance".

"Lazily, drowsily —" sketch from a life-model
done in the garden on Xmas day.

ones. Charles' work was very varied, ranging from the normal priestly activities of running the churches and meeting the parishioners, to seeking new converts, training African catechists and expanding the reach of the church. Marion ran the household and helped Charles with his work. Living arrangements were not easy, which increased the burden on both of them. On top of it all, the need to travel to different parts of Charles' areas of responsibility in conditions that were often uncomfortable (if not dangerous) made additional demands on their time and energy. Despite all this, they seem to have enjoyed their time in Zululand. References he made to it in later years suggest that it made a deep impression on them and established their love of Southern Africa, where they were to spend another ten years.

They still had time to relax. One of Charles' main forms of relaxation was painting wildflowers. As will be explained in detail in chapter 10, he painted about 300 fine watercolours of flowers he found growing wild in Zululand. This was a remarkable achievement by any standards.

were hospitable to European parishioners who drove into town to attend services. Charles refused to take a stipend, and asked for the money to be devoted to the fund he had set up for a church. The church was eventually built on the site of the rondavel, but Charles and Marion never saw it. They were planning to visit in 1930, but ill health caused them to cancel the trip.[102]

The eight and a half years that Charles and Marion spent in Zululand were busy

---

102 These facts were taken from an obituary in the *Zululand Times* that was reprinted in *The Net,* December 1930.

CHAPTER 6

ENGLAND AND FRANCE IN WARTIME

They did not stay long in Empangeni because Charles wanted to contribute to the war effort in France. He volunteered for the front and left South Africa in April 1917. However, the powers that be in the church in England had other ideas, and he was appointed vicar of Pontefract. There were many vacancies in English parishes caused by clergymen working at the front, and Charles was familiar with conditions in the West Riding of Yorkshire.

As it happened, his time in Pontefract was cut short by a bad attack of malaria. He had contracted it in Empangeni which had a climate more amenable to mosquitoes than Nongoma. He was ordered to take a complete rest, and left Pontefract late in 1917. He and Marion stayed with her sister, Kathleen Browning, in Purley until he recovered.

Anti-German sentiment was, of course, strong in the UK during the war. There were occasional riots, assaults of individual Germans (or people suspected of being German) and looting of shops with German owners (or owners with German-sounding names). Even senior clergymen succumbed to the general mood. Charles quoted in his notes from a letter in the *Daily Mail* from Bishop Welldon: "The evil which has plunged the world in misery lies deep down in the German nature; it is the doctrine that might is right – that everything, however immoral, is justifiable if done for the state. Until this evil is burnt out there can be no peace. Repentance, restitution, regeneration are the three lessons Germany must learn, and no sign that she has learned even the first so far."[103]

---

103 *Daily Mail,* 22 July 1918. James Edward Cowell Welldon (1854-1937) had been headmaster of Harrow (1885-1898), Bishop of Calcutta (1898-1902) and Dean of Manchester (1906-1918). He was a keen proponent of British imperialism.

The Royal Family responded to the anti-German mood by changing their name from Saxe-Coburg and Gotha to Windsor in July 1917.[104] Charles and Marion decided that they too had to escape from their German name. Charles therefore executed a deed poll on 20 November 1917 that changed their name from Hahn to Headley, the name of the village in Hampshire where he grew up.[105] His solicitors, Messrs. Foyer and Co. of Essex Street, supported his case with information about his family and their long history in England. Charles had been in touch with family members to collect information that Foyers could use. A letter from his cousin, Louisa Brownrigg, mentioned that, of the twelve children of their grandfather, George Henry Hahn, only one, Henrietta, could understand German.[106] The letter also referred to the "trouble and annoyance" that Charles and Marion had experienced because of their name. We do not know what this was but can imagine that it included anti-German comments and other unfriendliness.

By March 2018 he was well enough to work. He joined the Church Army as a chaplain and went to France on 24 March. He was based in camps in and around St Omer, which is about twenty-five miles south-east of Calais. It was well behind the front lines,

although within earshot of the heavy artillery at the front. It was, however, exposed to aerial attacks. Apart from two to three weeks' leave in England in September, Charles remained there until he returned to England for good in January 1919.

Army chaplains were commissioned and wore uniforms but did not carry arms. About 4400 chaplains of all denominations were recruited during the war, and 179 lost their lives. Their job was to conduct services, especially funerals, and provide spiritual guidance and sustenance. Most of their work took place in the camps in the rear, although they also visited the troops in the trenches at the front. Roman Catholic chaplains had the reputation of spending the most time in the trenches with the troops, with whom they established close relations. Anglican chaplains were perceived as being more distant, in part because they were more usually of a different class from that of the troops. Many of them reacted to this gap by blaming the remoteness of the Church of England from its parishioners at home. Such ideas contributed to reform movements in the church after the war.[107]

One Anglican chaplain who could relate to the troops was G.A.Studdert Kennedy, known as 'Woodbine Willie' for his practice of giving troops cigarettes. He was also a poet whose

---

104   The King's proclamation to this effect was published in *The London Gazette*, 17 July 1917.

105   Reported in *The London Gazette*, 25 December 1917.

106   Letter from Louisa Brownrigg to Charles Hahn, 16 November 1917.

107   A book of essays by Anglican chaplains contained several ideas about reform: Macnutt, Frederick Brodie, *The Church in the Furnace*, Macmillan and Co., 1917. Charles read it and made detailed notes.

poems revealed deep empathy for the troops and their families. Charles later acquired a copy of his *Peace Rhymes of a Padre*, containing poems written after the war.

Charles' work was fairly typical of most chaplains in that he spent most of his time in the camps behind the lines. St Omer was packed with wartime activity: lorries, cars, the occasional tank, guns, carts, mule carts and every other kind of transport; French soldiers in light blue overcoats and British soldiers in khaki; together with a "cosmopolitan throng" of "dirty-looking German prisoners, Chinese coolies, South African native transport drivers and turbaned Indians". Charles often escaped into the Jardin Publique, which kept its "air of mediaeval repose". The only military actions he saw were attacks by German bombers, usually at night. First, he heard the vroom, vroom, vroom of their engines. Then the warning sirens went off and the searchlights were directed onto the attacking planes. Next, the anti-aircraft guns fired, with fragments of shrapnel falling all around. On at least one occasion there was "a sudden rush and swirl of something big coming down, and the whole air shook with six or seven heavy explosions" one after another.

As explained later in chapter 10, in 1918 Charles started writing notes about nature which he bound into volumes entitled *In the Winds of Heaven*. He did not write much there about the war itself, or his work or his thoughts about it, at least not in anything that has survived. He noted in July 1918 that nature had already covered with flowers an abandoned training ground, which included overgrown trenches and mock-ups of German soldiers ("imitation Fritzes") swinging from a bar. In January 1919 he saw men filling in trenches that wound across the fields, having already removed the barbed wire entanglements. He was interested in the carrier pigeons that had been stationed in his camp for many months. Their keeper explained to him how they had to retrain them to return to the right place each time they were moved to a different station. Just before the Armistice in November he was in Hazebrouck, a town fourteen miles east of St Omer that had been within reach of the German guns. It had sustained serious damage and the inhabitants had all fled long before. "It looks like a person who is hardly through the crisis of a serious illness, and who is still so frail and feeble that his words are few and his voice only a whisper."

His spirits lifted as the end of the war came into sight, and he looked ahead to better times with a hope that was bolstered by his faith: "Through winter, sacrifice and death ever on to that new life of which times of darkness and stress are an essential part. Through all things there runs a deep undertone of joy and hope, because:

God's in His heaven,
All's right with the world."[108]

---

108 From *Pippa Passes*, a verse drama by Robert Browning.

He had a small leather-bound notebook with hand-written prayers. When he went to France he was issued with a miniature version of the New Testament, called the Active Service Testament. It was published for soldiers by the Scripture Gift Mission and the Naval and Military Bible Society, and had a message to the troops from Lord Roberts that began "I ask you to put your trust in God".[109] He collected wild flowers to decorate the huts where services were conducted. One outdoor service made him imagine that they were in a cathedral, with tall elms representing the columns, overhanging branches the arches, and a grassy mound, beneath which were two old dug-outs (the "crypt"), the chancel, with the altar on the highest part. Led by a military band, hymns such as "O God our help in ages past" and "Eternal Father strong to save" "went with a swing and go". Some people caught the spirit of the moment and were uplifted. For example, a burly Yorkshireman, who played football for Bradford City, said he had been "right touched, out in the open and all".

We can only speculate about his thoughts on the war and the role of the church, drawing on the tiny clues in the notes he wrote about the books and articles he read. (Chapter 11 explains his reading and note taking practices more fully.) He probably shared the general view of the Church of England that although violence and war were bad, the alternatives were worse. Once the war had started, clergymen and the church had to pray for and support the soldiers. Charles wrote notes from a sermon in Manchester Cathedral in August 1918 in which the preacher said that the choice on 4 August 1914 was "not between right and wrong, but between two great evils. War is wrong, but this war is necessary."[110] Looking to the future, the preacher said that we should never again put ourselves in the position of having to choose between two great evils. Charles did not record how he said this could be done.

After the war was over, the church was able to take a stronger stand. The Archbishop of Canterbury spoke in Geneva cathedral on 3 September 1922 at the opening of the Third Assembly of the League of Nations about the role of Christianity in preventing war. Charles summarised what he said as:

"Our great need is to get away from the warlike spirit. Up to the last war there were many who thought it was inevitable, and good; but very few can think that now. Statesmen have fashioned all sorts of delays to prevent the final clash. But the only real hope is the creation of new spirit. Public opinion must be whole-heartedly against war, and Christianity alone can give that spirit."[111] It is likely that Charles agreed with this view.

---

109   Field Marshal Frederick Roberts, 1st Earl Roberts (1832-1914), was one of the most successful military commanders of his time.

110   The preacher was P Green, and the date was 4 August 1918, the fourth anniversary of the start of the war.

111   The Archbishop was the Right Reverend Randall Thomas Davidson (1848-1930). He had ordained Charles in 1893 when he was Bishop of Rochester.

On a cold September day in 1919, he and Marion visited the new Cenotaph in Whitehall.[112] He was deeply moved ("the emotions were strangely stirred"), not because of personal loss, but rather because of "the mighty sacrifice that had been offered up amid pain and suffering and loss for a great ideal… ..A voice seemed to come from the unplumbed depths which …… awakened tremors which must have sprung from somewhere in the Great, Central, All-absorbing Unity". Charles was attracted by the idea of a Central Unity, especially when contemplating nature: "There is deep down in the eternal immensity a unity in which all beauty and goodness and glory meet, and the woods in spring seem to be full of the inarticulate expression of it in as far as our mind and senses are able to take it in". He perceived the Central Unity in some of Blake's writings, in which "time and space had no meaning. In his mystic outlook it was possible

To see a world in a grain of sand,
And Heaven in a wild flower,
Hold infinity in the palm of your hand
And eternity in an hour."[113]

For Charles, the Central Unity was God.

Charles followed the discussions among clergymen and other Christian thinkers about reforming the church and other religious matters. He read and noted *The Church in the Furnace*, the collection of articles by army chaplains that contained many reform ideas.[114] He seemed to agree with the criticism that the church was too institutional, pretentious and material, and out of touch with ordinary people. He noted Hankey's comment that army chaplains did not understand that the soldiers' dislike of the formalism and self-righteousness of the church did not mean that they lacked religion.[115] He took an interest in the growing debate about uniting the various Christian sects. Amidst the horrors of war, the divisions among Christian churches seemed so petty. Another interest was spiritualism which was attracting people who had to cope with the death of loved ones. Charles read works by both sides, those who believed that one could speak with the dead, and those who thought it was all bogus.

Charles returned from France at the end of January 1919. He rejoined Marion who had been living in a flat they had leased in

---

112 The Cenotaph was a temporary structure of wood and plaster designed by Edwin Lutyens for the peace parade in July 1919. It was replaced in 1920 by a permanent stone monument to commemorate those killed in wars. This was also designed by Lutyens and retained many features of the original structure that Charles and Marion saw.

113 William Blake, Auguries of Innocence.

114 Macnutt, Frederick Brodie, *The Church in the Furnace*, Macmillan and Co., 1917.

115 Donald Hankey, *A Student in Arms*, (1916 and 1917). Hankey (1884-1916) trained for the priesthood but chose instead to work with poor people in Bermondsey as part of the Oxford mission. He wrote about Christianity and its relevance for the poor and, after he joined the army, soldiers. He was killed at the Somme.

Prince of Wales Drive, overlooking Battersea Park. They planned to return to South Africa, but it would be a few months before Charles could arrange a suitable job there. In the meantime, while they spent most of their time in London, they also stayed with family and friends in the country.

They spent May and June with Charles' cousin, John Key, in Moulsford, a quiet village on the Thames between Oxford and Reading, where Key was the vicar. He and Charles had much in common as they had both been missionaries in Africa.[116]

In July they lived in Charles' Uncle Martin's second home in Selsey, on the Channel coast south of Chichester.[117] Martin's main house was in Bognor, where Charles and Marion also stayed for a few days. Charles had a younger cousin, Helen Hawes, in Bognor. She was the daughter of his mother's brother, George Ranking Walters, who had died the previous year. Helen, who was separated from her husband, lived with her mother and three young sons.[118] Although Charles had five aunts and uncles on his mother's side who lived to adulthood, Helen was his only first cousin on his mother's side.

They stayed in Hampstead for a few weeks in August. On the Heath, as on walks in Battersea Park, Regents Park, Kensington Gardens, Richmond Park and Kew Gardens, Charles delighted in being able to enjoy nature and the changing seasons in the city. One clear day he came over the brow of Parliament Hill and saw the whole of London spread out below. He could see as far as the Hog's Back, which was part of the North Downs to the west of Guildford, and Crystal Palace to the south. He observed in *In the Winds of Heaven* that coming unexpectedly upon "the whole panorama of the greatest city on earth .... was calculated to give a pleasurable thrill". Despite, or perhaps because of, his spending many years abroad, he was always proud to be English.

The war cannot have been far from his thoughts in the months after he returned from France. He continued to read about world events and the reactions of Christians and the church to the war. On 28 June 1919, when the Peace Treaty was signed in Versailles, "not many flags were to be seen in Moulsford" where Charles' attention was instead on the roses, pinks, carnations, Canterbury bells, delphiniums and Madonna

---

116 On returning from East Africa in 1904, Rev Sir John Kingsmill Causton Key became, first, vicar of Little Wittenham and then, from 1915, vicar of Moulsford, both in Berkshire. The Hahn and Key cousins kept in touch in other ways too. For example, John Key officiated at the marriage of Dorothy Louise Hahn (1893-1976), at St John's, Notting Hill, in 1917. Dorothy was the daughter of Frederick John Alexander Hahn, the first cousin of both John Key and Charles.

117 Martin Rawlinson Walters (1838-1926) was a younger brother of Charles' mother Helen (neé Walters).

118 Helen Maud Walters (1881-1930) was the daughter of George Ranking Walters (1846-1918), who was the brother of Charles' mother Helen (née Walters) and Martin Walters. She married Robert Hawes in 1905 in Bognor. She had been a bridesmaid at Emma's wedding in 1902 at which Charles officiated.

lilies in the villagers' gardens. He reflected on how sacrifice in nature - the bird risking its life for its young, for example - was akin to the patriot dying willingly for his country. And he speculated that "life through death and sacrifice is a fundamental law of nature". Regarding cruelty in nature, he asked "does it not look as if the spirit of evil which infects mankind is also at work on a wider sphere than the merely human?" One might read into these remarks his struggle to divine God's will in allowing so much death and suffering to take place in the war.

By September, the arrangements for returning to South Africa were falling into place. They were to sail from Southampton on the *Llanstephan Castle* on 30 September 1919. There was a morning mist that day as they drove to Victoria Station along the Mall, past the half-grown plane trees and the beds where potatoes grew during the war, and now red geraniums formed vivid masses of colour. The massive proportions of the Victoria memorial outside Buckingham Palace loomed into sight out of the mist. As it turned out, the *Llanstephan Castle* did not sail that day because a railway strike held up many of the passengers.[119] It eventually left on 2 October, even though a few passengers had still not arrived.

---

119 The strike was called to protest the government's plans to reduce the pay scales that had been introduced during the war. The government gave in after nine days and agreed to continue the existing pay scales for another year.

Robinsonites House at Charterhouse, 1886. Charles is fourth from left in the back row.

The Junior Common Room at Pembroke College, 1891. Charles is seated, first from left.

The clergy team at St Mary's, Barnsley, 1901-05. Charles is standing at left.
The vicar, Foxley Norris, is seated at right.

At the marriage of Charles' sister, Emma, to George Odling (later Odling-Smee), 1902.
Charles and Marion are the first and second from left. Charles' father, Theo, is standing seventh from left,
with George next to him and Emma seated in front of them.

On holiday in Norway, 1906.

In the Church Army, 1918

CHAPTER 7

CAPE TOWN

Charles was going to take up a job in Cape Town, but first he and Marion went to Zululand to collect some of their belongings and say goodbye to friends. The *Llanstephan Castle* took them all the way to Durban, where they arrived on 28 or 29 October, after a stop in East London. They stayed a couple of days in Durban, where Charles had time to visit the zoo, which had suffered during the war, although the birds were still a major attraction for him.

Then they took the train to Empangeni, where Charles had been priest-in-charge a few years before. Observing the natural scene closely, as always, Charles noted that the veld was still brown due to the season (early spring) and shortage of rain, although the pawpaws were abundant and the pineapples, bananas, oranges and apricots were coming. By contrast with the veld, the sugar plantations were yellow green. The cutting was coming to an end, but there were still long trains snaking round the narrow gauge railway to collect the cut cane. Oxen were pulling ploughs to prepare the ground for the next season, and African workers, dressed in old sacks, were hoeing to remove the "Farmers' Friend", a species of ragwort.

From Empangeni one could see the Umhlathuze Lagoon, a vast expanse of water eight to nine miles away on the coast, separated from the sea by a spit of sand. Charles observed that it might be possible one day to build a harbour for ocean-going vessels there. Other people, including the government, later had the same idea. As a result, the new port and town of Richards Bay were developed in the 1960s and 1970s, with the port becoming one of the biggest exporters of coal in the world.

After Empangeni, Charles and Marion

went to Eshowe, the centre of the area of which Charles had been Archdeacon, and a few days later, to Nongoma, where they had lived from 1909 to 1916. In those days journeys between Eshowe and Nongoma had been on horseback or horse- or mule-drawn carriage or cart. This time they travelled by motor car, which had the disadvantage that its noise scared away birds and animals that would not have been put off by horse-borne transport. Not completely, however: when the car was gliding quietly down a hill, two grey monkeys crossed the road in front without a concern, and watched it go by from the fork of a tree.

On a rise above the White Umfolozi valley, they saw the thorn bush below thickly dotted with aloes, plants with red spikes that stick straight up. Charles was reminded of the occasion during the Zulu war when an excited British officer saw a similar scene and reported that an attack by thousands of Zulus might be expected at any moment because they were spread out over the plain below as far as the eye could see! He commented in *In the Winds of Heaven* that the officer "must have had the wind up badly".

In addition to renewing their friendships with people in Nongoma and the surrounding area, Charles and Marion reacquainted themselves with the local flora and fauna that they enjoyed so much. There had, however, been a significant change in the latter as a result of the near eradication of East Coast fever. This was a cattle disease that was transmitted by ticks. It had come from East

Africa in the 19th century and devastated cattle herds. In the years since Charles lived in Nongoma, the government had introduced compulsory dipping of cattle to kill the ticks. As a result, there were more cattle on the veld. The herds were often accompanied by egrets which looked for grasshoppers and other small creatures that the cattle might disturb. To Charles' disappointment, there were fewer wild flowers than before because the cattle grazed on grass and flowers indiscriminately.

One morning in Nongoma, Charles was struck by the beauty of the views. "Not a breath disturbed the atmosphere, and all was so still and clear that the Ngome range stood out beyond the Vuma valley and the Mahashini Hills with every detail perfect. It was like looking through the purest and most transparent water, so clean and delicate were the blue-greens of the distant veld and the more decided blues of the places where the forest mounted over the crests and ran down into the ravines... Then above the range in the clear blue sky, soft, small, cotton-woolly clouds of pearl and opal, just touched with shadows of the finest grey, were gathering." He retained his painterly eye despite not having used a brush for over two years.

Charles and Marion returned to Eshowe after a couple of weeks in Nongoma, and from there went on to Durban on the branch line. Their train had only one passenger coach, but added trucks with cattle, sugar cane and wattle poles as it went along. After a day or so in Durban, where Charles admired the spring flowering trees and shrubs (flamboyant, bourgainvillea, hibiscus, jacaranda and oleander), they took the train to Cape Town. The journey took them through Bloemfontein in the Orange Free State Province and the Great Karoo, and took four to five days. The train made heavy weather of the climb up the escarpment to the high veld, at one point being split into two to lighten the load, and at another having a second engine pushing from the rear. The open plains between Bloemfontein and the Orange River were followed by the Karoo, whose immensity impressed Charles. The train took 24 hours to cross it; Charles thought that it might take a man over a month to walk the same route. The vast hot, parched, stony land was occasionally interrupted by farmsteads, with gardens irrigated with water pumped up by windmills from boreholes.

They arrived in Cape Town in early December 1919, and Charles took up his position as the editor of the *Church Chronicle for the Province of Southern Africa*, a fortnightly newspaper published by the Anglican church of Southern Africa from 1904 to 1935. The *Chronicle* contained both news relevant to Anglicans in Southern Africa, and articles of general interest. As editor, Charles wrote much of the *Chronicle* himself, while drawing on others for some of the material. An example of a general interest article was the one he wrote about science and religion in September 1920. Among other things, he explained how the theory of evolution was compatible with Christianity. The foreman at the works where the *Chronicle* was printed read the article and was much disturbed. He could not accept that man was connected to the animals. He believed that man was a special creation, because it was said that the Lord God made him from the dust of the ground. Fortunately, he did not sabotage the production of the issue containing the article, but Charles had a difficult job trying to persuade him of the compatibility of evolutionary theory with the scriptures.

In addition to being editor of the *Chronicle,* Charles was a sub-dean of St George's Cathedral in Cape Town. As such he conducted services in the cathedral, ministered to Anglicans in the diocese and visitors, and had administrative responsibilities relating to the cathedral. St. George's Cathedral was the cathedral of the diocese of Cape Town, which was created in 1847. It was also the seat of the Archbishop of Cape Town, who was the head of the Anglican church in Southern Africa. The foundation stone of the cathedral was laid in 1901 but building took place gradually over many years. It was still not completed by 1919.[120]

Charles and Marion lived in Newlands, a suburb six miles from the cathedral, round the side of Devil's Peak, which flanks Table Mountain on its east side. It was just a little beyond the suburb of Rondebosch where Charles had stayed on his visit in 1896-97. They named their house Nongoma, to remind them of their days in Zululand. There was a

---

120   In more recent times the cathedral was associated with the anti-apartheid movement, especially after Desmond Tutu became the first black African Archbishop of Cape Town in 1986.

garden in which they grew both vegetables and flowers. Charles did a considerable amount of garden work himself. He took a special interest in the vegetables, regularly recording their progress in *In the Winds of Heaven*.

While working in, and observing, the garden, Charles followed the activities of the creatures living there. There were many insects to watch, such as the bees, which loved the flowers of the eucalyptus tree, and the wasp which took a caterpillar it had caught for dinner into its hole which it carefully covered to prevent intruders. Some insects were pests which destroyed the vegetables. Others were subjects of wonder. He was fascinated by the spiders that spun their webs around the tomato plants. He never caught them actually spinning and wondered when they did the work. And why did they suddenly disappear, sometimes to be replaced by smaller versions of themselves? Perhaps the answer to this question lay in the thimble-size ball of webbing he found containing many small eggs. Once, when digging, he turned up a frog, and on another occasion found a chameleon.

He loved the birds and their songs and took pride in being able to identify them. He noted that the summer must be approaching when, on 1 September 1921, he saw the first swallow returning from summer in Europe. The restful cooing of the turtle doves, especially during mating season, was attractive. But they liked to eat his peas, which reduced his feeling of pleasure when "the voice of the turtle is heard in our land".[121] It was perhaps the flowers that he loved most. His passion for, and knowledge of, wild flowers was matched by his interest in the cultivated ones in the garden. Nature in the garden reminded him of a popular verse by Dorothy Gurney:

The kiss of the sun for pardon,
And the song of the birds for mirth,
We are nearer God's heart in a garden,
Than anywhere else on earth.[122]

Charles had a motorcycle and sidecar. He drove it to and from St George's Cathedral every day, and he and Marion went on excursions at weekends and on other holidays. There were two main routes he could take into town. One was the Peninsula Main Road, a fairly straight road that ran along the contour near the foot of Devil's Peak. The other was the mountain road that climbed over the shoulder of Devil's Peak. Charles nearly always took the latter, not because it was less busy than the Main Road, although it was, but because the views were spectacular, and the driving was more challenging. Many of the entries in *In the Winds of Heaven* drew on what he saw on his commute to work. Coming over the shoulder on his way into Cape Town, he saw the city with its red roofs below, Table Bay

---

121   Here Charles was quoting from the *Song of Solomon*.

122   From *God's Garden* (1913), slightly misquoted. Dorothy Frances Gurney (1858-1932) was a hymn writer and poet. She was the daughter and wife of Anglican priests, and converted, with her husband, to Catholicism in 1919.

and Robben Island beyond, Table Mountain and Lion's Head to the left, and the distant Drakenstein range and other mountains across the Cape Flats. Coming home he saw False Bay and the mountains running down the Cape peninsula. He loved the sense of freedom and exhilaration he had on the mountain road. Some verses reflected his feelings:

For the deeps are calling, calling,
And the clouds sail slow,
And the wild in my breast has wakened,
And I rise to go.
Over the great wide spaces
To the fields of morn,
To the hills and silent places
Where the clouds are born.
Over the seas and mountains
To the great world's end,
With the sun and the rain for my brothers
And the wind for my friend.

These lines came from a poem by J C Squire in his book of parodies. The poem was in a section of the book entitled *The Aspirant's Manual: Models for the Verse Writers*, and the poem was entitled *The Contempt-for-Civilisation-and-Geography-Fraternal-with-the-Elements-Plein-Air Piece*.[123] Although Charles recognised that it was a parody of a real "back-to-nature" peon, and slightly ridiculous at that, he was honest enough to admit that he identified with its message. Squire's book was published in early 1921, and Charles took his quotation from it in June 1921, showing that he kept up with new writings. Sir John Collings Squire (1884-1958) was a poet, writer, historian and literary editor.

The mountain road went past the zoo at Groote Schuur where he often saw apes and baboons, peacocks and wildebeest. They were not too troubled by the motorcycle, although one old baboon always rushed out to the end of his chain when he passed, and sat and jibbered, whether in scorn or admiration Charles did not know. The flock of crowned guinea fowl he often met foraging on the side of the road created a great commotion when he appeared and ran around before many of them flew away.

The motorcycle rides were not without occasional mishaps. A not uncommon problem was caused by the south-easterly winds that blew over Devil's Peak and created a strong headwind as he was driving home. His Enfield's 6 horsepower engine was barely

---

123 J C Squire, *Collected Parodies*, (1921). The first two verses of the poem help to explain its focus:
"We have had our fill, my heart,
Of the haunts of men,
We will tread the stones of these cities
Not ever again.
So I take the road to the sunset
My staff in my hand
To make my peace ere I die
With the sea and the land."

powerful enough to carry him up the hill while also battling against the wind.[124] On more than one occasion he had to dismount and push the motorcycle at the same time as he kept the engine revved up in bottom gear. Once, the strain of climbing the hill into the wind caused the back tyre to become displaced and ruin the inner tube valve. As the sun was setting, a roadside repair was not possible, so Charles pushed the motorcycle part of the way home and walked the rest of the way. The worst problem was a broken spindle in the front wheel which forced him to stop on his way to work, just after crossing the highest point. A passing ambulance driver promised to send for help, but it never arrived. With the help of a coloured man who walked by, Charles managed to push it downhill to a garage. He summoned his mechanic who fixed the problem in time for him to ride home that evening. In the meantime, he had missed a meeting and a service that he was due to take.

Charles and Marion had many outings, sometimes on the motorcycle and sometimes by other means. Given their love of flowers, a favourite destination was one of the two botanic gardens. Kirstenbosch, being started only in 1913, was still in its infancy. Nevertheless, Charles thought that there was "no other botanic garden in the whole world that can match it for beauty". It was set on the eastern slope of Table Mountain below its crags, with the Liesbeek river running down the middle, the Flats below stretching from one ocean to the other, and the blue line of the distant mountains beyond. Run since 2014 by the South African National Biodiversity Institute, it remains an important garden dedicated to South African plants. By contrast, the other botanic garden, which was in Cape Town itself, contained many plants native to the British Isles. Charles liked it both for that reason and because it provided a peaceful escape from the busy city. "There are only a few of οι πολλοι about to disturb the peace." (Charles only occasionally used Greek, Latin or French words or phrases in his writings, and he was obviously pleased that he could recall them. It is unlikely that he thought that hoi polloi had the derogatory tone that it came to have later.)

Given his love of physical exercise, and even serious challenges, it is not surprising that Charles and Marion tackled the climb up Table Mountain more than once. On one occasion they started by going up through the Kirstenbosch garden and ended up at the Kasteel Berg, a rocky headland on the south side of the mountain. On the way they passed the reservoirs that were being constructed when Charles was there in 1897. The remains of the aerial cableway used for the construction were still there. There were birds, animals and plenty of wild flowers to see and, in Charles' case, record faithfully in *In the Winds of Heaven*.

Their motorcycle outings took them on a tour round Table Mountain, as well as

---

124 Modern mopeds have 1-2 HP engines, and the smallest cars have about 70 HP engines.

down both the east and west coasts of the Cape Peninsula. The scenery was spectacular, especially on the west side where the mountains fell straight down into the sea. South of Hout Bay a new road, the Chapman's Peak Drive, was being constructed by creating a ledge along the mountainside. It was eventually opened in May 1922 by the Governor General of the Union of South Africa, HRH Prince Arthur of Connaught.[125] When Charles and Marion tried to drive along the completed section in October 1921 they were turned back because a strip of road had given way and disappeared into the sea during the winter. It was being repaired by a gang of convicts, who comprised the main workforce for the new road. A few months later, they hiked along a path above the sea on the same coast. Although the path was overgrown and difficult to locate in places, they managed to find their way, and also many plants of interest.[126]

Closer to home was Wynberg Hill, only two miles south of Newlands, from the top of which there was a fine view of False Bay. When Charles had passed it on his climb up Table Mountain in 1897, there had been an army camp there. Now it was more or less deserted, the last of the Imperial troops having recently been withdrawn. Carved on a huge boulder about 10 feet high at the top entrance gate were the letters: *Royal Engineers 1806-1921*, "thus proclaiming", Charles wrote, "the end of an old long-drawn feud and the dawning of a new era as one people for the two white races of South Africa". He was too much of a colonial to reflect on what the new era might mean for the non-white races.

In March 1922, a little over two years after they had arrived in Cape Town, Charles and Marion moved to South West Africa, where they were to spend the next six years. We do not know why they moved. There is no evidence available to us that the powers that be in Cape Town were dissatisfied with his work or presence there. More likely was that they wanted to return to a simpler life, and some of the adventures that came with it, and to have more contact with Africans. They may also have sought the opportunity to travel more, after two years in and around the city of Cape Town, and to experience a different part of Southern Africa. In addition, Charles may have been attracted by the prospect of effectively being his own boss. He was appointed priest-in-charge of Keetmanshoop with Luderitz and his formal superior was 310 miles away in Windhoek.

---

125 Prince Arthur (1883-1938) was a military officer and son of Queen Victoria's third son, the Duke of Connaught and Strathearn. He was Governor General from November 1920 to January 1924.

126 In *In the Winds of Heaven*, Charles called the crags above where they were Captain's Peak. From the context he was probably referring to Chapman's Peak but misnamed it. There does not seem to have been a Captain's Peak there, either then or later.

CHAPTER 8

SOUTH WEST AFRICA

Since the Versailles Treaty was signed on 28 June 1919, South West Africa had been a League of Nations Mandate Territory administered by South Africa. Before the war it had been a German colony, Deutsch-Südwestafrika, which was established in 1884. It remained so until an invading South African and British force led by Generals Jan Smuts and Louis Botha, who was also Prime Minister of South Africa at the time, defeated a German force in 1915. South West Africa was administered by South Africa from 1915 to 1990 when it became independent and was renamed Namibia.

When the war began in Europe in August 1914, the South African government immediately commenced plans to attack South West Africa. One element of the plan was to construct 278 miles of railway to link the South African railhead of Prieska with the southernmost railhead in South West Africa. The railway was built in record speed, on good days at over five miles a day, and opened on 25 June 1915, just a few weeks before the German surrender. It was along this railway line that Charles and Marion travelled in 1922.

They left Cape Town at the beginning of March 1922. On the final stretch of the journey, partly on the new line, they travelled with the Director of South West African Railways in his private coach. It was a historic coach that had belonged to Paul Kruger, and he had made his final flight into Portuguese territory at the end of the Boer War in it. They crossed the South Kalahari desert: "brown, stone-strewn earth with scanty brown, lifeless looking bushes scattered here and there". Occasionally there were outcrops of rocks, and beds of waterless rivers marked by lines of sturdy camel-thorn trees. Charles was delighted to see "a species of melkbosch of a refreshingly light green colour" in one place, and surprised that there were occasional signs of human habitation. They arrived in Keetmanshoop, their home for the next two years, on or about 8 March 1922.

The first missionaries in Keetmanshoop were Lutherans from the Rhenish Missionary Society. They arrived in the 1860s and in 1895 built a fine church which became a major landmark. The Anglicans did not have a significant presence until after South Africa took over the administration of South West Africa in 1915. The Reverend Nelson Fogarty was a chaplain in the South African military in South West Africa in 1915, and was appointed in 1916 by the Archbishop of Cape Town to be Archdeacon of Damaraland and his Vicar-General in South West Africa. Damaraland was the area in the central-northern part of the country inhabited by the Damara people. In 1924 the diocese of Damaraland was created to cover the whole of South West Africa and Fogarty was appointed the first bishop, based in the capital Windhoek.[127] Fogarty was therefore Charles' superior, first as Vicar-General and then, from 1924, as bishop.[128]

As priest-in-charge of Keetmanshoop with Luderitz, Charles' "parish" stretched from Luderitz on the Atlantic coast in the west to the South African border in the east, and from the Orange River (the other border with South Africa) in the south to about a quarter of the way to the northern border of South West Africa. It corresponds roughly to the modern Namibian region of Karas, which at 62,000 square miles, covers a fifth of South West Africa, and is slightly larger in area than England and Wales. Keetmanshoop, where Charles and Marion lived, was about 310 miles due south of Windhoek, the capital of South West Africa, 210 miles north of the Orange River, and 225 miles due east of Luderitz, the port on the Atlantic coast.

The topology of the "parish" changed from the coastal plain round Luderitz, which was the southern edge of the Namib desert, to the mountain range about eighty miles inland which rose to over 4000 feet above sea level, and the plateau beyond, on which Keetmanshoop was located, which averaged about 3500 feet above sea level. The land sloped down towards the south and the Orange river valley. Part of the Kalahari Desert was in the far east of the region.

The climate was hot and dry, being one of the sunniest places in the world. The average annual rainfall was only 6 inches in Keetmanshoop, and less on the coast. Only the Orange river ran year round, with other

---

127 The diocese of Damaraland was renamed the diocese of Namibia after independence.

128 The Right Reverend Nelson Wellesley Fogarty (1871-1933) was born and educated in England and went to South Africa in 1893. He was ordained priest in St George's Cathedral in 1896. After various positions in Rhodesia and South Africa, he was appointed archdeacon of Damaraland and Vicar-General for the Archbishop in South-West Africa in 1916. In 1924 he was consecrated the first Bishop of Damaraland, a position he held until he died in 1933. During his episcopate, St George's Cathedral in Windhoek was built.

rivers being seasonal and dependent on the rains. The deserts were barren and rocky, and the central plateau was semi-arid, with sparse vegetation, as Charles had seen from the train. Sheep and goats managed to remain healthy despite the limited vegetation, as did donkeys and oxen.[129] Charles observed this with surprise and attributed it to the nourishment that was contained in the camel thorns and other scanty bushes. He noted that, except in the driest periods, the farmers managed to produce milk and butter.

There was little economic activity beyond subsistence farming and a few small commercial farms. Keetmanshoop itself was a transport hub where the railway from Luderitz to the west joined the north-south railway. It was also an administrative centre.[130] Near the coast there was diamond mining. With such a large area and a poor economy, the population density in the southern part of South West Africa was very low. Then, as now, the bulk of the country's population was in the Windhoek and northern regions. The population of Keetmanshoop and Luderitz was 2600 and 2000 respectively in 1921. In the same year the population of South West Africa was 229,000, of which 19,400 were white, most of these being Germans or Afrikaners.[131]

Charles spent 2-3 weeks a month in Keetmanshoop, and the rest of the time in other parts of his "parish". He was usually in Luderitz in the first week of the month, with less frequent visits to other areas. The Anglican population was very small, comprising mainly English-speaking South Africans who had come since the establishment of South West Africa, and some local Africans. There were no permanent churches. Charles conducted services in private houses and other convenient places. For example, in May 1922, and perhaps on other occasions as well, he held a service in the station master's house in Klein Karas, eighty-seven miles south of Keetmanshoop. He started a fund to build a church in Keetmanshoop; it was built later in the 1920s after he had moved on.[132]

The distances were vast, and the trains that Charles and Marion took between the main towns were slow and unreliable. The journey from Luderitz to Aus, which was 4800 feet up in the mountains on the way to Keetmanshoop, took eight hours although it was only eighty-seven miles. On one occasion,

---

129 In more modern times, karakul sheep have done well in the region.

130 In the 21st century it is sometimes described as the "economic capital of southern Namibia", which remains a poor and sparsely populated region. It is still a transport hub and administrative centre. It is also the centre of karakul farming and attracts some tourists.

131 The population of Namibia in 2011 was 2,113,000. Despite rapid growth after independence, the population of Karas region was only 77,000 in 2011. The population of Keetmanshoop, the largest town in the region, was 21,000.

132 This was noted in the obituary for Charles in *The Net*, December 1930, written by the former Bishop of Zululand.

in April 1922, Charles' train was held up for three hours because a mail bag had been left behind and they had to wait for it to be sent on. On another occasion, the wheels of the engine came off the rails, causing a delay of over five hours. To reach places that were not on the railway, he had to travel on dirt roads by horse and cart or carriage, or occasionally by motor vehicle. Although he had his motorcycle, he rarely used it because it easily got bogged down in sandy patches on the road.

The heavy rains in the early months of 1923 caused havoc on the railways. The line from Keetmanshoop to Windhoek in the north was washed out in various places, and at one point an engine and its tender collapsed sideways across the line. No sooner had repairs been made to the track than another downpour would wash it away, in the same place or somewhere else. Some passengers who were trying to get from Keetmanshoop to Windhoek were delayed for over a month.

They eventually decided to take the train to Luderitz, after that route reopened, and then a boat up the coast to Walvis Bay from where they could reach Windhoek. The line from South Africa was also damaged: a train that was scheduled to arrive one Saturday evening did not reach Keetmanshoop until the following Friday. The line from Keetmanshoop to Luderitz on the coast was closed for a few weeks after the bridges across the Fish River were washed away at Seeheim. Soon after Charles' train had passed through on his way home from Luderitz, the river "came down in a wall over the railway bridges which are 30 feet above the river bed". The repair work took a few weeks, and the work of 400 men, who were brought from throughout the region. Some had come nearly 200 miles by trolley, covering fifty miles a day, because there were no trains to transport them. Charles was on the first train to go back to Luderitz after the line and bridges had been repaired. There were some anxious moments when they crossed the repaired bridges, and Charles took extra provisions in case they were held up in the desert by sand on the track because no one had passed that way for weeks. But all was well. Although the line was cut again by more rain while he was in Luderitz, it had been repaired again by the time he returned to Keetmanshoop. This journey was accomplished in the record time of 16 hours and 40 minutes, but Charles had to spend a rough night in the guard's van because the passenger coaches had stayed behind in Luderitz to accommodate people who were waiting to take boats. It is a good thing that he thrived on adventures.

For most of the year, the problem was too little water, not too much. Just before the heavy rains in early 1923, the boreholes up and down the railway line were running dry, and the trains had to carry extra water tanks to see them through their journeys. Even during the rains, which fell primarily on the mountains and inland plateau, the Namib Desert on the coastal plain remained dry. The only borehole in the diamond fields region where 5000 people lived was running low, and the water was too brackish to drink. They had to rely on water from the desalination plant at

Luderitz, but only a limited amount could be transported to the diamond fields because of an insufficient number of horses to haul the water tanks along the railway track.

The streets of Keetmanshoop were wide and open, with surfaces of loose sand. Both driving and walking were difficult, except where there were stretches of harder material. When there was a wind, dust and sand were blown along in a gritty cloud. There was no grass anywhere, and only a few trees. Charles believed that such an inhospitable place might have been chosen for the town when there was a vlei surrounded by shady trees.[133] The vlei had long dried up and the trees cut down, but the town remained. There was a park that was about the size of a football field. In the middle was a squat stone monument, surmounted by a crouching bronze eagle, in honour of those who lost their lives in various native wars in German times. The sandy paths were marked off from the sandy ground beyond by rows of whitewashed stones. The park was otherwise bare, apart from some trees, many of which looked rather unhappy.

The Governor General of South Africa, Prince Arthur, spent three hours in Keetmanshoop on 29 July 1922. A reception was held for him in the park the stones of which had been freshly whitewashed and which was enlivened by tea booths and decorated with festoons and bunting. Alas, as Charles noted, "even these were shorn of their full glory by a gusty hot wind which swept all the more flimsy part of the decorations away and brought plenty of dust along instead."

Like the park, the cricket ground, an essential feature of towns in the British Empire, was made of sand, with a covering of dust. "A man after the ball in the long field was lost in a cloud of dust." On hot, sunny days, which meant most of the year, the heat burned through the soles of Charles' shoes. When a wind blew up, the whole field would occasionally be blotted out in a dull yellow cloud and the bails would fly off the stumps. But the players were not put off by minor setbacks like this, and the games continued.

Charles was even less impressed by the location of Luderitz than he was by that of Keetmanshoop. "Luderitz, one would think, is one of the last places on earth that could have been chosen as a suitable site for a town." It was built on bare rock running down to the sea. Up and down the coast there was no greenery, only desolate grey white rock and shifting sand. The Namib Desert, which surrounds Luderitz and extends 1000 miles up and down the coast and up to 100 miles inland, was and is extremely arid. When Charles was there the average annual rainfall was less than one inch. This is primarily due to the encounter between moisture-laden winds that come from the Atlantic and hot air in the interior causing fogs rather than rain. The rain was also unpredictable. It rained at least four times in 1922, whereas Charles was told that it had not rained at all in the previous seven

---

133   Vlei is an Afrikaans word meaning a small, shallow lake, often seasonal or intermittent.

years. The temperatures were less extreme than at Keetmanshoop. Thus Charles was able to sit outside without a coat one June day, having just arrived from a cold Keetmanshoop in which there was ice on water in the shade. On one of his last visits, in January 1924, he painted a watercolour of the town and harbour. The plentiful bare rock and lack of any vegetation illustrate his disapproval of the site.

Except for fish, all food and other supplies had to be imported into Luderitz. The water supply was based on the desalination of sea water. Despite these disadvantages, Luderitz had been relatively prosperous before the war because of the readily accessible diamonds in nearby regions. The houses, built in German styles, were roomy and solid, and the shops were well stocked. There was, however, a lull in the diamond business due to wartime disruptions and the Soviet Union flooding the market with diamonds. Charles observed that Luderitz' excuse for existing would disappear if the diamond business did not revive. However, he need not have been concerned, because it picked up again during and after the years he was based in Keetmanshoop.

Charles always found something of interest in other towns in his "parish". Around Klein Karas, there were thousands of springbok (and a party of South African hunters when Charles was there) and the kokerboom tree, called the 'quiver tree' in English because the local people used its hollowed-out branches as quivers for their arrows.[134] Bethanie was founded by the London Missionary Society (LMS) in 1814, making it one of the oldest settlements in the country. Later the Rhenish Missionary Society (RMS) took it over and it became an administrative centre under the Germans. It was blessed with good supplies of underground water, enabling the cultivation of vegetables, fruit and flowers. Charles was there when the dates were ripe and, on another occasion, he admired the long avenue of oleanders, with their pink and white blossoms, in the Residency garden. Up in the mountains at Aus, Charles found many wild flowers that he had not seen before. When he was there one September day, a carpet of bright yellow Aus daisies filled the valley. The winter rains, and occasional snow, "had brought them into being and had made this spot a veritable oasis in the desert."

Warmbad, in the south of the "parish", had also been a base for the LMS, then for the RMS, and later a government centre. The main African people in Warmbad were the Bondelswarts, a group of Khoikhoi, called by Charles and other Europeans Hottentots, a term that later was regarded as derogatory.

The Bondelswarts started an armed uprising against the government in May 1922 because of a number of grievances, including police brutality, pressures to join the labour force, taxation, and the official status of their chief. The authorities responded with force, including machine gunners and aeroplanes, which Charles saw buzzing overhead in Keetmanshoop. After the uprising was defeated in June, the Bondelswarts were not treated well, although their cattle, which had been confiscated, were returned within a few months. Charles noted in November that their beehive huts in Warmbad were "mangy looking affairs compared with the neatly thatched erections of the Zulus".

Meanwhile, their ramshackle vehicles were still parked by the police camp in Kalkfontein, a place that Charles thought was "without distinction". The Commission that was set up to investigate the events surrounding the uprising concluded the following year that the South West African administration should have treated the Bondelswarts more sympathetically, both before and after the uprising.[135] Charles recorded approvingly that some coloured people who lived with the Bondelswarts had told him that the situation would have been

---

134   The kokerboom tree is a type of aloe, indigenous to Southern Africa, with a yellow flower in winter. A quiver tree forest near Keetmanshoop has become a tourist attraction.

135   The South African government sent three commissioners of the Native Affairs Commission (NAC), Alexander W. Roberts, Charles T. Loram and General L. A. S. Lemmer, to enquire into the uprising and how it was handled by the SWA administration. The NAC was set up to advise the SA government on African affairs, and to act as a communications channel between Africans and the government. The commission was unable to produce an agreed report. Roberts and Loram, who were generally sympathetic to African demands, were critical of the administration, and Lemmer, who was conservative on race relations, wrote that force was necessary to enforce the rule of law.

better if the British and not the Afrikaners had been in control of the Bondelswarts.

Day to day life in Keetmanshoop was not easy. The annual average daily temperature was 25°C. In the summer it would often be as much as 35°C during the day, with minimum temperatures being 10°C or less. (Charles kept daily records of temperatures, barometer readings and weather conditions.) Sometimes Charles would lie in the bath to cool off.

We do not know what food supplies were like, or what other supplies were available locally, but one can assume that there was not much choice. Charles and Marion had to bring many personal items with them from England or South Africa, or order them to be delivered, which would have involved long delays. We do know that Charles had plenty of reading material, both books and magazines, because he wrote copious notes about what he read.

Charles and Marion acquired a puppy, Toby, while in Keetmanshoop. In addition to companionship, Toby provided Charles with opportunities to speculate about animal behaviour and biology. Impressed by Toby's penchant for rolling in the remains of dead animals, Charles imagined that "these high-pitched odours reminded him of that delectable state" a few months before when he had stunk of "concentrated effluvium". He noted that some smells linger longer than others, and some can overpower others. He was struck by how a smell can bring back a memory, as Kipling wrote:

Smells are surer than sounds or sights
To make your heart strings crack.

In Charles' case, the scent of lavender took him back to childhood visits to the Walters family home in Bognor. The smell of eau-de-Cologne "always brings vividly before my mind's eye the frail figure of my grandmother sailing across the room in a full black silk skirt with a small lace cap on her head".

On one occasion, Toby gave an involuntary kick when Charles was stroking him at a particular spot on his side. Charles then became interested in the ways in which stimuli, such as the stroking, sent signals to the brain which responded in various ways, in this case a "conditioned reflex". Observing Toby playing with his younger brother who lived across the street, Charles wondered about the play of young animals. After consulting a book on psychology, he concluded that "play is just an exuberance of spirits, an overflow of the elan vital, the joy of life, by which all things live".[136]

There was a large insect community in Keetmanshoop. During wet weather, the mosquitoes were active. "The high-pitched skirl of the mosquito bagpipe band is continuous all around, varied by the individual squeak of one nosing round the net searching in vain for an entrance". In early 1923, Charles managed to derive some pleasure from watching them grow. He had been keeping the bath full of water because it only came on for an hour or two a day. The mosquitoes found it an

---

136   The book was William MacDougall, *An Outline of Psychology*.

ideal spot for laying their eggs. They looked like dots to the naked eye, but through a magnifying glass he could see bundles of 50 or so eggs. He transferred them to a tumbler and a day later the larvae were swimming around with spring-like jerks.

Mosquitoes were not the only insects in abundance. On one occasion, when Charles went to look for wild flowers outside the town, he was disappointed because grazing animals had got there first. However, there were plenty of insects – butterflies, beetles, locusts and grasshoppers – such that "an entomologist would have gone mad with excitement". Black clouds of locusts passed over from time to time, causing trouble, not only for farmers, but even for the railway. The swarms of locusts on the tracks could be so thick that the wheels of trains spun around until sand could be shovelled under them. The religious Afrikaners regarded plagues of locusts as Visitations from God and concluded that there was no point in trying to kill them. There was even a resolution passed in the South African Parliament calling on the government to proclaim a day of humiliation and prayer because calamities such as locusts, drought and cattle dying were caused by the sins of the people. Charles disapproved of the "decidedly Old Testament atmosphere" in which the supporters of such a resolution lived. He thought that they "would not have been able to survive in an Assembly imbued with a more modern outlook". One creature who welcomed the locusts was Toby, who enjoyed eating the voetgangers, as the young wingless locusts (nymphs) were called in Afrikaans.[137]

Whether or not Charles and Marion went to South West Africa for a change of scenery, they certainly got it. For most of the year, the landscape was brown and barren. Only after the rains was there much greenery. Sand and dust were pervasive features of life – we have already noted how they could intrude into cricket matches, not to mention the tea party for the Governor General. Charles, with his usual positive outlook, could see the beauty and mystery of the desert regions, and he was captivated by the flowers that appeared after the rains.

After 14 months in Keetmanshoop without a break, Charles and Marion left at the end of May 1923 for a holiday at the Victoria Falls. They went by train, which first took them 570 miles in a south-easterly direction to De Aar in South Africa. There they changed to a train going north through Kimberley, Mafeking, Bechuanaland (now Botswana) and Bulawayo in Rhodesia (now Zimbabwe) to Victoria Falls.[138] The whole journey was 1700 miles and took about a week. The route after De Aar formed part of Cecil Rhodes' grand scheme to build a railway from the Cape to Cairo. He dreamed that it would run entirely on British territory. Rhodes died in 1902,

---

137   Literally, a voetganger in both Afrikaans and Dutch, is a pedestrian.

138   At that time most of what became Southern Rhodesia and later Zimbabwe was ruled by the British South Africa Company. Only a few months later, on 12 September 1923, the Colony of Southern Rhodesia, a self-governing British Crown colony, was established on the lands between the Zambezi and Limpopo rivers. We refer to it as Rhodesia throughout the book.

aged 48, before the railway reached Victoria Falls in 1904. The route to Cairo was never completed.

Charles and Marion spent three weeks at the Victoria Falls Hotel, which had a fine view of the railway bridge over the Zambezi River, and the spray rising from the falls beyond. As usual, Charles wanted to learn everything he could about the falls: how they were formed (eg an earthquake or, more likely, differential erosion of rocks of varying hardness), the height and width of the falls, the volume of water, the depth of the gorge below the falls, the height of the railway bridge above the river, etc. He recorded it all in *In the Winds of Heaven*. Naturally, he was especially interested in the wildlife. In addition to many birds (including swallows, cranes, hornbills, red-winged starlings, toucans, woodpeckers, wagtails, hawks and snipes), there were baboons, monkeys, dassies (an African rodent) and crocodiles. He loved the rainforest trees, their lushness being in sharp contrast to the stunted and spare vegetation of South West Africa.

As explained in detail in chapter 10, Charles took up painting again during the trip to the Victoria Falls. Among other scenes, he painted the Falls and the surrounding country from twelve different vantage points.

Charles and Marion made a small detour on their way back to Keetmanshoop from Victoria Falls. They went to Rhodes' grave on the top of a hill about twenty miles south of Bulawayo in Rhodesia. Rhodes had chosen the site, which he called World's View, before

he died. The hill was solid granite and was covered with huge granite boulders. The grave had been carved into the granite and covered with a simple bronze slab with the inscription "Here lies the remains of Cecil John Rhodes". Charles was moved by the feeling of Rhodes' presence, just "as at Caen, the spirit of William the Conqueror still seems to dominate the place". "One can somehow come to feel his dreams and to understand his ideals more fully as one stands on that bare summit... One could enter into his world-wide vision and realise the high position which he would have his race hold and maintain among mankind. There was nothing mean or petty in his outlook; in all his work he had his face ever turned towards the future, and his wealth was to him but a means to an end. He wanted it for the power it gave him to make his visions for the future a reality. Solidity and simplicity were the marks of his life..." hence the choice of a grave carved into the solid granite of the hill top.

Charles' praise for Rhodes is not to his credit when judged by 21st century attitudes to colonialism and exploitation of native populations, even if one assumes that his reference to Rhodes' "race" was to the British rather than to whites as a whole. While not supporting the exploitative side of colonialism, Charles did believe in the civilising mission of the British Empire. He therefore admired Rhodes' contribution to the development of Southern Africa through the support of British-type political and legal institutions and administration, and encouragement of economic development.

Luderitz Location was a shanty township in a sandy, wind-swept hollow that was separated from Luderitz by a rocky ridge. Most of its population comprised African migrant workers and their families. They came from many parts of Africa, one man even from Togo, and spoke many languages. However, mostly they came from the Cape region of South Africa. The main employers were the factories for canning rock lobsters, which were called crayfish there. Charles thought that the township "was the last spot on earth in which anyone would choose to dwell", especially when there was a south-westerly wind whipping up the sand so "that it stings one's face". However, the people seemed happy, which Charles ascribed to the social life: dances, concerts and political meetings. Many of them, he wrote, were

believers in Marcus Garvey, a Jamaican-born black nationalist, and "are looking to him to fly over to South Africa with a fleet of aeroplanes and drive all the white people into the sea". Despite his pan-African writings and campaigns in America for Afro-Americans to return to Africa, Garvey never went to Africa. He was actually in prison in America on mail fraud charges at the time that Charles noted that he had supporters in Luderitz Location.[139]

There was an ongoing dispute in the Location while Charles was there between the education authorities who wanted the schools to teach African students in their own language, and the parents who wanted them to be taught in English, thinking that it would be useful in future. Charles was on the side of the parents because "the whole place is polyglot and a conglomeration of races" ("one child can answer back in seven languages"). It would be "inconsiderate" to insist on the mother tongue.

Charles and Marion had very few visitors in Keetmanshoop. However, on one occasion, Wilmot Vyvyan, the Bishop of Zululand and Charles' former superior there, came. In his obituary of Charles, Vyvyan wrote that Keetmanshoop was a hot and dusty place, and that Charles' work involved much travelling.[140]

After nearly two years in Keetmanshoop,

---

139 Marcus Garvey, born Jamaica 1887, died London 1940. He founded the Universal Negro Improvement Association and African Communities League (UNIA) in Jamaica in 1914. From 1916, he lived in the US, where he worked through the UNIA with other black nationalists and pan-Africanists. He was imprisoned in 1923 and deported to Jamaica in 1927. Although his ideas were not accepted by all Afro-American and anti-colonial leaders, he was nevertheless regarded as an important figure in their movements.

140 *The Net*, December 1930. Vyvyan wrote that the visit took place in 1926, but that was wrong because Charles and Marion left Keetmanshoop in 1924.

Charles and Marion went to England on leave in 1924. On returning, Charles took up a new position as Archdeacon of Damaraland and priest-in-charge of Swakopmund with Walvis Bay in the Diocese of Damaraland. Swakopmund was to be their home for the next three years and a few months, apart from the period in 1926 when they went to England on leave.

Swakopmund was similar to Luderitz in topology, climate and recent history. It too was squeezed between the Atlantic Ocean and the Namib Desert. It had a temperate climate, the average highs being in the range of 18° - 23°C all year, and the average lows being in the range 10° - 16°C. It was extremely dry, with average rainfall being less than one inch. It usually rained on only one or two days a year, and sometimes not at all. However, there were frequent fogs, caused by the cold air from the sea, driven by the Benguela current, meeting the hot air from the land. The moisture in the fog was sufficient to allow a few specialised plants to grow in the desert.

Like Luderitz, Swakopmund was created during the German period as a port, in this case to service the settlements in the centre and north of German South West Africa. A railway was built to the capital, Windhoek, which was 231 railway miles to the east. It was an administrative centre for its region. A number of fine German colonial buildings were erected in the first decade of the century for the courthouse, Lutheran church, hotel, trading houses, railway station and barracks. These are tourist attractions today. The population

was 1,800 in 1921, much the same as that of Luderitz (2,000).

As priest-in-charge of Swakopmund with Walvis Bay, Charles also spent time in Walvis Bay. It was only twenty-one miles south of Swakopmund on the railway and shared the topological and climatic characteristics of Swakopmund. But it had a different history because it was colonised by the British and administered as part of the Cape Colony and later the Cape Province of the Union of South Africa. It was never part of the German colony, in which it was an enclave. After the war, Walvis Bay came under the South West African administration and was governed alongside Swakopmund. Walvis Bay was a better site for a major port than Swakopmund, because it was protected by the Pelican Point sand spit to the south, thus creating a natural harbour. After the war, it was gradually developed into the main port for South West Africa, and Swakopmund became a seaside holiday town as well as an administrative centre. Whereas in 1921 Swakopmund was the larger of the two, with a population of 1,800 compared with 800 in Walvis Bay, by 2011 Walvis Bay had grown to 62,096 and Swakopmund to 44,725, over a quarter less.

Charles was also Archdeacon of Damaraland. As such, he travelled throughout his archdeaconry, which stretched in a north-easterly direction to Omaruru and Grootfontein. It was a large area, bordered in the north by the Ovambo region, which was next to the frontier with Angola, and stretching in the south almost as far as Windhoek. He conducted services and visited Anglicans, most of whom were white, of British or South African origin. Until German rule came to an end, there was no missionary activity by Anglican societies. This gradually built up during the 1920s, especially in the most northern parts of South West Africa, outside Charles' archdeaconry. The creation of the Diocese of Damaraland in 1924 was intended in part to strengthen the mission work.

Charles' and Marion's house in Swakopmund overlooked a lagoon formed by a sand bar that separated it from the Atlantic Ocean. They could see the waves rolling in from the sea. At times when the wind was coming over the desert from the east, it caught the crest of the waves as though "they were having their hair combed back". Sometimes the sea broke through the sand bar at high tides or poured over the top of the sand bar. This brought new water into the lagoon. On at least one occasion it came over the top with such momentum that the waves swept across the lagoon to the far side. There were times when the water in the lagoon ended up higher than the sea. At other times, the lagoon was cut off from the sea and shrank as its water evaporated. Its shape and size were always changing.

In summer, when the air and water were a little warmer, Charles and Marion swam in the lagoon. Other white people, both locals and people on holiday from upcountry, did the same. There was a springboard on the sand bar separating the lagoon from the ocean, from which one could dive into deep water.

But when the lagoon shrank, the springboard was marooned in sand with no water around it. And when the sea had pushed the sand bar inwards, the springboard might be stuck with its back in the sea. On at least one occasion high tides had washed an enormous quantity of refuse over the sand bar from the sea into the lagoon, which quite spoilt it as a desirable bathing spot. Charles noted that "for some time now the bottom has been unpleasantly slimy, and lately the water has had a grass-green tinge, which although it is a really beautiful colour when the light shines through the breaking ripples raised by the breeze, does not invite one to plunge beneath its surface".

Heavy seas drove a freighter, the *Cawdor Castle*, onto the beach about 100 miles south of Swakopmund while Charles and Marion were living there. It gradually sank into the sand and had to be abandoned, although some of its cargo of whisky, motor cars, pianos and Christmas goods were rescued.

Swakopmund was built on the north bank of the Swakop river where it met the sea. To the south of the river, all the way to Walvis Bay, there were massive sand dunes that later became an attraction for visitors to Swakopmund. The river was dry for most of the year but became very full when there were rains upcountry. Even when the river was dry, there was water to be found deep below the river bed. In fact, this was the source of the water supply in Swakopmund, and the reason why the town was built there.

Charles' and Marion's household after they returned from England included two dogs, a puppy called Blighty and his mother, Susan. Blighty chased anything that moved but could not understand why the foam blowing off the sea disappeared completely after he had jumped on top of it. As Toby had been in Keetmanshoop, both Blighty and Susan were "as thoroughly carried away by what is to me a regular stench as an old toper is by the sight of a drop of whiskey". They were therefore "much more enthusiastic when there are definite signs of a walk round the lagoon than they are when there is merely a visit to the town in prospect, for by the lagoon there is always something to be found in the way of a fish or a bird in a more or less advanced stage of decomposition." They also enjoyed walking on the river bed when it was dry because there were small sandy-coloured lizards and geckos there lying in the sun. When the dogs appeared, the lizards bolted for cover followed by the dogs, which dug energetically in the likely hiding places.

The trains from Swakopmund to Walvis Bay had to cross the Swakop river mouth at the beginning of their journey. The tracks were laid on a low embankment of stones and sand on the river bed, and trains could not pass when the river was sufficiently high to cover them. Worse still, when the river was flowing very fast, it could wash the tracks away altogether, necessitating repairs that could take a few days. There had been no water in the river for a few years until 1923 when heavy rains upcountry caused the tracks to be washed away. This happened again in February 1925, Charles' first summer there.

He and Marion realised that something was wrong when the water from the taps was "the colour of strong coffee". Then they saw that the sea was also dirt coloured, and "the great rollers coming in no longer broke a dazzling white in the sunlight but rushed ashore in a welter of pea-soup coloured foam."

Down on the river bed, the rails had been undermined and the sleepers tipped up almost on end. The gangers and their labourers were already at work repairing the track, even though it seemed likely that their work would be washed away again. Charles noted that "the gangers regard their job quite philosophically – it is what they are paid to do, and if all their work goes again, well, it goes". And it did, four more times that summer. The third time the gangers did not rebuild the embankment, but just laid the line on the river bed to simplify work in the event of another washaway, which duly came. On one occasion Charles was able to walk across the river using the sleepers as stepping stones. On another occasion, he waded across in his bathing dress, "but it was not much over my knees except in one place where I got into a hole of loose sand". The last washaway, in April, was the worst. "For 300 yards or so where the stream is coursing along in a broad expanse, the rails have been swept away, and for 500 or 600 yards beyond they are all twisted and hanging suspended over gaps and covered with debris right away to the further bank."

The inconvenience and cost of having the line over the Swakop mouth repeatedly washed away led to the decision to build a permanent bridge. Work started in the winter of 1925. Charles watched it proceed, recording the various stages and the engineering challenges encountered in *In the Winds of Heaven*. A big worry was whether the floods that were expected the following summer would damage the unfinished bridge. But the rainfall in early 1926 turned out to be well below normal, and even more below the 1925 amounts, so that the bridge could be completed without mishaps by April 1926.

Everything went well for a year. But heavy rains upcountry in April 1927 led to rushing water that first washed away the buttress of heavy stones protecting the end of the railway embankment, and then, more seriously, hit the first concrete pillar holding up the bridge, causing it to sink into the sand almost a foot. No train could cross it in that condition, although some men were able to push trucks carrying cattle over to the other side, where they were hitched to a waiting engine. Within a few days, workmen jacked up the pillar and put blocks of timber under it so that trains could cross again.

After crossing the Swakop river, the line to Walvis Bay ran between sand dunes and the sea. "On one side lie the sand dunes, the colour of ripened oat fields against the blue sky, sweeping up into hills and mountains as smooth as driven snow. Sometimes when the wind is blowing freshly, the sand is streaming over their summits, making each crest appear as if it was the top of an active volcano with the smoke pouring from it... On the other side the long Atlantic rollers come tumbling in white foam on to the shore."

While there were passenger trains between Swakopmund and Walvis Bay, they were not frequent. Charles therefore sometimes travelled in the guard's van on a goods train, or on a motor trolley, a small petrol (or diesel) engine trolley used by maintenance workers. The only other mode of transport on land, through the sand dunes, was a camel, which was used by the police.

Charles' first impression of Walvis Bay was that he was in Norway, because of the wooden houses. They were built on stilts rising out of the sand which was below sea level in many places. Although a sandbar held the sea back, the stilts were a necessary precaution in case the sandbar was breached and the sea flooded in. Walvis Bay had been discovered by Bartholomew Diaz in the 15th century, but was not settled by Europeans until the 19th century, when a whaling station was opened. It had three jetties which were used by lighters that chugged back and forth to ships anchored in the bay. A major infrastructure project was under way to build a wharf for ocean-going ships and thereby avoid the need to transship. Charles took an interest in it and checked on progress from time to time. It was completed late in 1926, with the first freighter docking in October. Charles was there when the first passenger ship, the SS *Usambara* of the German African Line, arrived in a sandstorm in November.

He was also there on 3 August 1927 when the Governor General officially opened the wharf. The Governor General and his wife arrived in the morning on the royal white train.[141] The wharf and shipping were gaily festooned with bunting but there was "hardly sufficient wind to keep the pennons fluttering". In opening the ceremony, the Administrator spoke "as if the South West had been unfairly maligned, being in reality the finest country in the world with infinite possibilities extending before it, but now, being put in direct touch through this new port with the world's markets, had a chance of pursuing its natural course of development; all of which somewhat amused those who had thrown in their lot with the land and knew what they were up against; however a bit of optimism on such an occasion was not out of place."[142] By the time the Governor General departed later in the day, the breeze had freshened and even "the heavy Union Jacks were well extended in full display".

Charles did not find the town attractive. From the sea, before the sheds were built on the new wharf, it looked like "a line of low-lying shanties rising apparently out of the water" backed by sand dunes and surrounded by "a waste of sand". The biggest buildings were the harbour goods sheds and the Imperial Cold Storage works.[143] The sanitary arrangements in the main settlement area, which was expanding rapidly, were primitive.

Dirty water thrown out of the houses did not dry properly because the water table was high. Sanitary bins and buckets were uncovered until inadequately buried a short distance away. Charles blamed these conditions, and the flies which took advantage of them to breed freely, for an outbreak of enteric fever. The locals, on the other hand, were inclined to blame the outbreak on the bluish sand that was being dredged up during the harbour works and dumped to raise the ground.

One day there was a terrible smell in the air in Swakopmund. Charles and Marion could not work out what it was. Then they heard about an explosion under the sea bed which had occurred in Walvis Bay a few days before. It had stunned all the fish which washed up in millions all along the shore. Despite efforts to bury the rotting fish, the smell persisted for quite a few days. There were many theories about the cause of the disaster. Charles favoured the theory that there had been a "sulphur" explosion of a volcanic nature somewhere beneath the sea.

A year later, in December 1925, there was another submarine explosion with more dead fish. Charles' tentative explanation was that decaying vegetable matter brought down over the years from inland regions and deposited in

---

141 The Governor General was the Earl of Athlone (1874-1957), a British army officer and brother-in-law of the King. He succeeded Prince Arthur as Governor General in 1924. His wife was Princess Alice, a granddaughter of Queen Victoria.

142 The Administrator of South West Africa from 1926 to 1933 was Albertus Johannes Werth. He had previously been a National Party member of the South African Parliament.

143 The Imperial Cold Storage company was a South Africa company that distributed meat and meat products to the major towns of South Africa.

the sea around Walvis Bay had given off gases, including hydrogen sulphide which people could smell, which gave rise to an explosion. He explained the fact that the explosions occurred only in December by the fact that this was the month when the atmospheric pressure was lightest and underwater gases were not held down. He revised this theory the following year. There were again dead fish in December, but the atmospheric pressure was not especially low. While abandoning the pressure explanation, he continued to believe that there must have been some rhythmic movement behind the submarine explosions.

A few weeks later, in January 1927, there was a sulphurous smell out in the bay, but no dead fish. Charles came up with a new theory. The Kuiseb river joined the sea at Walvis Bay and, though usually dry, was running at that time. Perhaps it had been flowing underground and broke through somewhere out at sea, thereby causing a disturbance? It was typical of Charles to want to have a scientific explanation for an interesting natural phenomenon.

Walvis Bay was not always unattractive, diseased or smelly. In February 1926, he wrote: "the last two mornings have been perfectly beautiful: the sunrise across the sand dunes lighting up the blue waters of the lagoon and the white masses and dots of flamingos gathered there with a clear and radiant glow, while a soft and almost imperceptible breeze from the north has had a bracing touch of coolness in it. This morning the flamingos

were standing about in the shallow waters in immense numbers – there must have been well over 3000 of them – and were apparently welcoming the coming day in a general chorus of croaks which sounded like geese cackling. Sometimes a flock would rise and fly off to another pitch with extended legs and necks, and as they did so the sunlight fell upon the red vermillion of their wings."

Charles spent half to two thirds of his time in Swakopmund and Walvis Bay. Every month he went to other parts of his archdeaconry for one to two weeks. This took him to the central plateau of South West Africa where the climate and vegetation were very different from those of the coast. It was much hotter for most of the year, although it cooled down at nights when there might occasionally be a frost, something unknown in Swakopmund. There was a rainy season in the summer and early autumn, and a dry season in winter. In most places and years, there was plenty of rain. Farming was therefore a common activity, although delays in the annual rains in some years could create difficulties. The population density was significantly higher than in the southern areas around Keetmanshoop, and even more so compared with the empty desert around Swakopmund and Walvis Bay.

The first town one reached travelling inland from Swakopmund was Usakos.[144] It was a railway centre, with repair workshops that were put up by the company that built the railways in the 1900s. The houses stood

144   In 1978 a new town, Arandis, was built closer to Swakopmund for the workers at the nearby mine at Rossing, the world's largest open pit uranium mine.

on a bare and stony rise above the river bed, which was often dry. There were hills on three sides, with the Erongo mountains lying some distance away to the north. Charles thought it was best to see it by moonlight. "It is when the moon is shedding its softening beams over all that Usakos looks its best, for then the barren and uncared for appearance of the place, which is so obtrusive in the glare of the day, is hidden."

There was a football field in the river bed at Usakos. The soft sand made running quite exhausting, but it was not as bad as the loose stones on the previous field, which were dangerous if one fell on them. Charles once found himself travelling from Windhoek to Usakos with a happy and jovial crowd of members of the Wanderers Club, a sports club in Windhoek founded in 1920, going to play a rugby match against the Usakos railwaymen. As he had time before his connecting train left for Swakopmund, he watched the match. Conditions were not ideal as a fresh breeze blew grit into one's eyes and mouth, and the scrums were obscured by clouds of dust. At least the ball did not burst when kicked into the surrounding thorn trees, as it had often done on other occasions.

Mining was an important part of the economy, accounting for 85% of total exports in 1925 (agricultural products accounted for another 15%). Copper was mined in Tsumeb and vanadium in Grootfontein. Together with Otavi, these two towns formed what was known as the Otavi Triangle. The ore from these mines was exported through Walvis Bay (during German times, through Swakopmund) to which it was carried on the narrow gauge (2 feet wide) railway that was constructed for that purpose in the 1900s. The Erongo mountains were also a source of minerals and contained good-quality marble that had been quarried in the past. But it turned out to be uneconomical to send it to South Africa, and South West Africa was not "as yet in a position to build marble halls". In the foothills of the mountains there was a small plant to extract tin from the soil. Charles observed the crushing and separation operations that produced the black oxide, containing 77% white tin. The next, more difficult step for the company was to find the reef from which the alluvial tin had come. In the same area there was a short-lived business collecting bat guano from caves where it had been deposited for centuries. While the guano appeared on the surface to be rich in nitrates, it turned out not to be so rich below the surface.

The Otavi Triangle was also good for farming, especially cattle and maize. The best land was held by whites, who were mostly Afrikaners or German speakers. On his first visit in December 1924, Charles observed that Grootfontein was by far the greenest place he had seen so far in South West Africa. The green trees and bushes were a perfect paradise for birds. As for the abundance of wild flowers, he declared that they "would send a botanist mad with excitement". Without searching hard, he saw various species he had never seen before.

On the return journey on the same trip, the train passed into a region where there had been very little rain and the vegetation was brown and dry. Charles was surprised when an old Afrikaner farmer from South Africa assured him that it was a good place for sheep. It turned out that he was referring to "the sparse clumps of dry grass rising from the bare sandy-yellow earth like short and scrubby tufts of hair". Charles thought that ostrich might do better than sheep. Indeed, at a halt an ostrich appeared and trotted briskly up and down the carriages, poking his head in the window demanding attention. When the train started, it ran alongside for quite a distance.

Farming was a precarious occupation, even in the Otavi Triangle, because of the uncertain rainfall. Charles thought that "they have to be endowed with a full measure of the gambling spirit, combined with an indomitable hope". On another visit to Grootfontein, he walked out to a farm with its owner, Grayson. The maize did not look too bad to Charles, especially the field that had been treated with phosphates, but Grayson said it would yield only 700 bags, compared to the 2000 bags he would have had if the rains had come at the usual time. More surprising was the devastating impact of the frost that had occurred the previous night. The tomatoes and cape gooseberries were ruined, and the leaves on the fig and mulberry trees were shrivelled and brittle. Nobody there had previously experienced a frost so early in the year.

North of Otavi, after winding through a narrow passage between the ranges of two high, steep hills, the railway came into a valley which Charles named the Happy Valley. It was a "wide and smiling valley... a delectable spot... the Land of Promise". Quoting from the Psalms that "the pools are filled with water", he went on to lament that mosquitoes carrying malaria also inhabited such pools. Not such a Happy Valley after all. Even when the mosquitoes did not carry malaria, they were a menace. At Omaruru a few days before, Charles was "fairly eaten up by them round the ankles and on the fingers and wrists".

Insects of all types could be quite troublesome. Charles had to cut short his sermon at an evening service in Swakopmund "as everyone in the congregation was anxiously watching the rapid gyrations of the insects round the room, the ladies being in a state of nervous tension lest a beetle might get entangled in their hair or crawl down their necks, and I felt that I might be hit in the eye any moment". Sitting on the veranda at home afterwards, insects gathered round the electric light in even denser numbers. One was the biggest beetle Charles had ever seen. "It flew so dangerously close at times that we knocked it lifeless, and on measuring it found that it was just four inches long and over 1½ inches across the shoulders." There was also a "lusty mosquito band" squeaking that night, and "next morning a large party of industrious little ants was wrestling with the body of the beetle".

When he first went to Swakopmund, Charles' travels around the archdeaconry were dependent on the railway, as more generally was life in Swakopmund and elsewhere. In his last year or two he was able to make a few journeys by car. The heavy rains in the winter of 1925 caused many problems on the railway. The Orange River had flooded and at one point was eight feet above the bridge at Upington in South Africa, which trains from South Africa to South West Africa had to cross. (Damaged girders from the bridge were later taken to Usakos to be repaired.) As a result, mail and newspapers from South Africa were held up for many weeks until the river subsided. The only way to get things from outside the country was through the ports, chiefly Luderitz and Walvis Bay. Coal stocks were running low, which affected the train service, the mines and other things. The only supply in the country was the stock of Welsh coal kept as a reserve by the British Admiralty at Walvis Bay. As it was needed at a time when the railway across the Swakop mouth was washed away, men had to carry 50lb bags of coal for half a mile or more across the gap to get it to trains that could run upcountry.

The line from Swakopmund to Windhoek, the first part of which Charles had to take to reach the narrow-gauge railway, was washed away. A number of people who were coming the other way to catch the boat to Europe from Walvis Bay were stuck the other side of the washaway. Although it was repaired in a few days, only one or two trains passed through before another flood swept away all the repairs, and moreover derailed an engine.

The narrow gauge also had washaway problems. In the summer of 1925, a bridge over a river bed collapsed when the river flooded. One stone supporting pillar sank six feet down into the sand, and another toppled over at an angle so that the girders and rails were twisted. By the time Charles got there a few weeks later, the line had been rebuilt through the river bed, which was now dry. At the northern end of the narrow gauge, the rain washed the ballast out from beneath the sleepers in places, causing the rails to sink down unevenly when a train passed over them. Charles was going north on a train that "gave such a sudden lurch sideways that for a moment I thought it was over". On the return journey, the bogie wheels of the engine jumped the line; luckily the driver was able to pull up in time. The "brake boys" jumped down from their perches on the trucks of copper ore and got out jacks with which they lifted the flanges of the wheels back over the rails. (The "brake boys" were men who sat on the trucks and operated the brakes as well as carrying out urgent repairs.) The whole thing took only 20 minutes. Charles witnessed the aftermath of a more serious accident in which, without any warning, an engine swerved off onto the veld and toppled over. The fireman jumped clear, but the driver and one other man were badly injured. The trucks were all jammed together at all sorts of angles. The line was closed for four days, after which the train carrying Charles was able to get through on a deviation line that went past the breakdown gang collecting up the wreckage.

The rains in the summer of 1926 did little damage, but in the summer of 1927 the Omaruru river washed away the narrow gauge line. Further north, Charles heard that about ten miles of line had gone. His monthly trip to other parts of his archdeaconry had to be postponed until repairs were made.

There were many other problems on the narrow gauge. After the rains in 1925, the grass had grown up so rapidly and spread over the rails that the engine wheels slipped and there was a risk of derailments. Insects were a problem. A plague of locusts on the line, where they were piled up six inches deep in some places, necessitated sending men out to sit "on the front of an engine armed with hosepipes driving arsenic solution into them". In one place termites had "secretly hollowed out a large and roomy cave beneath the permanent way". After the rain had softened the roof of the cave, it collapsed just after an engine had gone across it. "The trucks following were hurled into the cavity and fell in a confused heap by the side of the line".

The distance from the railhead at Grootfontein to Usakos, where the narrow gauge ended and joined the main line from Windhoek, was 272 miles. The journey was usually divided into two ten-hour stretches so that the "brake boys" could take a rest in the middle. On a trip in February 1927 there were trucks carrying livestock. The door of one truck burst open and a couple of oxen fell out. "The train stopped as soon as it could, but the animals did not seem much the worse for their experience, and both immediately started to graze, displaying a decided antipathy to resuming their journey." They were left to themselves as there was no time to round them up.

A few months later, also returning from Grootfontein, Charles' train was held up because the axle on a truck on a train coming the other way on a single-track section had broken. First, they had to replace the broken axle, and then a rail that was damaged when the truck broke down. The train eventually arrived at its destination four hours late.

The frequency of washaways, breakdowns and other mishaps meant that the railway company always had to be prepared to carry out emergency repairs to keep the service going. Gangers travelled with the trains, which also had a number of labourers, among them the "brake boys". As some of Charles' stories show, they were able to get the trains moving again fairly quickly, even when the initial problems were severe, such as washaways removing sections of line. Charles accepted all the inconvenience with good humour. He took advantage of unexpected delays on a trip to examine and write about the local flora and other features of interest. For him, it was always a bit of an adventure, a part of his jolly life.

Charles usually travelled in a passenger coach when he went round the archdeaconry by rail. But sometimes he had to go in the guard's van on a goods train if a coach was not available, or if the goods train could get him to his destination earlier. A journey of many hours in the guard's van was a different proposition from the short trip to or from Walvis Bay. He recorded one such trip overnight from Usakos, a distance of about ninety miles. "The only place to lie down amid the stacks of cases, parcels, motor tyres, beer barrels etc. was a narrow strip between a pile of ox carcasses and sacks of potatoes which, judging from their odour, were well on the way to decay." While the smell was bad enough, the noise in the van was terrible: "a concentrated concatenation of clamour as would fill the heart of any jazz band master with envy. The door set up a piercing shriek like a wheelbarrow in need of oil, and kept at it; somewhere else a kind of grating noise commenced, as of the high-pitched yapping of an excited terrier, only much louder; a shrill squeak proceeded from another part; chains rattled and clanked; and each wheel seemed to have a nobble on it so that it came down with a bang on every revolution." Despite all this, Charles managed to sleep for about six hours. It was a good thing he enjoyed adventures – and writing about them afterwards – as there were plenty of them in South West Africa.

A couple of years later he went to the station at Karibib to catch the passenger train to Usakos, where he intended to change, after a wait of many hours, to another passenger train going to Swakopmund. When he got to Karibib station he found that a goods train that was running late was setting off for Swakopmund. He immediately joined it and settled comfortably among the overseas mail bags in the guard's van. As a result he arrived home about 12 hours before he would have done if he had gone on the passenger trains.

Travelling by railway had problems, but road transport could be more difficult. For two months in the winter of 1925, the supply of vanadium ore for the boats calling at Walvis Bay was interrupted because the ore could not be brought from the mine to the railhead in Grootfontein, twenty-five miles away. It came on wagons, but the wagon tracks were quagmires in places. However, the roads improved during the time Charles and Marion were in Swakopmund, and Charles sometimes went by car instead of train. The roads were unpaved and not well marked, so that drivers had to follow tracks in the sand.

When the weather was hot, they sometimes travelled at night, which made navigation even more difficult. One night journey from Swakopmund to Karibib in November 1927 took 8½ hours to cover about 100 miles because the driver did not know the route, and a passenger who took it upon himself to act as navigator instructed him to go the wrong way. Charles "began to think something was wrong when, after making a magnificent sweep round on the desert, we entered the town again at the top end of the same street by which we had lately left at the other end". Their next attempt to find the correct route took them almost to Walvis Bay, due south of Swakopmund, whereas they should have been heading east. Charles' intervention eventually helped to get them onto the right route. Other adventures included getting stuck in wet sand in a river bed, bumping along on rocks and stones where the sandy covering had been washed away by rain, and, of course, many punctures.

Charles and Marion kept up with family news from England. They were saddened by the deaths of three close relatives in a short space of time in 1926. First, Charles' brother-in-law, George Odling-Smee, the husband of his deceased sister Emma, died aged only 52 on 24 March in Guildford, after having been unwell for many months. Then, Charles' Uncle Martin died in Bognor on 30 March at the age of 87. Four weeks later, his cousin, John Key, died in Oxford following an accident on his bicycle. He was 72.

At the beginning of 1928, Charles and Marion had been in South West Africa for almost six years. They decided then that the time had come to leave for good. It is likely that there were health reasons for this. The main evidence is the remark by Bishop Vyvyan in Charles' obituary that "owing to his wife's ill-health, he was not able to stay in that trying country, and eventually returned to England".[145]

145   *The Net,* December 1930.

CHAPTER 9

ENGLAND AND ELSEWHERE

Charles and Marion went to England on leave twice during their six years in South West Africa. The first time was in 1924, when they had been nearly two years in Keetmanshoop. The second time was in 1926, when they were about half way through their time in Swakopmund. The first time they sailed from Luderitz on 20 February 1924 on a Dutch cargo ship that was going to Cape Town heavily laden with goods from Europe, including British-made steam lorries, live animals (pedigree bulls, cows and rams), oil drums and dried fish. In Cape Town they transferred to the *Llanstephan Castle*, a Union-Castle line ship that was returning to England via the East Coast of Africa and the Suez Canal.[146] They had taken that route once before, in 1910, and Charles wanted to see the changes that had occurred in the meantime. They left Cape Town on 23 February, and six weeks later disembarked in Genoa from where they took the train to London.

The first part of the journey, calling at Port Elizabeth, East London and Durban, was familiar from their days in Zululand. After that, they called at Lourenço Marques (later

---

146   The Union-Castle line was the main shipping line for passenger and cargo services between the UK and South Africa. The company was formed by a merger in 1900 between two separate companies, Union and Castle. It ran weekly passenger services between Southampton and Cape Town, a voyage of three weeks. In 1922 it started a Round Africa service, a nine-week voyage calling at twenty ports en route. Alternate sailings travelled out via the Suez Canal and out via West Africa. This was probably the service Charles and Marion took in 1924. Their previous voyages had also been on Union-Castle ships: *Tintagel Castle* in 1908, *Garth Castle* in 1910, *Gloucester Castle* and *Guildford Castle* in 1914 and *Llanstephan Castle* in 1919. In 1896 and 1897, Charles had travelled on *Grantully Castle*, before the Castle line had merged with the Union line.

renamed Maputo, the capital of independent Mozambique), Beira and Mozambique in the Portuguese territory of Mozambique. Only in Beira did they have much time to explore the towns and environs, although Charles was able to visit the zoo in Lourenço Marques where he admired the marabou storks and pelicans.

They were delayed in Beira by the need to load a cargo of chrome iron ore that was destined for Marseille. It had come from Rhodesia on the railway that had been opened in 1900 for the main purpose of exporting minerals from there. Despite the busy port, Charles noted that there had not been much progress in Beira since 1910. He saw only one car, although the road surfaces were harder than the sandy ones of 1910. The town of Mozambique was the first to be settled by the Portuguese. who built a fort that was still there after 400 years. Charles reflected on the reasons why the Portuguese Empire had not been as successful as others, despite their explorers, Bartholomew Diaz and Vasco da Gama, having opened up so many territories in Africa and the East to Europeans. He concluded that, after the first 100 years, they had been too slow to innovate and so lost their lead, and some of their territories, to the Dutch and later the British and French.

After the Portuguese territory came the British ones. The ship called at Dar es Salaam, Zanzibar, Tanga and Mombasa, but spent time only in Mombasa. Dar es Salaam was in Tanganyika Territory, a former German colony that the Versailles Treaty gave to the UK. There were still many signs of the fighting during World War I, including damaged buildings and rusty hulks that had been sunk across the entrance to the harbour. In Zanzibar the ship picked up a cargo of cloves. Boys swam around calling for coins. Charles noted that copper coins were prized, whereas in 1910 they had not been. The ship stopped at Tanga very briefly, but long enough to offload four horses.

Mombasa was the major port on this part of the trip. Compared to 1910, it was bustling, with new sheds and cranes, and an ongoing project to build new wharves for shipping. There were cars, mostly Fords, on the streets, whereas before the main means of transport for people who did not want to walk had been on trolleys that were pushed along rails by African men. Charles took a walk through the old, narrow streets, in which men in fezzes looked after their shops amid wandering chicken and other animals. Goods were being transported in carts, some pulled by men and some by camels. When the ship left after a few days, it had acquired a small menagerie in the shape of two lion cubs, four or five leopards and some monkeys.

The next leg of the voyage, over 1600 miles to Aden, was the longest of the whole trip. They occasionally saw the cliffs on the barren Somali coast. Aden shared with Luderitz a bare rocky location, in which drinking water had to be obtained from condensing sea water. Charles, ever aware of the colours in nature, observed that the rocks in Aden were reddish brown and looked as though they had been "blown up from below by some gigantic force", whereas in Luderitz they were grey and gave the appearance of having been "formed by a flow of lava".

The long journey up the Red Sea to the Gulf of Suez was broken by a call at Port Sudan, where Charles was impressed by the strength and agility of the men who carried sacks of grain onto the ship, chanting together all the while. Reminders of the war returned when they were passing through El Kantara on the Suez Canal. It had been a major base for the Sinai and Palestine campaigns led by General Allenby against the Ottomans. Lines of abandoned horse sheds could still be seen. The railway that had been built to move armies and their equipment now went all the way to Jerusalem. Port Said at the end of the Suez Canal was built on a sandbank extended by earth and mud dug up when the canal was built. There were flies everywhere in the market in the Arab section – "the fourth plague of Egypt" as Charles called them. "Egyptian ladies all dressed exactly alike in the regulation Mahomedan style" of black burqas with only their eyes showing were shopping for linens. Charles observed many arguments among local men and concluded that they were a more excitable people than the easy-going East Africans he had seen in earlier weeks.

The final non-stop leg of the trip across the Mediterranean to Genoa was over 1400 miles long. The journey was stretched over six days because the ship reduced speed after hearing from Genoa that there would be delays in their being attended to there. The animals that had come on board in Mombasa had been joined by some Egyptian dogs "of the sort that Arabs take with them for food on their long camel journeys". The monkeys enjoyed being stroked, while the leopards snarled and swore "at any attempt at conversation". There were many sightings of land, notably Crete, and Italy and Sicily as they sailed through the straits of Messina. There was snow on Mount Etna and the mountains in Calabria. The damage from the earthquake in 1908 in Messina was still quite apparent. They passed Stromboli, which had been "hurling forth stones and ashes" only two days before and was covered by dense clouds of vapour, as always.

The long voyage from Cape Town and the numerous ports of call had given Charles many opportunities to study the birds and fishes, as well as the sea and the sky. He managed to name many of the birds he saw. Of the sea animals, the most impressive were the sharks. They often appeared when the ship was anchored off a port, and food waste was being thrown out of the galley. Charles was impressed that they knew not to grab a hunk of meat that had been attached to a hook in Mombasa, and he admired the scene when a shark in Dar es Salaam rolled over and the "light shining up from his white belly through the water flashed a transparent bluish emerald green".

It was not only the sharks whose colours caught Charles' eye. Near Port Sudan, the shallow water in a coral lagoon on the seaward side of the harbour sandspit, with "the white sand reflecting upwards through it making it a transparent crystal green, extended outwards for some distance. Towards the centre it deepened through a vivid emerald green to a dark turquoise blue, while the outer rim of the lagoon was so near the surface that it gave quite a reddish tinge to the water flowing over it and causing it to break into little white wavelets. Beyond the rim lay the indigo-cobalt of the open sea".

Two things struck Charles most on his first day or two in Genoa: the green shuttered houses "swarming down the crowded, narrow streets" and the ubiquitous evidence of the Christian faith, so different from South Africa. "Black-cassocked priests stroll among the people gathered round the posters announcing the latest results of the elections which have put Mussolini firmly into power once again. Habited monks wearing little black silk caps to keep the draught off their tonsure hurry down the crowded streets. Old churches rear their heads among the mass of buildings. The Cathedral is particularly rich in relics, possessing among various other carefully preserved treasures: the remains of St John the Baptist, the charger in which his head was presented to Herod, an arm of St Anna, the head of St Barnabas, a thorn from the Crown of Thorns, fragments of the cross, and the original Holy Grail!" There was more than a touch of Anglican scepticism about Roman Catholic beliefs in this comment.

The train from Genoa took Charles and Marion to Turin and on to Paris. They crossed the Channel from Boulogne to Dover and arrived in London on 10 April, seven weeks after leaving Luderitz. As the train covered the last stretch from Dover, they felt the warm familiarity of the neat English countryside, as Britons who have lived in less developed, and more sparsely populated, countries always do when they return home.

Charles and Marion stayed with family and friends during most of their six-month leave in England. Two relatives in particular hosted them for many weeks each. Charles' Uncle Martin lived in Bognor, and also had a second house in Selsey. He was 85, a widower with a housekeeper, and not in very good health. He no doubt welcomed Charles' visits both for the company and because Charles was to be his executor and would in due course take over the final disposition of the Walters family money from Martin. Marion's sister Kathleen was widowed and was living with her 31-year-old unmarried son in Purley. She was the closest sister to Marion in age. Having raised three sons, one of whom was killed in the war, in the same house, there was room for Charles and Marion to stay.

They also stayed for a week or so with Charles' brother-in-law, George Odling-Smee, and his family in Guildford. Charles and Marion had taken a special interest in the children ever since their mother, Emma, Charles' sister, had died in 1911. The youngest, Barbara, who was 14 in 1924, was Marion's goddaughter. Despite being away in Southern Africa for most of the time, Charles and Marion kept in touch as best as they could from a distance and spent time with them when in England. They wanted their nephews and niece to know that they would always be a supportive uncle and aunt.

They took several trips round southern England in Charles' motorcycle and sidecar. They went twice to Oxford, the second time combining it with a few days in Stratford and Henley. Another trip was to Salisbury and Stonehenge. Yet another was to Cirencester and the New Forest. Some of the trips were heavy on nostalgia. This was certainly the case with Oxford, where punting on the river and dozing when the punt was tied to the bank brought back happy memories. Boating on the Thames at Henley reminded Charles of the regatta in which he had rowed for Pembroke College over 30 years earlier.

Other trips were to places Charles did not know. He took these visits seriously. He studied the guide books, and took a special interest in the history and architecture of the places. Even after going home, he would follow up with further study, for example of the history of Petworth House and its owners, the Percy family, and the origins of the name of Oxford and of its university. The guide books sometimes irritated him, as when that on Stratford referred to Holy Trinity Church where it said "Shakespeare sleeps". Charles wrote in *In the Winds of Heaven* that it would be more truthful to use the language of the old refrain about John Brown's body because the soul of Shakespeare, of all people, surely went marching on while his body was mouldering before the altar in Holy Trinity. He was not attracted by the Shakespeare tourist industry in Stratford, although the many fine old gabled

half-timbered houses "stirred one's dormant proclivities of sketching to the depths".

Charles' adventurous spirit was reflected in his choice of a motorcycle to get around. It was not without mishaps, of which the sharp flints on the road across Salisbury Plain that cut up the inner tube was only one. He wanted to visit Friday Street, an isolated village in the Weald not far from Dorking, where there was an attractive mill pond left over from the long-abandoned iron works. He had some difficulty finding the road into Friday Street and ended up going down a cart track that "was not only worn into deep ruts in which were concealed various snags in the way of rocks and tree roots, but it was tipped up at an angle sideways. A bank rose so sheer up from the rut on the off-side that I was afraid to let the sidecar wheel run in it for fear of catching in the various projections, so the machine had to do its best in the lower rut. Once or twice I thought that the foot-rest would be torn off, and every now and then it seemed as if the side-car was coming over on top of me, but we pulled through."

Riding on a motorcycle, he was exposed to the weather. A number of trips were postponed or shortened because of rain. It was, in fact, quite a rainy spring and summer. Charles, in his usual passion for recording facts, every day wrote down the temperatures (minimum and maximum), rainfall, barometric pressure and general condition in London. In October he totted up the totals: 73 days with no rain, and 101 days when it rained, "so the summer has been more than usually damp. Moreover, the temperature has only reached 80° on three occasions."

We do not know what Marion thought of the adventures on the motorcycle, although, sitting in the sidecar, she would have been more protected from the rain than Charles. But she had gone along with his adventures her whole life, starting with summer holidays together with Emma, and culminating in many years in testing conditions in Zululand and South West Africa. She must have had some spirit of adventure herself and was surely attracted to Charles in part because of his love of adventure.

Their leave came to an end, and Charles and Marion sailed from Tilbury on the *Grantully Castle* on 9 October 1924.[147] They arrived three weeks later in Cape Town, where they spent a few days seeing old friends and making business and other arrangements. The setting of Cape Town was as spectacular as ever. Among the rocks on the slope of Table Mountain "were masses of pink pelargoniums in full blossom, and thick-set proteas bearing large pin cushions of yellow flowers at the end of their branches".

The train to South West Africa from Cape Town passed through the Karoo, where the river beds were dry, and crossed the Orange river which, by contrast, was in full flood from the upcountry rains. The water was "surging along, a turgid, brown-yellow flood, twice the width of the Thames at London Bridge, right up to the top of the stone pillars which carried

the line across". The train passed through Keetmanshoop where they had lived for over two years, but they continued to Windhoek, the capital of South West Africa, and the centre of the Diocese of Damaraland, the Anglican diocese covering the whole of South West Africa. They spent a few days in Windhoek, where Charles had business with the Bishop of Damaraland, who was his superior, and other diocesan priests and officials. They then took the train to Swakopmund, where they arrived on 19 November and where Charles was based for the next three and a quarter years.

Half way through their time in Swakopmund, they again went to England on leave. They left on 7 May 1926 on the train to Cape Town, a journey of 1614 miles that took 3½ days. As Charles observed, the most impressive feature of the country they went through was its vast monotony. Until they left the Karoo, there was no sign of any cultivation, except at Upington, where they crossed the Orange river, and spasmodic attempts on the Karoo itself. The most interesting part was in South West Africa, south of Windhoek, where the wide plains of the uplands gave way to stony bush-strewn hills.

On one of the three days they were in Cape Town, the House of Assembly passed the Mines and Works Act, known informally as the Colour Bar Act, which required certificates of competency for skilled jobs, and was designed to reduce competition from blacks for jobs usually held by whites. Presciently, Charles

---

147   The ship was a successor to the older *Grantully Castle* on which he had sailed in 1896 and 1897.

noted that "it may well be the beginning of the doom that will fall upon the back-veld Boer when the native people are educated enough as a whole to overwhelm him". As it turned out, the National Party, which represented the interests of the Afrikaners, was able to postpone that day of reckoning for nearly 70 years, in part by restricting educational opportunities for Africans.

They sailed from Cape Town on 14 May on the *Balmoral Castle* for the 5987-mile journey to Southampton. The only pause on the journey was an eight-hour stop in Funchal, Madeira. It was the first time Charles had been there since 1896. He and Marion went ashore to look around. After admiring the jacaranda trees that were blooming and the Public Gardens, they took the railway to the top of the 3300-foot mountain, where there were spectacular views over the town and harbour. They came down by carrinho da cesta, which translates literally as basket cart, a suitable name for a two-seater wickerwork chair fixed to wooden runners that slid easily over the knobbly paved road. It was steered with ropes down the steep, curvy route by two men running alongside. The journey was more exciting than they might have wished, as they nearly ran into a heavily loaded sleigh coming round a corner, and "finally dashed into the town travelling at a record pace".

The drizzling rain and mist in the Bay of Biscay gave them "a taste of the old homeland" when they arrived in Southampton on 31 May. As on earlier occasions, returning to England stirred warm feelings in Charles. "The first day back in the old country is always a day of wonder, as however bright one's memory vision of it may be, it is never quite as satisfying as the real thing." The "white billowing clouds", the cows "grazing in buttercup-bestrewn meadows through which the full-brimming Hampshire trout streams were winding their way", the "leafy foliage of the trees and the greenness of the grass and the brightness of the wild flowers" all moved him. Early next morning the cuckoo called from a neighbouring copse. Charles shared Kipling's sentiment in *The English Flag*: "What should they know of England who only England know?".[148] He added: "One has to come from the desert or to return after many years absence in far different lands to feel and really to enter in to the wonder and fair beauty of it all".

As they had done when on leave in England in 1924, Charles and Marion based themselves in Purley with Marion's sister Kathleen, and Bognor. Charles' Uncle Martin having died just a few months before, his house in Bognor might have been available to Charles, who was his executor. Charles also had a cousin in Bognor, Helen Hawes, the divorced daughter of his Uncle George, and he and Marion might have stayed with her. Uncle Martin had left his house in Selsey to his housekeeper, Miss

---

148 Kipling's poem *The English Flag* (1891) was an implied criticism of what he saw as the blindness of the English to their Empire and the men that served and defended it. Charles slightly misquoted it, writing in *In the Winds of Heaven*: "What do they know of England who only England know?".

Plumbley (known as Plumb in the family), and Charles and Marion stayed there briefly on a couple of occasions.

They stayed at the Odling-Smee home in Guildford a couple of times. With the children having lost their mother fifteen years before, and now their father earlier in the year, it was especially important that they should spend time with their nephews and niece and their stepmother. They made other short visits to friends and relatives. One person was Annesley Harold Brownrigg, the son of Charles' deceased cousin Louisa Brownrigg. He lived in Milford, near Godalming, and was an architect and surveyor.

As in 1924, they took a number of trips around Southern England with the motor cycle and sidecar. The longest one, lasting 2½ weeks, was to Oxford and the New Forest. As they liked to do in Oxford, they went boating on both the Thames and the Cherwell, stopping for picnics on the bank or even on the punt. Although we cannot be sure, they were probably joined for at least part of the time on this trip by their nephews and niece, the three Odling-Smee children. After Oxford, they went to the New Forest, staying in Ringwood, just on the other side of it. While there they visited Emily Key, the widow of Charles' cousin John Key. She lived in Southbourne, near Bournemouth.

Charles and Marion visited many churches, both grand cathedrals, such as Winchester and Christchurch, Oxford, and small village churches. The church at Tangmere, just north of Chichester, was distinguished by having an ancient stone communion table, which Charles thought was probably made of Petworth marble. He was also intrigued by a quaint, rough carving on the outside wall of a figure, perhaps the priest, "whose head is about the same size as his body and whose cassock is as short as the ladies' skirts at the present day".

On a visit to London, Charles went to the Hudson Memorial Bird Sanctuary in Hyde Park. The new memorial to "that great outdoor naturalist, W.H. Hudson" had been opened in 1924. Charles liked the setting with rose bay and plume thistles in full flower, a privet hedge behind and lawns in front, but not the stone carving by Jacob Epstein. It was meant to represent Rima, the child goddess of nature who featured in Hudson's novel *Green Mansions*, published in 1904. But, Charles asked, "what is there of Rima, the delicate spirit of the forest, clothed in gossamer woven for her by the spiders, to be seen in that crude, naked figure of exaggerated angles and enormous hands?" Could Epstein ever have read Abel's eulogy in *Green Mansions*: "Listen, Rima, you are like all the beautiful things in the wood – flower, and bird, and butterfly, and green leaf, and frond , and little silky-haired monkey high up in the trees"? Maybe he did read it, but decided to go to the opposite extreme, and design something so strong and rough that everyone would be able to see how different his conception was to that of Hudson's.

When Charles and Marion were preparing to return to South West Africa, Charles gave his motorcycle to his nephew Bill Odling-

Smee. One of the first long trips that Bill took on it was to Scotland, where he went for an engineering job on a road project in Glencoe.

Charles and Marion left Southampton for Cape Town on the *Kildonan Castle* on 10 September 1926. It was a sunny day, and their "last impression of the old country was one of greenness – green trees and hedges and meadows". As they sailed down the Solent, the setting sun showed up the various coloured strata on the cliff side of Alum Bay: pink, brown, claret, yellow, light ochre to cream.

Charles and Marion went ashore when the boat called in at Funchal. They opted for a quiet time at the Palace Hotel rather than more adventures comparable to those when they had been there only four months earlier on their journey to England. Many flowers were open in the bright sunlight, including red hibiscus, purple bougainvillea, light blue plumbago, creamy honeysuckle, red and pink geraniums, and white cactus. Charles and Marion idly watched the moths probing the flowers for nectar, and the lizards basking on the warm rocks. After this brief break, the rest of the voyage was smooth and uneventful.

They arrived in Cape Town on 27 September and took the train to South West Africa a few days later. The contrast between the desolation of the Namib desert on the final stretch into Swakopmund and the green fields and hedgerows of England still struck Charles, even though he had been back and forth between the two many times. Anyone going to sleep in England and "waking up for the first time in the Namib might easily conclude that he had been mysteriously transported to some desolate region on the moon or on one of the outer planets".

They were in Swakopmund for another year and four months and then they left for good. As we have seen, this was probably because of Marion's poor health at the time, which may also explain why they treated themselves to a two-month holiday in the Canary Islands on their way home to England.

Charles and Marion travelled directly from South West Africa to Las Palmas de Gran Canaria on the SS *Ussukuma* of the German African Line. They sailed from Walvis Bay on 1 February. The ship was carrying 2000 tons of copper ore from the mine at Tsumeb and a cargo of fishmeal. Although it called briefly at Luanda, the passengers were not permitted to disembark. They looked out at the town built on a high, sandstone bluff with an ancient Portuguese fort at the southern end, and a low-lying sand spit with thatched huts half hidden among tall coconut palms, quite a romantic tropical spot, Charles thought. Without any further stops, they arrived in Las Palmas on 16 February. As it was approaching 11pm when they disembarked, there were no Spanish customs or immigration officers to check their arrival. They therefore took a car straight to their hotel.

For the next few weeks, they stayed in Santa Brigida, which is up in the hills about ten miles from Las Palmas. They explored the hills around, mostly on foot. Their walks took them all over the central part of the island, including up to the Pico de Bandama, an old volcano, and down into its caldera. The views from the high points were spectacular. They could see not only all around the island of Gran Canaria, but at one point also across to the island of Fuerteventura, sixty miles away. They observed the primitive farming and household management practices: oxen pulling ploughs, pack mules (and a few camels) carrying loads, and women carrying laundry on their heads after washing it in the streams and laying it on rocks to dry. As usual, it was the plants that Charles was especially interested in. On one walk he collected 53 different wild plants. He was able to name most of the plants he saw, or at least to locate their genus.

The main edible fruits being grown were grapes, bananas, oranges, dates and prickly pears. Charles had not tasted prickly pears before and decided that they were not worth the trouble of eating. First, he had to deal with the little bunches of bristles which, "unless one is careful, stick into one's fingers". Then there were the hard pips within. "But the juice, what there is of it, is quite refreshing, and is of a bright carmine pink colour such as might appeal as a lip stain to the females of today's decadent world".

They were in Santa Brigida for Carnival. The first they knew of it "was on Sunday when an otherwise staid and sober old Spanish gentleman walked into lunch at the hotel with a false nose on". After that they could not get away from the music, dancing and "people in fancy dress larking about with one another".

They ran into a "jazz band party wearing night gowns with bits of curtain lace over their faces, playing on mouth organs, with empty petrol tins for drums and using their lids as cymbals – they were a jovial and noisy crew." They also "met parties in fancy dress, mostly with guitars, visiting villas and cottages on the surrounding hills. The whole countryside was given up to revelry. In England the nearest approach to such a spirit of abandonment is when 'arry and 'arriet change hats for the time being on a Bank Holiday."[149] The partying continued until Tuesday, "when things worked up to a climax".

After nearly four weeks on Gran Canaria, they took the boat from Las Palmas to Santa Cruz on the island of Tenerife, a journey of about five hours. They then went by car across the island to Puerto de la Cruz, twenty-six miles from Santa Cruz. Puerto de la Cruz is near the mouth of the Orotava valley, where Charles and Marion stayed for the next two weeks. As on Gran Canaria, they took many walks. They were "regarded with so much interest that one feels almost as important as a travelling show". Heads appeared at windows, women gathered at doorways and stared, and children followed them, "more often than not for the purpose of demanding cash, a hopeless errand for they never got it".

Charles wondered about their Christianity. Many buildings, secular as well as religious ones, even gateways, had crosses on top. Shrines were used for various purposes, in one

---

149   'Arry and 'arriet was a slang expression for the generic Cockney man and woman.

case to store lumber; in another, empty wine bottles were standing on the bare wooden shelf before an old cross from which the paint was peeling off. "It is hard to know what to make of it, for taking it at its lowest, superstition does not die easily, and especially so among an uneducated people, as is evinced by a cross set up in the Iglesia de la Concepcion in Orotava with the undertaking attached that whosoever should kiss it and say a paternoster before it shall be remitted 200 days in purgatory." There was a mixture of condescension and Anglican superiority in this remark, which was not uncommon among English travellers in Catholic countries at the time.

After Orotava, they returned to Santa Cruz, where they stayed for another two weeks. Nelson lost his arm there in 1797 when he led the British fleet in an unsuccessful assault on the town. The Plaza de 25 de Julio commemorated the date that the Spaniards "regard as a red letter day in their history". The verger of the church pointed "with some pride to the two flags which were captured from the English landing party and are now carefully preserved in two long glass-fronted cases in a side chapel of the church".

Their holiday in the Canaries ended on 12 April, two months after they arrived. They embarked on the *Buenavista*, a cargo boat loaded with bananas, potatoes and tomatoes. After calling at Las Palmas on Gran Canaria to pick up more cargo and passengers, it sailed directly to England.

The *Buenavista* sailed up the Thames and Charles and Marion disembarked at Greenwich on 19 April 1928, two and a half months after leaving South West Africa. While delighting in all the signs of spring, Charles noted that there did not seem to be "the same freshness in the growth of spring such as has been so immediately impressive on first landing in the old country on former occasions". He explained this partly by their having already had a foretaste of spring in the Canaries, and partly to a cold snap that had been "holding the country in its grip".

Charles did not have a job when he arrived in England. Until one became available, he and Marion lived in Selsey. Charles now had a car, so they did not have to ride around in a motorcycle and sidecar as in earlier years. They went on outings both locally and further afield, the latter including trips to the New Forest, Canterbury, Purley to visit Marion's sister Kathleen, and Guildford to visit the Odling-Smees. They also went twice for a few days to Kensworth in Bedfordshire where they stayed with the vicar, William Challis, an old friend from South Africa.[150] On one of these occasions Charles took some Toc-H members from Kensworth to Luton to visit people in hospital.

Charles enjoyed driving and recorded the routes and road and traffic conditions in

---

150 Rev William Adams Challis was about five years older than Charles. He had also spent ten years in parishes in industrial Yorkshire before going to Zululand. He worked in Zululand and Swaziland from 1901 to 1918 and in the Cape Province from 1920 to 1926. He was vicar of Kensworth from 1926 to 1937.

detail. He could be frustrated by heavy or slow traffic and loved the open road where he could choose his own speed. In the New Forest he drove on a "magnificent highway" with tarred macadam, which "in years gone by would have been smothered in clouds of choking dust". While "one got closest in touch with the country" when walking, "in motoring through it, it is possible very really to appreciate the joy which comes from:

The sweep of English uplands,
The sigh of English trees,
The laugh of English rivers,
The breath of English breeze."[151]

Charles went to London from time to time for business. He found it took a little time to get "used to the rush and crowds of London once again". But after a few months he could say that "walking about in the streets of London is quite a fascinating occupation. All the change and variety, the constant movement going on around, the glide and rush of the motor traffic, and the concentrated vigilance required in crossing from one pavement to another, all tend to add to the general effect." Nevertheless, he usually sought the relative peace of St James Park, which was a short walk from his solicitor's office at Charing Cross.

For most of the time in the first few months that Charles and Marion were back in England, they stayed near their home in Selsey. They took many walks, accompanied sometimes by their dog Jack. They loved to watch the changing vegetation, with Charles, of course, focused on the flowers and, to a lesser extent, the birds. On their outings, whether locally or on their motoring trips, they often took picnics and found beautiful spots from which to admire the scenery while eating their lunch.

As usual, Charles followed the weather closely, keeping detailed records and commenting in *In the Winds of Heaven* on the more interesting developments. It was unusually hot in July, which reminded him of Spenser's lines:

Then came hot July boiling like to fire
That all his garments he had cast away.[152]

There had been no rain for some time, and, as happens in England, people were worrying about the possibilities of water shortages. For Charles, "it is difficult to get used to the idea, after living in South West Africa, that when it has not rained for a fortnight, a state of drought has become established".

After a few months, Charles was offered a position as a Public Preacher in Chelmsford Diocese. This presumably required him to conduct services but without having any responsibilities in particular parishes. He and Marion went to Essex in early August to meet his future superiors and colleagues, and to find somewhere to live. They stayed in the village of

---

151 Cicely Fox Smith (1882 – 1954). She was about 16 years old when she wrote the poem from which these lines are an extract.

152 Edmund Spenser, *The Faerie Queen*, Book VII, Canto XXXVI.

Great Warley which had a fine modern church built in Art Nouveau style in 1902 (and which much later was listed Grade 1). Charles, who was suspicious of departures from traditional styles, thought that "although its appearance tends towards the opulent, it is not too blatant to be offensive... The whole church is full of symbolism, and, as the novelty of the decoration wears off, the more one is able to appreciate it." There was a Saxon church in Greensted, a nearby village, which Charles seemed to like better, perhaps because of its long history and simple interior.

They found a house to buy in Hutton, a village further out from London than Great Warley, and closer to Chelmsford. In the two months before they could move in, Charles went to two church conferences. The first was the fourth meeting of the Continuation Committee of the Life and Work movement, which had started with a conference in Stockholm in 1925. The aim of the movement was to promote the church's role in finding solutions to economic, industrial, social and moral problems. It was ecumenical, including most Protestant and Eastern Orthodox churches, but not the Roman Catholic Church. While it encouraged co-operation between churches, it recognised the leading role of the World Alliance for Promoting International Friendship Through the Churches in that area. The Life and Work movement was one of the organisations involved in the agreement in 1937 to set up the World Council of Churches which came into existence in 1948. There had been three annual Continuation Committee

meetings before the fourth meeting which Charles attended in Prague on 3-5 September 1928.

We do not know whether Charles was there as part of a Church of England delegation, or whether he attended as an individual. He had taken quite an interest in ecumenical developments, which had flourished after the war.

Various leading figures in the movement gave reports on issues relating to youth, theology, the press, social morality, alcoholism, gambling, disarmament, and the strength of Life and Work groups in individual countries. Resolutions were passed, but they were largely expressions of hope (for example, one supporting all efforts towards cooperation between employers and employees) rather than ones that would lead to actions by participants. Following a controversial discussion about how to respond to the Pope's recent allusion to Life and Work, a resolution was passed that there should be no response now but that the committee of theologians should define the position of Life and Work on the issues raised by the Pope.

In a private discussion, the secretary of the US Federal Council of Churches, McFarlane, told Charles that the Anglican Church was regarded with some suspicion, except for some individuals such as the Bishop of Winchester. "They talked a good deal but got no further." McFarlane said that they would lose their position in the general movement if they did not show they were in earnest.

The conference lasted three days, but

Charles was in Prague for six days, probably on his own. He saw as much of Prague as he could, although hampered by not having an English language guidebook. The special exhibition of desert plants in the botanical gardens introduced him to many "old friends" from Southern Africa, although they were mostly smaller than the ones he knew. St Vitus cathedral was being renovated, with the floors taken up, scaffolding all around and general disorder. Charles remarked that it looked "as if it has been suffering from a severe attack of the complaint which the saint to whom it is dedicated is supposed to cure".[153] His trains to and from Prague took about a day. On the way back he had to endure conversations with, first, a German man who had known South Africa in the early days, and then an English lady who had been to Marienbad for the waters and mud baths. She seemed to Charles to have "spent a lot of money without feeling much better".

The second conference Charles attended was the Church Congress of the Church of England held in Cheltenham in early October. The Congress was an annual meeting of clergy and laity to discuss religious, moral and social issues, without any legislative consequences. The Cheltenham Congress was the next to last one; there were no more after the one in Newport in 1930. Again, we do not know whether Charles was there to represent his diocese or other constituency, or on his own account.

He and Marion made a little holiday out of the trip to Cheltenham. They first went to Oxford, where they stayed for three nights. As was their habit there, they took a boat down the river, and pulled into the bank for a picnic. After Oxford, they drove through the Cotswolds to Upton St Leonards, their destination for the next week. Charles went into Cheltenham for the sessions of the Congress, but otherwise they had plenty of time to walk in the countryside and visit Gloucester, Painswick and other places of interest. In Cheltenham itself, they saw people drinking the waters regardless, Charles observed, of the warning in the epitaph:

Here I lie and my three daughters
Died through drinking Cheltenham waters;
If we had stuck to Epsom salts
We shouldn't be in these here vaults.

They broke the journey back to Essex to spend three days at the White Hart Hotel in Buckingham. The first day was market day, and the hotel door was "blocked with country farmers discussing the qualities of cattle with the same fervour as any wealthy Zulu headman… In the evening the Salvation Army came out to bear their witness, endeavouring to enliven their proceedings with tambourines and a couple of wheezy wind instruments very much out of tune, without any success". A walk in the park that was the seat of the Earls and Dukes of Buckingham until the line died

---

153   The aid of St Vitus was invoked against chorea, also called St Vitus dance, a disorder characterised by rapid, uncoordinated jerking movements.

out in 1887 but had been owned by Stowe School since 1923 was frustrated by locked gates and threats to prosecute trespassers. Charles grumbled to himself in *In the Winds of Heaven*: "Why should a boy's school be enclosed with all the strictness of a nunnery?"

Arriving in Essex a few days before the completion of the purchase of their house in Hutton, they stayed in the White Hart Hotel in Brentwood. Completion took place on 13 October and they moved in on 16 October. The house, which dated from 1906, cost £1700. It was called Trevone, but they changed it to Newlands, the name of the area of Cape Town where they had lived from 1919 to 1922. It was at the end of a muddy track which could be very slippery after rain.

There was a large garden, with a grass tennis court, an orchard with apple, pear and plum trees, flower beds, a vegetable garden, and berry bushes (gooseberries, currants and raspberries). Charles was enthusiastic about the opportunities, and within a few weeks of taking up residence was digging over a section three spades deep. He built a shed for tools out of the packing cases that brought their things from South Africa. In the spring he planted vegetables, including potatoes, cabbages, broad beans, French beans, peas, turnips, carrots, parsnips, beetroots, spinach and lettuce. The resulting crops were good, apart from the damage from rabbits, birds (which liked the peas and berries), caterpillars (which got into the cabbages) and wasps, which attacked the ripening plums and other fruit. Charles found the hole in the ground where the wasps lived and poured a mixture of sugar and water with potassium cyanide into it.

Charles and Marion explored the towns and villages in Essex in the car. Charles read up the history of each place and recorded it in *In the Winds of Heaven*. He was intrigued by the church at Laindon because a two-room priest's house had been built onto the west end in the 13th century. It "certainly is very different to the white elephant rectories of a later generation". Blackmore Village was where Henry VIII's mistress Elizabeth Blount lived and where she gave birth to his illegitimate son Henry Fitzroy. The church had an unusual wooden tower. Charles was struck by the number of religious houses there appeared to have been in Essex before the Reformation. "No doubt, in the height of their prosperity these places did much good in helping the country people... and moreover they were the chief centres where the lamp of learning was kept burning. But they had their day", and were wiped out completely by Henry VIII and "his unscrupulous ally, Thomas Cromwell". "Although none of them were very rich, yet owing to their number, the King netted a good round sum from their endowments with which to fill his pockets and to bestow upon those who had been useful to him." The road to Brentwood from Hutton, Hanging Hill Lane, was so named because it was the "hanging spot of those condemned to death at the court of the abbot of a monastery". Near the centre of Brentwood was another spot where a 19-year-old boy "was burnt at the stake in 1555 during the Marian persecutions for reading the bible!"

Charles went to London at least once a month while living in Hutton. Most were one-day trips for business. He attended a meeting in the Chapel of Henry VII in Westminster Abbey to inaugurate a new phase of the work of the Life and Work conference, following the Prague meeting. He usually visited St James Park and sometimes the zoo in Regents Park. He joined a crowd outside Buckingham Palace in December 1928 to read the bulletin about the King's health, about which there had been much anxiety. On May Day the following year he was in Hyde Park when a procession of about 2000 communists arrived. "Beyond their fiery speeches, no incident worth reporting seems to have taken place – very different to Berlin where the communists barricaded the streets and fighting still continues."

Charles and Marion travelled elsewhere in Southern England, but much less than they had done in the months before they moved to Hutton. Their main holiday was a three-week stay in Selsey in May 1929. They spent a few days with the Odling-Smees in Guildford in September 1929. One day while there they indulged in one of Charles' favourite activities: boating on the river – in this case the Wey – with a couple of members of the party going for a swim in the river after a picnic lunch on the bank. They also stayed twice with William Challis in Kensworth, and made a day trip by train to Southbourne to call on Emily Key, the widow of Charles' cousin, John Key.

When he was driving around, Charles appreciated the improvement in roads in recent years. But at the same time, he deplored the impact of the new arterial roads and by passes on the countryside. Ribbon developments with their clusters of bungalows and shanties sprang up along the new highways, and "the beauty of many an old village is in danger of being overwhelmed by the incongruous erections which are rising around them".

A new building in London was a special object of Charles' disapproval. The District Railway was building new offices for its staff at 55 Broadway, above St James Park underground station. At the time it was the tallest office building in London. Its height and the massive base caused Charles to deplore the "great pile" encountered as he left St James Park by Queen Anne's Gate. He reserved his greatest scorn for the sculptures by Jacob Epstein, Eric Gill and others carved into the walls. The figures by Gill and others represented the four winds and were "strange and uncouth. One of them is like a female figure having her legs distended with dropsy energetically swimming the Channel." Epstein's two figures representing Night and Day had limbs "out of all proportion as if Epstein hated anything that in any way resembled the beauty of Greek statuary... Their general repulsiveness has led a much ruffled critic to declare that they are nothing but a throwback to the savage art of the Aztecs." He admitted to finding "something quite attractive about the face and figure of Night" but could "not get over the real ugliness of Day with her sightless wide open eyes, flat cranium and tree trunk legs". The modernism and graphic nakedness of Night and Day created a public outrage, and Epstein was forced to modify Day. Vandals had already tried to tar and feather her, a fate the "grotesque representation" of Rima in Hyde Park (another of Charles' bêtes noires) had suffered a few days earlier. Charles was not alone in his dislike of modern sculpture.

Soon after Charles and Marion moved into their house in Hutton, he had an attack of Africa nostalgia. The shortening days and raw and chilly wind made it "impossible not to hear soft voices calling from far away across the sea. Just as in the burnt-up wastes of South West Africa, there sometimes came the lure of the English spring, so now, amid signs of the departing season, the wide expanses of the sunlit land are singing their siren songs." After quoting South African poets who wrote about "the call of the veld", he fell back on Kipling again:

There's a whisper down the field where the year has shot her yield,

And the ricks stand gray to the sun,

Singing: -- "Over then, come over, for the bee has quit the clover,

And your English summer's done.

You have heard the beat of the off-shore wind,

And the thresh of the deep-sea rain;

You have heard the song -- how long! how long?

Pull out on the trail again![154]

But he resisted the urge to pull out again – it had, after all, been a year with much travel. "Like Ulysses of old, we have metaphorically to fill our ears with wax and turn away."

But reminders of Africa kept appearing. After a gale that broke off bits of trees, the sticks lying in the road at night reminded them of snakes on the paths in Zululand. In December it took "some getting used to being boxed up so much indoors with no daylight at all for at least two thirds of the time" after so many years of open-air life. The canna lilies in St James Park in August were "quite a reminder of the brightness of Durban". When autumn came round again, his thoughts "involuntarily ran back to Africa" and to the words of a poet (unnamed):

When autumn leaves are falling, and England's summer wanes,

I see the veld reviving beneath the early rains.

Yet now once more in England, my fickle memory flies

To Africa's wide spaces and Africa's blue skies.

In Southbourne, the waves breaking on the sands with "a boom and a hiss" reminded him of "the South Atlantic rollers thundering in at the foot of the sand dunes on the South West African coast."

With Africa never far from his mind, it is not surprising that Charles looked for an opportunity to return there. By 1929 Marion had recovered from whatever illness had prevented them from remaining in South West Africa in 1928. They therefore decided to visit Cape Town to explore possibilities. In October, Charles had been a Public Preacher

---

154   From Rudyard Kipling, *The Long Trail.*

in Chelmsford Diocese for a year, which may have been the period of his engagement or, more likely, a respectable time after which he felt that he could leave. They moved out of their house in Hutton on 14 November, and sailed from Southampton a week later, on 22 November, on the *Armadale Castle*. There was a strong gale and rough seas during the first few days, which slowed the boat down. As a result, it arrived in Cape Town three hours late in the morning of 9 December 1929.

They found that Cape Town had changed quite a bit since they were last there three years earlier. There were more vehicles on the streets, including motor buses which were taking business away from the railways and trams. The town was creeping up the steep hillsides of Table Mountain. Massive buildings were going up in the city centre. Crowds of bungalows had appeared in Newlands, where Charles and Marion used to live. The university had moved out to a new campus on the slopes of the mountain near Groote Schuur.

"But the greatest shock of all is the excrescence which has appeared right on the summit of the western buttress of Table Mountain, breaking the clear line of the ridge." He was referring to the cable car terminus. The aerial cableway had been open for only a few months and had already carried 20,000 passengers. It was likely to be a financial success, which was going to disappoint those Cape Town residents who, like Charles, disapproved of the "desecration of the mountain" and "have half hoped that it will not pay its way".

One thing that had not changed was the wind, the 'Cape doctor'. It still whipped round the side of the mountain and over the Cape Flats. One Sunday evening violent gusts of up to seventy-eight miles per hour were registered at the docks. Charles was in Somerset West, a small town to the east of Cape Town, at the time. "The wind played tricks with the electric light, for twice during the evening service the church was in darkness owing to the swaying branches outside causing temporary short circuits." There were many fires in the whole area because sparks were fanned into flames. A few days earlier Charles had attempted to sketch at the Strand, a seaside town near Somerset West. "A tearing South-Easter was rushing along sweeping billows of sand along with it in savage gusts quite in an old-fashioned Walvis Bay style." His brushes and water were swept away more than once, and his paint box was hurled to the ground. "What with the riotous wind, flying sand and hot sun, it was quite a business to produce any picture at all."

We know that Charles was able to complete two pictures, because they are still in the possession of the family. They were painted in February 1930, and depicted the Rhodes Memorial, one from below with the Devil's Peak in the background, and the other from behind the statue of Physical Energy, with a view across the Cape Flats to the mountains beyond. Charles thought that the Memorial "must be one of the most satisfying in existence". The site, on the slopes of the mountain, "in view of the two oceans, with the everlasting mountains in serried

ranges stretching away in far blue distances beyond the Flats" is certainly exceptional. But the design of the Memorial itself, by Sir Herbert Baker and Francis Macey, with its Grecian temple, eight seated lions and bust of Rhodes, is similar in character to many other monuments in the British Empire and elsewhere. Charles was moved not only by the site and the design, but also by his admiration for Rhodes. "The solidity and simplicity of the whole design, from the statue of Physical Energy at the base of the wide flight of steps, flanked by four complacent looking bronze lions on either side, to the massive granite pillars of the shrine on the top, set among the pine trees with the crags of the Peak towering up 2000 feet above, and facing northwards towards the great lands far away beyond the mountains, not only express the manner of man he was, who once thought out his great schemes on this spot, but seems to be instinct with his very spirit." (The final phrase does not make sense. Perhaps he intended to say "instilled with his very spirit".)

Charles and Marion went to an exhibition of rock art by San people.[155] The San were nomadic hunter gathers without possessions of their own. They could not understand that something might be the particular property of someone else. As a result, early European settlers called them thieves and pushed them out, often brutally, from their lands. By the 1920s, there were very few San in South Africa, and only small numbers in South West Africa, mostly in the Kalahari Desert. Charles thought that "soon their cave paintings will be all that is left of them… as they cannot settle down to a civilised life". However, he was aware of the views of George Stow, who argued that the wrongs inflicted on them by the Boer colonists, including having their hunting grounds taken away, led them to retaliate with atrocities. "They were as susceptible to right treatment as any other section of the human race."[156]

Bishop Vyvyan, who had been bishop of Zululand when Charles and Marion lived there, retired in 1929. His successor, Charles Arthur William Aylen, was consecrated Bishop of Zululand by the Archbishop of Cape Town on 2 February 1930 in St George's Cathedral, Cape Town. Charles participated in the service as one of the chaplains of the Archbishop.[157]

155 They called them Bushmen, the term used by Europeans, but which was later regarded as derogatory.

156 George William Stow, *The Native Races of South Africa: A History of the Intrusion of the Hottentots and Bantu into the Hunting Grounds of the Bushmen, the Aborigines of the Country* (1905).

157 The Most Reverend William Marlborough Carter, Archbishop of Cape Town, 1909-30.

Bishop Vyvyan, who was also at the service, thought that Charles looked very well. But Charles told him that he could not return to live in South Africa because of "some internal trouble".[158] He was presumably referring to a problem with his health. We do not know what that was, but it must have been serious as it turned out that he did not have much longer to live.

Charles and Marion sailed from Cape Town on 1 March on the *Armadale Castle*, headed for Southampton. As the sun dipped towards the horizon, Charles' last view of South Africa was "a delicate rose madder glow [that] lighted up the fast fading Twelve Apostles and the Lion's Head". The voyage was uneventful, although heavy seas off the Portuguese coast caused a "wholesale glissade of all the knives, forks, plates, tumblers, etc., down the tables, and in the extra bad rolls a general crash onto the floor". When passing the Canary Islands and Madeira, Charles reflected on the decline of the Spanish and Portuguese empires from their peaks. "It is remarkable that these islands should still be in possession of the Spaniards... and the Portuguese seeing how far both these nations have lost their spirit of adventure and enterprise by which they were so fully possessed in the 15th century". He was reading a book by J H Curle, an engineer and eugenicist with racial views, who suggested that the decline was attributable to the celibacy of the priesthood and, even more, to intermarriage with natives in Latin America and, in the Portuguese case, also Africa. In Portugal, "the race has lost its fibre and will power. The nation is slowly sinking, and there are probably not enough pure-blooded individuals remaining to raise it again".[159] We do not know whether Charles agreed with this view.

They arrived in Southampton on 17 March. They went to stay with Marion's sister, Kathleen, in Purley, from where they made short visits to central London. On one of those, they saw an exhibition of objects from the ruins of Great Zimbabwe at the British Museum. Charles recorded the signs of spring, which were slow in coming because of the cool weather, in *In the Winds of Heaven*. The final entry was made on 25 April. Given his love of flowers, it is fitting that he recorded seeing 22 flowers in bloom on his walk that day. While he may have written notes on later days, the notes that he bound into the final volume of *In the Winds of Heaven* concluded with the entry for 25 April.[160]

The absence of any written material after April suggests that Charles' health was deteriorating. He died in St Paul's Hospital in Endell Street in Covent Garden on 16 September 1930. The hospital specialised in diseases (including cancer) of the genito-urinary organs and skin. He had prostate problems: his death

---

158   Obituary of Charles by Bishop Vyvyan in *The Net*, December 1930.

159   James Herbert Curle, *To-day and To-morrow: The Testing Period of the White Race* (1926).

160   The entry for 25 April ends mid-sentence at the foot of the page, indicating that there was at least one more page that remained unbound.

certificate cited an operation for enlarged prostate as the secondary cause of death. The primary cause was cardiac failure with phlebitis. These may have been complications from the prostate surgery. He was buried at Bandon Hill Cemetery, Beddington, on 19 September 1930.

CHAPTER 10

NATURE IN WATERCOLOURS AND WORDS

Charles' love of nature and the outdoors has been a theme of this story of his life. He and Emma spent much time when they were growing up observing the wildlife and flowers in and around Headley. They collected flowers and sketched the local scenes. On his solo trip to South Africa, Charles painted some fine miniatures of wild flowers as well as townscapes and landscapes. During his holidays with Marion and Emma in England, Wales, France and Norway he continued to paint, although mostly landscapes rather than flowers.

His painting of flowers shifted up several gears after moving to Zululand. Between 1908 and 1916 he produced a phenomenal number of botanical paintings. The subjects were the native flowers which he found all around him in Zululand. He started with rough pencil outlines and then painted them with watercolours. He dated each painting and recorded where he had found the plant. He added the botanical and common names when he knew them. Although the paintings were accurate enough to match those of a good herbarium, he produced them for his own pleasure rather than for any scientific purpose. However, the two motives tended to come together in Charles, who was much given to chronicling the natural world.

He produced perhaps 300 botanical paintings during this period. His productivity was remarkable, completing as many as three or four paintings a week during parts of 1911 and 1912 when he was most active. More than thirty paintings have remained in the family. The bulk of the rest, 235 paintings, were purchased at auction in London in 1986 and then or later belonged to David Cope, John Wessels and Mrs Nancy Claire Foster. Cope

Oct. 1911.   118

Irideae gladiolus

and Wessels showed them to two botanists, John Rourke and John Manning, at the National Botanical Institute, Kirstenbosch, Cape Town, who were so impressed by the quality and accuracy of the paintings that they took monochrome photocopies of them which they deposited in the Compton Herbarium at the Kirstenbosch National Botanical Garden.[161] They described and documented the paintings, together with a short biography of Charles, in an article in 1992 in *Bothalia*, a South African botanical journal.[162] We do not know what happened to the originals, but Cope and Wessels were hoping to sell them.[163]

When he went to England in 1917, he felt that he could not continue to paint outdoors because of wartime security concerns. He therefore launched a new venture. He began to write notes about nature which he collected and bound later in a volume entitled *In the Winds of Heaven, a Diary of the Open Air, together with Thoughts on the Problems of Nature*. He thought of the notes as "descriptive sketching". He wrote them to satisfy his urge to capture something of what he saw for future contemplation and recall. He was also motivated by a wish to find the best ways to express what he saw. In the introduction to the first volume, he reflected on the differences between sketching and writing. Words can describe changing scenes,

---

161 The National Botanical Institute and the Compton Herbarium were subsequently incorporated into the South African National Biodiversity Institute.

162 J P Rourke and J C Manning, "The Venerable Charles Theophilus Hahn, a Hitherto Unknown Edwardian Botanical Illustrator in Natal, 1908-1916", *Bothalia*, Volume 22, 1992.

163 From a communication from John Rourke.

such as a storm developing, as well as smells and sounds, in ways that pictures cannot. And they can convey impressions and suggestions. On the other hand, they cannot capture the sight of a scene, its colours and shapes, like a picture does.

There were eventually three volumes that he bound from loose pages of notes. The first covered five years, 1918 to 1922, the second 1923 to 1927, and the third 1927 to 1930. Each entry, in his neat handwriting, was usually between half a page and a full page. There were several entries each month, each numbered sequentially and most of them dated. The total number of entries in the three volumes altogether was 1628. He made very detailed subject indexes in the first two volumes, and separate indexes of the numerous quotations in all three volumes.

He had, of course, been writing diaries and logs for 30 years since he was a student. But whereas the early diaries focused on what he was doing, *In the Winds of Heaven* described the natural world around him, rather than his place in it. There was much about the weather and the changing skies. There were also detailed descriptions of flowers and plants in which he showed a love for, and deep knowledge of, wild flowers. He saw God in the beauty of nature, as shown by his choice of this saying of Gregory the Great for the title page of the first volume:

"If we look attentively enough at outward, material things, we are recalled by them to inward, spiritual things. For the wonders of visible creation are the footprints of our creator; himself as yet we cannot see, but we are on the road that leads to vision when we admire Him in the things that He has made."[164] At various times during the twelve or so years he was writing notes in *In the Winds of Heaven* he asked himself whether he had the time and energy to continue. He admitted that he wrote merely "with a view to my own delectation". Some notes "are articles more for my own special reference than for anything else, and others have been put together I suppose with the object of clearing the air in my head". He quoted approvingly from a writer in the *Times Literary Supplement* who stated that "the good anthologist is he who follows his bent, who puts nothing in because he ought, but everything because he will… In an anthologist, self-indulgence is a cardinal virtue."

Fortunately, for those of us who want to know about his life, he found time and energy to continue the notes. While living in Swakopmund, he admitted that writing the notes, and the reading that lay behind some of them, "helped to a large extent to make existence tolerable… as there is so much leisure in the style of life that falls to one's lot in this country". Unfortunately for us, he did not write about the people he met and lived and worked with. On the same occasion in Swakopmund, he wrote: "there are, of course,

---

164 St Gregory the Great was pope of the Catholic Church from 590 to 604 AD. He was famous for sending a mission, often called the Gregorian mission, under St Augustine, to evangelise the pagan Anglo-Saxons of England.

all the human associations, which these notes do not touch on, that are the main part of the interest of the life in this land from one's work point of view".

Charles was a fluid writer, whose style had become smoother and less self-conscious over the years. The very first sentence in the first volume of *In the Winds of Heaven* shows how far he had come. At Bognor in January 1918:

"The smoke from the chimney-stacks was rising up straight into the cold, frosty air; while, on the sea, the surface was just disturbed by the lightest of swells, which only revealed itself as it rose and fell with a gentle, oily swirl above the sunken rocks, and finally spent what energy it had in quiet little wavelets which broke with a perceptible effort on to the ribbed sand."

The painterly power of observation is apparent here. While it is understandable that the first sentence of his new venture would be a little overwrought, his painterly eye never deserted him. He recorded the colours of some fields in France in July 1918 almost as though he was planning to sit down and paint them when he returned home:

"In the little hedgeless fields the crops are marked out from one another by their distinctive shades of colour. There is the dull sea-green of the patches of broad beans next to the lighter green of the oats and the browner green of the wheat. The grass of the pasture lands where the cattle are feeding are of a dirty brown green, while the fields where the hay is being gathered are more of a light yellow brown, and the newly growing clover lands a brighter green. Dotted everywhere are the little red-tiled and brown-thatched cottages and barns, and rows of trees, right away to the horizon, where the trees appear as rows of little dots against the sky, and church spires rise up, and here and there a tall thin chimney is giving forth its smoke."

His descriptions of the sky were especially vivid, as in this one from early morning on New Year's Day in 1919, also in France:

"Lines of luminous, rosy-pink cloud streamed across a porcelain blue background which toned down towards the horizon into an emerald green. Above floated a sea of little alto-cumulus cloud-balls all flushed with the morning glow; and higher still long wind-blown streamers reached up towards the zenith."

One could easily miss from the forty or so pages he wrote during his time in France the fact that he was there as part of an army engaged in a major war. These notes were essentially about nature in his part of France. Whether he deliberately focused the notes this way to distract himself from the war, or because he did not want to have a record of it, we do not know. Whatever the reason, they create the impression that he had time to spend walking in the countryside around St Omer and the villages to its east, enjoying the natural scenes and the activities of the French farmers during the growing and harvesting seasons of 1918. An indication of his intense engagement with nature was that he spotted and named forty-five wild flowers that he saw in the first week of November, and later the twenty-two he saw in the first week of December. Even in January he was able to find eleven species. Thus his lifetime urge to chronicle every detail was not interrupted by the war. The same applies to the weather and the sky, which he watched carefully and recorded faithfully.

Back in England in 1919, he and Marion stayed with his cousin John Key at Moulsford in Berkshire. He was delighted that the spring flowers were at their peak, and the meandering river provided a pleasing backdrop. He was moved to recall favourite lines from the poets, such as:

Along the shoare of silver streaming Themmes,

Whose rutty bancke, the which his river hemmes,

Was paynted all with varyable flower [165]

His wish to capture the visual impact of a scene in writing comes through in a note he wrote when living in Cape Town. He called it *A Study in Blue*: "On the way up to Bishopscourt, the sunlight was glinting through the pine trees and falling in bright patches on the road, while the blue-green foliage of the pine needles met high above forming a series of lofty arches through which was visible the deep cobalt blue sky. The tall straight trunks running up on either side – the supporting pillars of the long-drawn aisle – seemed to have caught the tone of blueness in all around, and their pink-brown bark was touched with a shade of blue. The same prevailing tint came from the further trees, and through them could be seen the towering buttress of the mountain on which a great cap of cloud, shining white where the sun fell upon it, was resting. Beneath the cloud the crags and precipices were in shadow, and the only colour that could have painted them, would have been a mixture of indigo, cobalt and Antwerp blue, so deep and intense was the blueness." [166]

When he and Marion were living in Keetmanshoop, a moment of homesickness one April reminded him of Robert Browning's *Home Thoughts from Abroad*. [167] He pondered on how "the renewal of life after all the bareness of winter in the old country is one of the ever-fresh wonders of nature". But then he remembered the compensations of Africa, including the dry air and the hot sun, the greenery and flowers after rain, and the width and freedom of the desert and the veld. "Africa has a fascination that is all her own. The great open spaces of the mighty veld give full advantage for the display of aerial scenery on the most extensive scale. Where

---

165   Extract from *Prothalamion* by Edmund Spenser.

166   *In the Winds of Heaven*, entry in late November 1920. Bishopscourt was the residence of the Archbishop of Cape Town. It was in a suburb with the same name about one mile further away from the centre of Cape Town than was Newlands where Charles and Marion lived. The buttress of the mountain was the eastern flank of Table Mountain.

167   *Oh to be in England, now that April's there.*

184

the country rolls away for eighty miles to the nearest mountains, with not even a bush or a tree to impede the view, there is nothing to distract the attention from what is going on above… Truly the land is wide, and the desert spaces have a soft and mysterious grip." As often when contemplating the beauties of nature, Charles felt that God was close: "the unseen Presence sometimes seems very near in the mysterious depths of nature". His moment of homesickness was banished when he found a South African poet who had the answer to Browning:

Yesterday you had a song,
I could not choose but hear,
'Twas, Oh to be in England
Now that April's there.
But I have found a new refrain
I cannot choose but sing,
'Tis, Oh to be in Africa
Now summer's on the wing.[168]

In 1923, over five years after he had stopped painting, Charles returned to it. As we have seen, he and Marion went to Victoria Falls on holiday. At wayside halts on the train he found himself busy with his pencil. He had given up sketching and painting in England in 1917 because of wartime security concerns and had started *In the Winds of Heaven* with its "descriptive sketching". In Victoria Falls he reflected that "having given up sketching during the war, the spell had passed from me, and I was beginning to think that I was altogether free from its influence. But those pencil marks in the train were the incipient symptoms of the smouldering malady. This has now broken out again with all its old-time fury, perhaps even in a more concentrated form than it ever existed before through having been suppressed for so many years." The "leaping waterfalls, dancing rainbows and mighty chasms filled with curling mists and spray" called for an attempt to capture "such fleeting impressions of Beauty" permanently.

During the three weeks at Victoria Falls, Charles completed twelve watercolours, each from a different vantage point. Some showed the falls themselves, sometimes with rainbows shining through the spray. Others showed the gorge beneath the falls and the railway bridge. Still others were of the superficially placid river as it flowed unknowingly towards the falls. With typical tidiness, he also drew a map of the area, with numbers to indicate the vantage point for each painting. While the paintings were completed away from the falls, his work on the preparatory sketches in many of his locations was made more complicated by the spray that was falling. The paintings are now in the possession of the family, but it is possible that Charles gave them to Wilmot Vyvyan, the former Bishop of Zululand, and Charles' superior when he was in that region. In the obituary of Charles, Vyvyan wrote that "he was no mean artist, and I have one of his paintings of the Ubombo mountains at the Mkusi drift with me, and many pictures he made in South Africa, notably a set of the Victoria Falls, which Mrs Headley and he

---

168   Perceval Gibbon, *An Answer.*

visited some time ago".[169] If these are the same pictures now in the possession of the family, it is likely that Vyvyan, or his estate, gave them to Marion at some point after he wrote the obituary.

Although he had resumed painting at Victoria Falls, he did not produce botanical paintings on returning to Keetmanshoop as he had done in Zululand a decade earlier. Nor did he discontinue writing notes in *In the Winds of Heaven*, the original excuse for which had been to record aspects of nature that he could no longer capture in paintings. The notes continued to be full of painterly descriptions of flowers, skies and the natural environment in general. Thus, he observed in Luderitz "the cerulean blue of the sea standing out in contrast to the monotonous yellow-ochre of the bare and desolate coast all around". Climbing to the top of a kopje[170] near Aus during an enforced stop because the train from Luderitz to Keetmanshoop had broken down, he saw "large cushions of magenta mesembryanthemums that make bright patches of colour among the prevailing yellow-ochre of the rocks around". On a visit to Windhoek in July 1923, he admired the "vistas opening out to blue ranges of

---

169   *The Net*, December 1930.

170   A kopje is a small, rocky hill. (this is at present on next page)

mountains far away or to those of a delicate yellow-pink hue in the nearer distance". There was "a species of Michaelmas daisy all massed together in straggling clumps on a hillside and these throw quite a violet sheen of colour over the rough ground".

Charles found the blue Erongo mountains to be one of the redeeming features of Usakos, which he often passed through going north from Swakopmund. With his painterly eye he observed that they gave "just that touch of colour which is needed to break the general monotony of ochres shading off from a whitish yellow to a dull reddish brown all around". Their huge mass of primitive rock stood out, when the sun shone on them, "a delicate rose-madder pink deepening into shadows of a soft chalky blue". Capturing these colours on paper would be very difficult, but worth the effort "as the green acacias down by the river bed would work well in with the brown and stony foreground."

We do not know whether he ever did paint in Usakos. Apart from one of Luderitz, none of the paintings he made anywhere in South West Africa have survived, as far as is known. He found that it was more difficult to capture the colours of the desert than he had expected. It was not just a matter of "plenty of yellow ochre with a touch of burnt sienna in it and perhaps a little aureolin, and the thing is done". The whole effect of the sun in a blue sky shining on the yellow sand with patches of a dark dust here and there "was of a wonderful softness which was really impossible to attain out in the open with a shower of fine sand blowing over with every wisp of wind that came along".

After moving to Swakopmund, Charles derived great pleasure from observing the birds on the lagoon and the sand bar. He stood on his veranda with his field glasses and watched their antics and comings and goings, which he recorded in *In the Winds of Heaven*. During the first year or so in Swakopmund, he watched pelicans, flamingos, herons, grebes, gannets, duikers, curlews, cape cormorants, gulls, terns, teals, ducks, pochards, avocets, sand plovers and sand pipers. Given the sparsity of wild plant life, the birds provided the main source of joy he derived from the natural world in Swakopmund and the surrounding desert.

There were many fewer birds around in December 1927, which Charles thought was due to two factors. One was that the sandbar had been pushed right back into the lagoon, which had split into two small pools. These no longer had the fish and other attractions for the birds. The second was that the jetty had been turned into a promenade. When Charles and Marion first came to Swakopmund, the iron jetty built by the Germans had two huge overhead cranes. A large colony of white-breasted cormorants, which Charles called duikers (Afrikaans for divers), built their nests in the cranes. Even after the cranes were dismantled as port activity disappeared, the cormorants remained. But they could not accept the disturbance caused by opening up the jetty to human beings, so they left. Charles bemoaned the loss: "In spite of municipal enterprise blossoming out in various directions, such as in the gardens on the way down to the mole, the broad flight of steps leading up to the Herero war monument and the jetty walk, Swakopmund has lost its chief attraction." For Charles, nature was a top priority.

Very few plants were able to survive in the Namib desert. One was the "window" mesembryanthemum. It has brown leaves that are flat on the ground and act as windows that let light through to enable green leaves to form underneath. They are difficult to find, but Charles was given a root by a German botanist which he planted in the sand in his garden. An extraordinary plant unique to the Namib desert is the welwitschia. It takes in water from the dew through a network of fine roots close to the surface, as well as any groundwater there may be from a taproot that can go down three metres It has only two leaves that grow continuously, but slowly, for a very long time. Some welwitschia are thought to be over 1000 years old. A kind of gourd, *Acanthosicyos horridus*, grew near sources of groundwater. It has no leaves, but its system of thick tap roots can extend up to 50 metres down. It can survive many years without water. Without vegetation, animals could not survive in the desert. There were a few mangy jackals that Charles thought must have lived on what was thrown up by the sea.

In Swakopmund, plants grew quite well if assisted with enough water. Charles thought that the cemetery must be "the greenest and most flower-bedecked spot in the whole of the Namib desert". When he and Marion first arrived, their own garden was just a bare sand bank flanked by manitoka trees. With a lot of attention and water, they created a fine flower garden. The main part comprised mesembryanthemums, which are indigenous to Southern Africa and like the sun. Also growing were mallows, carnations, and white and yellow daisies. Alas, after returning from a five-month trip to England in 1926, they found "dying trees, withered plants, rusting tins half buried in the sand". However, two months later, after regular watering, it was making a good recovery. The manitoka trees were flowering, the mesembryanthmums, which Charles had divided and planted out, had taken root and were beginning to flower, and the seeds of the previous season's daisies and mallows, which had hidden themselves in the sand, had germinated where some water had been applied. A line that he had recalled somewhat desperately on returning from England was now more appropriate: "*A garden is a lovesome thing, God wot!*" [171]

As we have seen, Charles was very interested in the weather and its fluctuations, and the changing skies. He approached it from both a scientific and a practical point of view. In the

171   This was the opening line of the poem My Garden by Thomas Edward Brown (1830-1897). Charles liked the poem for its affirmation of God's hand in the beauty of gardens, as in the final lines:

...the fool contends that God is not –
Not God! In gardens! When the eve is cool!
Nay, but I have a sign;
'Tis very sure God walks in mine.

latter case he needed to take account of the weather in managing the plants in his gardens, and in making decisions about travel, whether on public transport or his motorcycle. He always looked at the sky and the land under it with a painterly eye. One of many descriptions of the sky in Cape Town was: "The clouds yesterday assumed an unusual shape. Instead of moving across the sky in broken fragments or swelling up in puffy cumulus, they lay in solid, straight-edged masses. A great sheet of cloud hung high up over the mountain. Further away a huge block, something after the shape of a side of bacon, floated alone. Southwards over Constantia rose up a white mountain of cloud with a sloping, clean-cut outline against the blue sky; while somewhere over False Bay a round balloon-like mass with a car attached below seemed to be revolving as if in a great eddy of air. As the sun went down, it was lighted up with a glowing salmon pink, dove grey on the shady side, and it seemed to be encircled with a grey band after the manner of the ring round Saturn. It foreboded wet weather, for today the rain has been teeming down."[172]

He often wrote about sunrises and sunsets, which could be spectacular in Cape Town against the backdrop of Table Mountain, the sea, and the distant mountains to the north and east. One example was this description of a sunrise as seen from the shoulder of Devil's Peak. "A faint blue sky overhead deepened to purple towards the horizon, while a large mottle-faced moon paling from silver-yellow to silver-white in the growing light was sinking to rest in the nek between the mountain and the upstanding conical head of the Lion. As the sun drew near the summits of the Eastern ranges, a few wisps of cloud above the Head were the first to catch his glory and were filled with a fiery crimson. Then the great square western buttress of the mountain saw his coming, and flushed a rosy red. Next the Head was suffused with a ruddy glow which, even as one looked, passed away, and soon the world around was filled with brilliant light."[173]

A brilliant sky caused by a different phenomenon occurred one evening when Charles was walking home from a service at a coloured mission church on the Flats. The crickets were stridulating, the crescent moon was shining, Venus was not far away with a peculiar liquid brilliance and ahead Table Mountain loomed up darkly into the star-dusted sky. Suddenly the whole scene was lit up as a glowing mass of white fire passed horizontally low down across the sky behind him. Its track was marked by a line of greenish light which persisted for some seconds after the meteor itself had disappeared.

In Swakopmund, looking back over the previous six months, he wrote in February 1926:

---

172 *In the Winds of Heaven*, entry on 20 June 1920.

173 *In the Winds of Heaven*, entry in late March 1921. The Lion and the Head both refer to the Lion's Head, the mountain that flanks Table Mountain, at a lower elevation, and runs south to north, hence catching the sun as it rises in the east. 'Nek' is a South African word for a mountain pass.

"For the last six months I doubt if a more equitable climate could be found anywhere else in the whole world. The blue night and the red day lines [that recorded minimum and maximum temperatures in his daily weather report] run along through the months with an almost monotonous straightness. Only one short shower has fallen (Oct 14th), and the mists have only been light, very seldom having partaken of the real Scotch variety. On two occasions the winds have been registered as strong, and the sunshine hours have altogether outdone those of cloud." But the weather was not always benign in Swakopmund. For example, a storm on 24 February 1925, the last time it rained before the shower on 14 October mentioned in the February 1926 summary, inspired the following entry in *In the Winds of Heaven*:

"Yesterday afternoon, a magnificent storm gathered across the desert. Massed blue-black clouds gradually mounted up towards the zenith, and the whole horizon was hidden in an advancing yellowish haze of flying sand. Occasionally a dazzling flash twinkled down through the gloom, and as it drew nearer the thunder rumbled through the dark canopy and a few large drops of rain began to fall. But the storm took a long time developing, and in the evening the sun descended across the sea in a blaze of splendour embowered in literal showers of gold sweeping down from the heavy clouds around, which a few moments later were all lighted up with a glowing fiery red as they caught the last kiss of the vanishing orb of glory. It was not until past midnight that the storm broke overhead and the rain came down in a deluge."

The roof leaked badly and Charles' study "was converted into a swimming bath".

The sky often attracted his painterly eye. In Swakopmund again: "Each morning as he [the sun] rises, the darkness fades down into a dusky blue above the western horizon surmounted by a dull pink band, and this melts into a soft primrose yellow as his rim looks over the desert hills, while the white waves flash momentarily with a delicate rose; and then in the evening as he sinks below the sea in a golden blaze, the same dusky blue band with the dull pink fringe begins to mount above the eastern sands."

Such a sunset a few weeks later was especially inspiring:

"Every now and then one comes across a scene which brings one up short with a thrill, and one becomes instinctively aware that beauty must all be a part of the eternal glory. It was so this evening. The sun had gone down over the sea – a perfect orb in a clear sky – and as the wings of night folded across the zenith and gradually descended, a delicate pale green-blue luminosity merging into a band of soft apricot light below glowed over the dark horizon of the waters."

At the end of this entry Charles wrote "beauty is one of the great main roads to God", a thought that was never far from his mind.

As well as the sky, the ever-changing sea was also a source of wonder and delight. Not only the sight of it, but also its sound. "Each time I return from my up-country trips to our home on the shore of the lagoon, where the waves are ever breaking on the sandbank beyond, I am aware of it, and feel there is some haunting but elusive meaning in their hush and hiss." He reflected on the sense of eternity that the waves evoked, their sound having existed since before the first man, and set to continue for the long ages to come. As he often did when contemplating the mysteries of the natural world, he turned to poetry:

Though inland far we be,
Our Souls have sight of that immortal sea
Which brought us hither,
Can in a moment travel thither,
And see the Children sport upon the shore,
And hear the mighty waters rolling evermore.[174]

Charles kept up his notes on nature in *In the Winds of Heaven* on his and Marion's trips to England. When they went in 1924, they had not been there for over four years, their longest time away. The flowers and lush greenery of spring and summer in England were in sharp contrast to the bare open spaces of South West Africa. In May, Charles wrote: "I do not know if it is the effect of having come from the barren wastes of the South West or whether it is the result of the frequent rains, but I have never been so impressed by the abundance and vividness of the green before". He found an echo of Africa in the view as he was driving to Oxford in September. "The view from the edge of the Chiltern Hills overlooking the far-spreading Thames valley to the north is always exhilarating... Its expanse is attractive to the eye accustomed to the wide open spaces of the African veld."

He wrote about the flowers he saw, the crops in the fields and the farmers' activities, the trees, the birds and small animals such as red squirrels and hedgehogs. He delighted in being able to name the flowers, and recorded most of the ones he saw – over twenty-five different wild flowers on one drive over the South Downs to Bognor. He improvised a theory that early spring flowers tended to be white, while later in spring they were purple and pink, and in high summer yellow was the most conspicuous colour. He knew many of the gardens in Purley and Selsey and watched the flowers there grow.

While Charles and Marion spent most of their time in the country (Purley, now a suburb, still had open spaces with wooded copses and large gardens), they made a few trips to Central London in 1924 where they usually visited the parks. In May, Charles noted that sheep were grazing in Hyde Park. The lake in St James Park, which had been drained and covered with temporary buildings in the war, was now restored, with pink rhododendrons around it and the pelicans in residence. In September, the animals in Regents Park Zoo were enjoying some sunshine, "which had an exhilarating effect on a young giraffe who was

---

174 William Wordsworth, *Ode: Intimations of Immortality from Recollections of Early Childhood.*

galloping round and round his paddock in an ungainly fashion".

In June 1926, the first month of their next visit to England, Charles was overwhelmed by the beauty of the countryside with all the flowers and colours of spring. Being up on the ridge of the South Downs was "altogether beautiful". "Down on the Weald there are green carpets of growing corn, buttercup meadows where dun-coloured cows earn an easy living, and along the densely clothed hedgerows the large creamy discs of the elder stand out in contrast among the green, and dog roses are in bloom here and there." On that occasion, he thought of Blake and "England's green and pleasant land", but then remembered the "deadening back-courts and sordid alleyways in the purlieus of the towns", and the deadlock in the coal strike.[175] To him these were clear indications, among others, that "desperate efforts in the way of mental strife and sword brandishing are still required before Jerusalem is really built in this delightsome isle".

He watched the sky all the time and was always interested in both the shape and colour of the clouds, both for their beauty and for what they meant for the coming weather. While in England he continued his practice of recording the temperature, rainfall, barometric pressure and general weather conditions every day. He noted that there had been more days without rain than days with rain, which was the opposite of the experience of 1924. There were also more hot days: seven days when it was over 80°F compared with only three in 1924. Nevertheless, he was often caught in the rain on outings on the motorcycle, a situation he accepted philosophically. Not that he enjoyed it. Coming from a hot and sunny climate made it more difficult to adjust to the rain than it was for stay-at-home English people. "People living in England are queer folk, for they seem positively to enjoy damp and chilly weather in preference to the warmth and sunshine. When it is getting to what is to us a tolerably comfortable temperature, there are more complaints and abusive language about the heat and how unendurable it is than one ever hears on a really rainy day."

The winter of 1929, when they were living in Hutton, was the first English winter they had experienced for many years. Charles was especially interested in watching nature adjusting to the winter and, even more so, responding to the approach of spring. There was much to observe, and write about, in the garden and on the walks that he and Marion took. He was able to name all the birds and plants he saw, with one exception. One day, he found a wild flower he had never seen before, growing among the garden weeds. He could not find it in the first flower book he

---

175 The coal miners were on strike to protest wage reductions and worsening conditions. In their support the Trades Union Congress had called a general strike in May. It ended in defeat on 12 May (when Charles and Marion were in Cape Town on their way to England). The coal miners remained on strike for many more months, but their main demands were not met. Charles may have been thinking of the Yorkshire towns where he lived before going to South Africa when he wrote about the back courts and alleyways.

consulted, but identified it in the second book as *Claytonia Perfoliata*.[176] It was a native of North America, and it was a mystery how it had "secured a footing as a weed in the garden".

The weather in England was a constant preoccupation. The winter of 1929 was cold, but fairly dry although there was some snow. One day in January when the bright wintry sun shone on the fresh snow was, for Charles, perfect. He wrote: "Thine eyes shall see the King in his beauty."[177] It took some time for the temperature to rise and the ground to warm up in the spring. The lack of much rain in the first half of the year disappointed the farmers, whose crops were lighter than usual. But for others, the hot summer was very pleasant.

With his enthusiasm for nature, Charles found much of interest in the different flora and birds he found on his and Marion's, usually very brief, stops in the Canary Islands and Madeira on their voyages between England and Southern Africa. Just one example, from their extended stay in the Canaries in 1928, illustrates this. Much of the land had been given over to the cultivation of bananas, which were a major export, going mainly to Spain, the UK and Germany. As Charles observed, "there are bananas everywhere, on the terraced hillsides… they are growing on every shelf, and where the slope is not so steep, they are spaced out in large plantations which extend down to the edge of the cliffs". He did not like it. While the mountains on one side and the sea on the other provided some relief, the bananas "deprived the place of most of its interest by their sheer monotony, like the cane farms on the Natal and Zululand coast, but even so the comparison does not altogether hold for they are not of the same fresh and cheerful green as the sugar cane". He found that the prickly pear in Tenerife was of a different species from that in Gran Canaria. The cochineal insect lived in it, and "before the discovery of aniline dyes, raised the islands to a height of prosperity they have never again attained". Even the requirements of the British Army for red tunics before it switched to the more serviceable khaki, and the fact that no aniline dye could match the cochineal for permanency of colour, were not enough to save the cochineal business.

---

176 The two books were Anne Pratt, *Flowering Plants of Great Britain* (1855-66) and Rev C A Johns, *Flowers of the Field* (1900).

177 *Isaiah*, chapter 33, verse 17.

CHAPTER 11

KNOWLEDGE AND BELIEFS

Charles was a keen reader. He liked to keep notes about the books and articles he read. He wrote them on loose pages which he periodically sorted roughly into subject groups and bound into volumes. The notes helped to cement his understanding of what he read, and also provided an easy source of information. On the title page of Volume VII he wrote "Litera Scripta Manet", meaning "the written word remains". He thought of the volumes as his Books of Knowledge, and inscribed Incwadi Yokwazi, which is Zulu for Book of Knowledge, on the cover of Volumes VII and VIII, which were bound together. He produced eight volumes altogether, but only the last three, covering the years from 1916 to 1928, have survived, together with some loose pages that he had not bound. We do not know

when he began the notes, but it was probably while he was living in Zululand. Volume V, which covered 1913 to 1916, contained 700 pages, as did volume VI, which covered 1916 to 1924. Volumes VII and VIII, covering 1923 to 1928, contained only 500 pages between them.[178] His writing was small and very neat, with remarkably few corrections. He managed about 400 words a page, so that Volumes V and VI each had about 280,000 words. In the years covered by Volume V, he was averaging nearly one page a day, assuming that he wrote for five days a week.

The extent of his reading and notetaking varied with the intensity of his other activities. His notes were prolific when he was in Zululand. Then the move to England, his bout of malaria and war service left him with little

---

178   The dates of the notes in the volumes overlapped a little because of the way in which he chose to group the loose pages for binding into volumes.

time and energy for reading and writing. In Cape Town in 1920-21 his job as editor of the *Church Chronicle* involved so much writing that he had little appetite for doing more in his spare time. He read and wrote more again during the years when he was in South West Africa, except in the months when he and Marion were in England on leave.

He read both books and articles. The latter came from a variety of sources, including the *Times Literary Supplement, Strand Magazine, Encyclopedia Britannica, Children's Encyclopedia, Discovery, The Interpreter, The Challenge, Conquest, Nature, The Guardian, Modern Churchmen, Church Quarterly Review, Church Chronicle* and *Christian Express* (the latter two were South African publications). He collected some of these while on home leave in England, and others were sent out to him, or borrowed from other people. The notes cover only his non-fiction reading. We do not know what fiction he read.

The notes are essentially summaries of the books and articles he was reading. He almost never expressed an opinion about what he read. Although we therefore lack the insights into his thinking that such opinions would provide, his choice of reading gives us some idea of his interests. Naturally religion, Christianity, the bible and the church were major interests. Especially after the war, he read and kept notes about international relations, the history and politics of combatant countries (Germany, Italy, Russia) and the Empire. Social and economic affairs interested him mainly insofar as they created problems, such as poverty, broken homes, alcohol abuse and gambling, for ordinary people. (His reading on these subjects related primarily to the UK, and sometimes the US.)

He had two other interests that did not intersect directly with his calling as a priest: science and literature. He read books and articles about chemistry, biology, geology, astronomy, genetics and natural selection, and was even acquainted with modern developments in the atom and relativity. His love of poetry dated back to his younger days. We have already seen the way in which he enlivened his account of his trip to South Africa in 1896-97 with lines from favourite poems. He continued the practice in *In the Winds of Heaven* and copied out many poems in his Books of Knowledge. He also made notes about a few famous writers and their works.

When he was freed in February 1922 from "having to consider the best way of expressing oneself without ruining the circulation of the paper" (the *Church Chronicle*), he started to write a log of current affairs. He kept it up for nearly five years, but with gaps in 1924 and 1926 when he and Marion were staying in other people's houses in England where it was difficult "to settle down to any making of notes". At the end of 1926 he had to admit that "the spirit of the log seems to have passed, so it is not much good trying to keep it going… There are so many things to occupy one's time that something has to go." He started again at the beginning of 1929 "as there seems more time on hand for doing things", but only managed to keep it up for four months.

In addition to notes on readings, Volume VI contained daily weather reports from 1 December 1915 to 12 April 1917, just before he left for England. There were also reports for two weeks in December 1919 after Charles returned to South Africa. From June 1920 until November 1929 he kept daily weather records in *In the Winds of Heaven* wherever he was in Southern Africa and England, except when he was away from home. From 1924, he even kept records of the weather on the voyages between England and Southern Africa. For each day he recorded barometer and thermometer readings, when they were available, the wind direction and strength, and a summary note (eg clear, cloudy, rain, etc.). As he noted where he was each day, we can trace his travels between the various parts of his bailiwicks in Zululand and South West Africa, and his trips within England. He had a lifelong interest in keeping track of the weather, as we saw earlier during his holidays in England and the Continent, and on his first trip to South Africa in 1896-97.

Much of his reading was directed at understanding the natural world around him. His interest in the weather, the changing skies, the stars and the movement of the planets led him to read books and articles about the atmosphere, meteorology and astronomy. He was up to date with current knowledge about the causes of weather patterns. He was excited when Pluto was discovered in 1930, noting – correctly as it turned out – that "it may not be a planet after all".

He made notes about the flora and fauna of Southern Africa. He consulted these and his books on the same topics whenever he wished to identify a bird or plant that he had seen or find out more about it. He read about the geology of Southern Africa and made detailed notes of the geological periods. He read theories about continental drift and how it might explain the rupture of Gondwanaland.

He was not afraid to try to approach the limits of what was known in physics, as described by leading scientists such as Arthur Eddington, J J Thomson, James H Jeans and Sir Oliver Lodge.[179] He spent part of the voyage from the Canaries to England in 1928 thinking and writing about relativity. This was a continuation of thoughts he had had during the voyage to the Canaries two months before. Then, he had concluded that Einstein's two postulates (about the relativity of motion and the constancy of the speed of light) led him (Einstein) to "embark on soaring flights of abstract reasoning which leaves ordinary non-mathematical mortals all of a whirl when toiling in his wake". Now, encouraged by something Smuts wrote to the effect that the implications of Einstein's theories could be understood apart from the abstruse mathematical process itself, he was determined to "try again to see

---

179 Among the books he referred to in his notes and presumably read, in whole or in part, were Arthur Eddington, *Stars and Atoms* (1926), J J Thomson, *The Structure of Light* (1925), James H Jeans' Presidential Address on *Space, Time and the Universe* at the Royal Astronomical Society on the award of a gold medal to Einstein, *Nature* Feb 27 1926, and Sir Oliver Lodge, *Ether and Reality* (1925).

what we can make of it".[180] In *In the Winds of Heaven* he wrote clear notes about the space-time continuum, gravity and acceleration, and the curvature of space. This was quite an achievement for a clergyman who had not spent much time in scientific environments, and it was a measure of his intellectual curiosity about the natural world. However, he himself admitted a couple of months later that his understanding was limited. "The vision is only here a little and there a little… Until some simpler form of explanation can be produced, it looks as if it can remain the property only of a few enlightened minds."

He also read about particle physics.[181] On the voyage from England to South Africa in 1929 he found himself thinking what a saving would be effected "if it were possible to make use of the concentrated energy stored up within the atom instead of merely using the outer electrons of the carbon compounds in combination with the oxygen in the air", as was the case in the steam engine propelling the ship. He went on to write about Moseley's demonstration that the atomic number of an element is equal to the number of free protons in its nucleus. Moseley was killed in the war when he was only 27: "It was a bad day for science when Moseley fell from a Turkish bullet in the trenches at Gallipoli."[182] He wrote about the differences between Bohr's and Schrodinger's theories of the atom. "Both theories work satisfactorily up to a point in that each explains something that goes on in the atom that the other does not." He noted that there were also competing theories of light – whether it was waves or particles. And quoted approvingly a comment of Sir William Bragg's: "For the moment we have to work with both theories. On Mondays, Wednesdays and Fridays we use the wave theory; on Tuesdays, Thursdays and Saturdays we think in streams of flying energy, quanta or corpuscles."[183]

His main interest in biology was evolution. He accepted the central ideas of Darwin, especially relating to natural selection, and read recent writings about evolution.[184] But he could not accept that it could be "merely a mechanical process". The "recognition of a Designer and Controller at the back of all

---

180 From Jan Christian Smuts, *Holism and Evolution* (1927). Smuts was prime minister of South Africa from 1919 to 1924. He was influential in the creation of the League of Nations and the British Commonwealth of Nations. Charles' readings about relativity included E A Fath, *The Elements of Astronomy* (1926), James H Jeans, *Space, Time and the Universe,* Presidential Address at the Royal Astronomical Society on the award of a gold medal to Einstein, *Nature*, Feb 27 1926, and Bertrand Russell's writings, possibly *A B C of Relativity* (1925).

181 For example, J A Cranston, *The Structure of Matter* (1924).

182 Henry Gwyn Jeffreys Moseley (1887-1915) was an English physicist who showed that atomic numbers have a firm experimental basis in the physics of their X-ray spectra.

183 Sir William Bragg (1862-1942) was a British scientist who shared the Nobel prize in physics in 1915 with his son Lawrence Bragg.

184 For example, H S Jennings, *Prometheus, or Biology and the Advancement of Man* (1927).

things" was a necessity. "The slow but ever advancing movement through the long ages of evolution, like a great tide coming in, must be the working out of some wonderful purpose which could only be conceived of by a Creative and Directive mind. The very appearance of life from non-living matter, in whatever way it first came into existence, seems impossible to explain apart from this; and the self-conscious human mind with all its moral and spiritual perceptions is even a greater difficulty if a First Cause be not admitted." In this he was in line with the views of many Anglicans, including the Bishop of Birmingham, whose remarks in a sermon at Westminster Abbey in 1927 Charles recorded in the Book of Knowledge: "Observed facts force us to the conclusion that God has been active throughout the evolutionary process".[185]

His reading and writing about evolution were only one aspect of his recurring interest in the question of what science meant for Christianity. As science increased our understanding of the world, for example through advances in atomic theory, relativity and radiation, he could agree with J J Thomson that "Great Are the Works of the Lord".[186] He never saw the advance of science as a challenge to his belief in a Christian God.

It did, however, cause him to re-examine his views about how God's will was exercised. He felt that the dividing line between the animate and the inanimate was becoming thinner. He imagined that the Creator must be working to the same plan at every level, from the atom to man. Just as man had free will to choose to do good or evil, so, in the inanimate world, outcomes were not predetermined. "The violence of the flood and earthquake, the unimaginable fiery heat of the stars, may all be manifestations of the freedom of action within limitations pervading the whole of nature." Charles was not referring to the uncertainty principle of quantum mechanics, of which he was probably unaware, and he recognised that his ideas were highly speculative: "Is this all mere fancy?" But they helped him reconcile his belief in God with the growing ability of science to explain natural phenomena. "There is much in nature that is not in accordance with the purpose of God (as there is also in human nature)... but He allows it because it is part of the outcome of the principle of freedom with which He has endowed the whole of creation."

This last sentence was included in his thoughts about the rise of science, but it would also have been in place in his comments on

---

185   The Rt Rev Ernest William Barnes, FRS, (1874-1953) was a mathematician and scientist who later became a liberal theologian. He was appointed Bishop of Birmingham in 1924.

186   "As we conquer peak after peak, we see in front of us regions full of interest and beauty, but we do not see our goal, we do not see the horizon; in the distance tower still higher peaks which will yield to those who ascend them still wider prospects, and deepen the feeling the truth of which is emphasised by every advance in science, that 'Great are the Works of the Lord'." From the Presidential Address by Sir Joseph John Thomson to the annual meeting of the British Association for the Advancement of Science in Winnipeg, 1909, *Science*, volume 30, 1909. Thomson was a British physicist and Nobel Prize winner who discovered the electron.

cruelty in nature, another of his philosophical concerns. He explained such cruelty as part of the struggle for existence and noted that man was close to the animals in that social life was "organised on the lines of strife and competition". He suggested that having to cope with conflict might be a necessary part of moving towards perfection. He quoted both St Paul and Isaiah to support the view that "With the final conquest of evil in man, the whole of creation will be uplifted. For man, while he touches God on one side, is intimately connected with nature on the other."

Charles reflected that Tennyson had also been upset about the contradiction between the cruelty and wastefulness of nature and the goodness of God:

Are God and Nature then at strife,
That Nature lends such evil dreams?
So careful of the type she seems,
So careless of a single life.
I falter where I firmly trod,
And falling with my weight of cares
Upon the great world's altar stairs
That slope, through darkness, up to God,
I stretch lame hands of faith and grope.[187]

In the end, the advance of science and the cruelty of nature, and of man, especially as seen in the war, were not enough to dent Charles' faith. His love of the beauty of nature outweighed all dark features of the world. "There is so much of surpassing wonder and beauty in Nature, one cannot help believing that there must be a Divine Intelligence behind it all, whose attribute in the end is perfection. With our limited outlook and knowledge there is much which cannot be explained, but yet somehow, although it is not possible fully to justify our belief, there is enough evidence to convince us that our intuition of the perfection of God must somehow be right. There are signs of his presence everywhere – in the grandeur of the mountains and the storm clouds, in the glory of the sunset sky and in the beauty of the wild flowers." He added that "Wordsworth knew it when he wrote:

I have felt
A presence that disturbs me with the joy
Of elevated thoughts; a sense sublime
Of something far more deeply interfused,
Whose dwelling is in the light of setting suns,
And the round ocean and the living air,
And the blue sky, and in the mind of man:
A motion and a spirit that impels
All thinking things, all objects of all thought,
And rolls through all things.[188]

---

187 Alfred, Lord Tennyson, *In Memoriam A. H. H. Obiit MDCCCXXXIII: 55*. Charles quoted only the second and fourth verses, and the first line of the fifth and final verse. The rest of the fifth verse reads:
And gather dust and chaff, and call
To what I feel is Lord of all,
And faintly trust the larger hope.

188 Extract from William Wordsworth, *Lines Composed a Few Miles above Tintern Abbey, On Revisiting the Banks of the Wye during a Tour. July 13, 1798.*

Some years later he returned to the question of the place of religion in a world in which science was explaining more and more. He was tempted by the Kantian idea that knowledge could be divided into two compartments, one in which science ruled and the other which belonged to moral considerations. But he worried about how the two could meet. "Both science and religion have had to suffer from the unnatural separation – science from having to work to the rule that there is no mind or consciousness behind nature, and religion from being supposed to stand on an irrational basis." He could not accept the position of rationalist thinkers, that "everything would eventually be explained in mechanical terms". "Materialism, epiphenomenalism, positivism, agnosticism and pluralism each and all fail in some way or other to cover the whole ground." "The only satisfactory explanation of the whole of existence is that there is one eternal, objective Ultimate Reality", namely God. We can know nothing of the inmost nature of the Supreme Being, "but he has revealed himself to us by means of those three chief values we have the faculties to apprehend: Goodness, Truth and Beauty." "They each mark out a particular path upwards: the Good, the way of all moral endeavour; the Beautiful, the way of all true Art; and the True, which is the end of all scientific research."

This is perhaps the clearest description that Charles wrote of the basis of his faith. He wrote it sitting in his house in remote South West Africa, surrounded by books and articles that he read carefully. We have to admire him for continuing to grapple with these large philosophical and theological questions when his day-to-day life was taken up with managing the affairs of his "parish", coping with the inconveniences of life and travel in an undeveloped country, and relaxing by observing (and writing about) the natural world around him.

In reflecting on life after death, while sceptical of most claims of spiritualists, he tended to accept the ideas of the scientist and promoter of spiritualism, Sir Oliver Lodge, that the individual does survive the shock of separation from the body.[189] Charles' conclusion was that "we ourselves in fact are distinct and can exist apart from our bodies". Separately from this, his belief in life after death came from his faith. Man's "spiritual experiences are so crammed with meaning that this life is all too short to comprehend them. They demand nothing less than eternity for their satisfaction. If death is the end of all, then there can only be vain imaginations."

One philosophical question that he pondered was whether there was such a thing as objective reality. Or were the phenomenalists correct to believe that the only knowledge is that which is presented to our senses? The latter view led some people to argue, in the

189   Sir Oliver Lodge (1851-1940) was a physicist who did original work in electromagnetism and radio. Charles read an article of his on Psychic Science in J Arthur Thomson (ed), *The Outline of Science, Third Volume* (1922). He also read two of his scientific books: *Talks about Wireless* (1925) and *Ether and Reality* (1925).

words of Jung, that "God is but a function of the unconscious... the divine effect springs from our own inner self". Unsurprisingly, he took the view that acceptance of the reality of objects is the only practical way forward, even if it cannot be proved to the satisfaction of all philosophers. The common sense behind this position was illustrated by Ronald Knox's famous limerick, which he misquoted as:

There was a young man who said "God
Must think it excessively odd
That a sycamore tree
Just ceases to be
When there is no one about in the Quad.[190]

Charles' reading was not confined to theological and related subjects. He was also interested in social and economic matters, and science and nature. In 1927 he read *The World of William Clissold* (1926) by H G Wells. It was a large, rambling novel that was as much a statement of Wells' views on a wide range of topics as it was a story about the titular Clissold. It led Charles to reflect on the sexual impulse and the role of marriage. Clissold favoured "temporary mating" to provide an outlet for the violence of his sexual desires. He thought that marriage was the quaint social survival of the backward suburbs and the provincial towns. Wells himself had affairs and children with many women. Charles thoroughly disapproved, partly because the permanence of marriage created stability in society. The true marriage union, he believed, rested on the spirit of unselfish giving for the good of others. It was not built on a "fleeting basis of sensual gratification or a passing obligation to children so produced, but on a truth which can transfigure human life, and which is eternal". His optimism about the perfectibility of man led him to elevate the spirit of unselfishness to a leading role in solving society's problems. "On a larger scale, it [the spirit of unselfishness] is the basis of all social life, both industrial and political, and civilization will not settle down

---

190   The version in the *Oxford Dictionary of Quotations* is:

There was once a man who said "God

Must think it exceedingly odd

If he finds that this tree

Continues to be

When there's no one about in the Quad".

An anonymous response, usually attributed to Knox, was:

Dear Sir, Your astonishment's odd:

I am always about in the Quad.

And that's why the tree

Will continue to be,

Since observed by Yours faithfully, God.

Ronald Knox was an English Anglican priest who converted to Catholicism.

peaceably until it comes to be the dominant idea in human life rather than that of the struggle for existence which we have brought up with us from our long past ancestry."

With regard to race relations, as a missionary he regarded Africans as equal to Europeans in the eyes of God. But he probably did not think that they were yet ready to have the same political and civil rights as Europeans had. Missionaries and other Europeans who worked with Africans generally preferred a slow rather than a fast path to more rights for Africans, and it is likely that Charles shared this view. In the late 1920s a British teacher at a mission school wrote: "it is a very big question, of course, as to how far the Native is fit to have the Franchise put in his hands" but "there is no doubt that the day is coming when the Native will ask for his rights, and that God has given him the right to ask for those rights". Later in the same article, the writer was blunt about why Africans were not yet ready for leadership roles. "No native has much power of creating, or originating; therefore there must be the white man to lead, to inspire, to see the vision, to hoist the flag."[191]

When Charles was editing the *Church Chronicle* in Cape Town in 1920-22, he kept up with the growing debate in South Africa about the "Native Question". He took copious notes from the book by Charles Loram, a teacher with a liberal view of African rights.[192] Loram was later appointed one of the commissioners on the enquiry into the Bondelswarts uprising that took place in 1922 when Charles was in Keetmanshoop.[193] Together with Roberts, the other liberal commissioner, he blamed the South West African administration for creating the conditions that had led to the uprising. The third commissioner, General Lemming, placed all the blame on the Bondelswarts, who deserved all they got. Charles quoted an editorial in the *Cape Times* stating that "there are still many South Africans who are wholly sceptical about the possibility of native progress. To them the degradation of the Bondelswarts is a natural fate, their discontent a mere semi-animal unruliness to be kicked or clubbed into submission, their grievances impudent presumption upon the white races".

"A gulf yawns" between the different views about the Native Question. Loram and Roberts were English speaking while Lemming was an Afrikaner. The Afrikaners were the main supporters of the National Party which set up the apartheid regime many years later.

Charles' own views were closer to those of liberals like Loram and Roberts than to those of Lemming. As we have seen, he recorded approvingly that some Coloured people who lived with the Bondelswarts had told him that the situation would have been better if the British and not the Afrikaners had been in control of

---

191   Muriel Balmain, "The Worth of the "Nigger"", *The Net*, December 1929.

192   Charles Templeman Loram, *The Education of the South African Native*, (Longmans, Green and Co., 1917).

193   The uprising and the Commission of Enquiry were discussed in Chapter 8.

the Bondelswarts. In general, he disapproved of what he perceived to be the harsh treatment of Africans throughout the country by the South West African administration, which was dominated by Afrikaners, many of whom had come from South Africa. He was well aware of the growing pressure for Africans to be given some political power. Towards the end of his and Marion's time in Cape Town before moving to Keetmanshoop, he wrote about the glorious setting of the city with its surroundings of nature. But he added that there was no doubt a "great colour problem of this country looming up in the future".

CHAPTER 12

CONCLUSION

The family after Charles

Marion lived for another 24 years after Charles' death in 1930. At first she lived in Belsize Park. She visited South Africa in 1931, and again in 1936 on her way back from India. She had gone to Calcutta for the wedding in St Paul's Cathedral on 22 December 1935 of her goddaughter Barbara (Barbie) Odling-Smee to Derrick Oliver (known as Dick), who was in the army in India. She also went to the Continent, including Norway and Italy, in the 1930s. From the late 1930s to the end of World War II she lived with Barbie and her children in East Lavant, near Chichester, as Dick was away in the war. The house belonged to Dick and Barbie.

She moved into London after the war. In the 1950s she shared a flat in Earls Court with Charles' cousins, Hilda and Helen Brownrigg and Esme Key. (They were actually first cousins once removed, Hilda and Helen Brownrigg being the daughters of Charles' first cousin Louisa Brownrigg, and Esme Key being the daughter of Kingsmill James Key, Louisa's half brother.)

Marion, who had no children of her own, was always ready to help other women with theirs. She helped Bill Odling-Smee's wife Katharine in the 1930s when she had three young children. And, as we have seen, she lived with Barbie and her children during the war. She was asked to be the godmother, not only of Emma's daughter Barbie, but also of two of Emma's grandchildren, David Odling-Smee and Barbara Oliver, and she was happy to accept. She was much loved by the grandchildren, especially the Oliver girls, with whom she lived during the war and for shorter times afterwards. She was remembered for her distinctive personality and lack of interest in possessions.

Marion and the Brownrigg sisters invited some of their teenage cousins to stay with them in 1953 so that they could watch the Coronation procession. There were six of them: Mary and David Odling-Smee, Susan and Sally Oliver, and Michael and Roderick Brownrigg. The first four were Emma's grandchildren. Michael and Roderick were the grandchildren of Hilda and Helen's cousin, George Worthington Brownrigg, who had emigrated to Argentina in 1889. They were born and brought up in Argentina and came to London for the Coronation. They all stayed in the Earls Court Road flat, sleeping in the attics which Marion and the Brownriggs rented to single women on other occasions. Marion had a friend who arranged for them to stand on the roof of the Playhouse Theatre in Northumberland Avenue from which they watched the procession go past after the coronation in Westminster Abbey.

Marion took the six teenagers to Northumberland Avenue on the tube. London was packed and the six youngsters protected Marion, who was almost 81, from the crush. Unfortunately, they could not defend her against the wind which blew the hat off her head and along the tunnel in the tube station. It looked rather like a man's hat, and Marion commented philosophically that one day some man would find it and be happy to wear it. Even at that age, she was still the strong woman who had survived many difficulties in Africa and elsewhere. Marion died in St George's Hospital at Hyde Park Corner in 1955, aged 82.

When Charles died, Bill Odling-Smee, Emma's oldest child, was working as a civil engineer, as he had been since graduating from King's College, London, in 1925. He was, however, wondering whether to become ordained and change careers. He loved engineering, but the carnage of World War I led him to think that he should become a clergyman to spread Christianity and the love of God more widely in the population and change people's thinking about war. Charles had similar views about war and Christianity, and it is quite possible that Bill, who admired his Uncle Charlie, was influenced by him, even to the extent of changing careers and becoming a clergyman. Bill went to theological college in Cambridge in 1939 and was ordained in Ripon in 1940. For the rest of the war he was a curate in Headingley, Leeds, where he reluctantly came to terms with the country being at war again. From 1945 onwards he was the vicar of rural parishes in Ripon Diocese. He had married a Scottish doctor, Katharine Aitchison, in 1934 and they had four children, William, Mary, David and John. He died in Brearton near Harrogate in 1990.

Emma's other two children were Jack and Barbie. Jack went to Sandhurst from which he graduated on the same day in July 1925 as Dick Oliver, Barbie's future husband. Jack and Dick were gazetted in the Royal Sussex Regiment on the same day in September 1925. They both served in India during the 1930s. Jack served in Europe in World War II and retired from the army after the war. He settled in Devon where he ran a market garden for some years. He had married Nancy Bowles in 1933 and had two sons, John and Peter. He died in Cornwood, Devon, in 1987.

As already noted, Barbie married Dick Oliver in Calcutta in 1935, with Marion representing the family. They had three children, Susan, Sally and Barbara. Dick served in Burma during the war, and, unlike Jack, remained in the army after the war. He was posted to Palestine in the 1940s and to Kenya during the Mau Mau uprising for a few years in the early 1950s. The family, having lived in Sussex during the war, lived in Hampshire and Wiltshire afterwards. Barbie inherited the house, Cotlands, in Selsey from Plumb (as Miss Plumbley, Charles' Uncle Martin's housekeeper, was called) in 1956, but they did not live there. Barbie died in Chitterne, Wiltshire, in 1988 and Dick died there in 1992.

A late echo of Charles' life was the appearance of his botanical paintings at auction in London in 1986. As we have seen, this gave rise to an article in a South African botanical journal.[194] Following this, entries for Charles appeared in the Biographical Database of Southern African Science and Wikipedia.

Summing up

There are various ways of summing up a person's life. Biographies of public figures focus on their achievements in their careers. One aspect of achievement is a legacy that lives on, such as a building for an architect, a painting for an artist, a law for a politician, or a company for a businessman. Another less tangible aspect is the impact of the person's life and work on others. A doctor might save a life or ease the suffering of patients. Teachers often have a marked influence on their students over and above the formal transfer of knowledge. Less visible still is the influence of parents on their children, and friends and family on younger generations, but this too is a form of legacy. One can also sum up a person's life from the point of view of the person himself or herself. Did he feel fulfilled? Was he happy? We shall look at Charles' life from these various angles.

Charles' career as a clergyman was moderately successful. In England, he was a curate for 14 years before becoming a vicar, which was perhaps slightly longer than average. During this time, he impressed his superior in Almondbury and Barnsley, William Foxley Norris, who himself rose in the church, ending as Dean of Westminster. In both Zululand and South West Africa, Charles was an archdeacon, which involved responsibilities over and above those for his own areas. In Cape Town he was a sub-dean of St George's Cathedral and editor of the Anglican church newspaper, the *Church Chronicle*, two important positions. His attendance at the Prague ecumenical conference on economic and social issues

---

194   J P Rourke and J C Manning, "The Venerable Charles Theophilus Hahn, a Hitherto Unknown Edwardian Botanical Illustrator in Natal, 1908-1916", *Bothalia*, Volume 22, 1992.

suggests that the Church of England saw him as a suitable representative (that is, assuming he was there for the C of E rather than as an individual).

He was hard working and thorough in his work. His wish to have good order and record everything that happened helped to give structure to the work of the church in his areas. In Africa, he was willing to put up with much physical hardship, not least in travelling around his "parishes". While his sermons may not have been inspiring – he himself sometimes doubted whether they were effective – there was no question about his commitment to the ministry and his congregations. His views on the broader social and political issues of the day were middle of the road, C of E views. He understood the difficulties of the working class in Yorkshire and the Africans in Southern Africa. He did not favour socialist remedies in England and was not involved in social or political movements. In Africa, he saw the dangers of the separation of Europeans and Africans, and the denial of opportunities for Africans to advance, economically and politically. But he accepted the state of affairs as given and saw his role as being to help them come to God and live Christian lives.

Obituaries tend to emphasise the positive, but his bishop in Zululand, Wilmot Vyvyan, was probably close to the truth when he wrote that Charles was "a devout and devoted priest, wholly unselfish, a good comrade, gentle and humble, and loved by everyone, European and Native alike". Someone who knew him in Empangeni wrote that "his death is a loss both to the church and the world outside, for men of his selfless devotion are rare in any age".[195]

Turning to physical legacies, he built a brick cottage in Inhlwati and a house in Nongoma, the latter of which he gave to the diocese. He started funds for churches in Empangeni and Keetmanshoop, with generous contributions of his own. Both churches had been completed by the time he died. He produced a remarkable set of about 300 watercolours of South African wild flowers. Most of them probably still exist, although we do not know where they are, apart from the 30 in the family's possession. He also wrote copiously in his diaries, journals and notebooks about his activities, travels, readings, and observations of nature. Without these, this biography could not have been written. His writings, and this biography itself, can therefore claim to be part of his legacy.

It is more difficult to pin down his legacy in the form of influences on other people. The most important person was Marion. She and Charles had a close relationship stemming from their shared interests. They both loved nature and the outdoors, and enjoyed hiking, cycling and other outdoor pursuits, at least in their younger days. Marion easily fitted into the role of clergyman's wife, helping Charles in his work in both Yorkshire and Africa. Charles had the stronger personality, and Marion benefited from his leadership and drive. They had a happy marriage which

---

195   Both this comment and Bishop Vyvyan's obituary appeared in *The Net,* December 1930.

was mutually supportive, especially in their illnesses of later years.

Charles' relationships with his nephews and niece, Bill, Jack and Barbie Odling-Smee, were important to them. Although he was working in Southern Africa for most of their lives except the earliest years, he and Marion always spent time with them on his lengthy leaves in England. Bill was the closest to him and his decision to become a clergyman after training and working as an engineer was partly influenced by Charles' example. Along with Marion, he was the executor of Charles' estate. Barbie was close to Marion, who was her godmother

It is a pity that we do not have any record of Charles' influence on the many people outside the family with whom he interacted. Did the lives of his parishioners in Yorkshire, his congregations in Africa, his clergy colleagues, servants in England and Africa, or other friends and acquaintances change in any way as a result of knowing him? One would love to know. Perhaps the closest we can come to understanding this is in the words of the person in Empangeni who has already been quoted: "A man of deep religion, but with broad tolerant outlook, fond of the simple things in life, Hahn was of a most attractive and lovable nature."[196]

From his own point of view, Charles had a good life. The world around him may have been changing in ways that he did not like: the growing labour movement in England, World War and the decline of the UK as a major world power, rising secularism in England (though with a reverse movement during and after the war), and the growing strength of segregationist sentiment among the European rulers of South Africa. On the other hand, science and technology were changing the world in beneficial ways, most importantly for him in making travel and communications easier. But it was in the simpler things that he found happiness, not least his marriage, the natural world, travel and the adventures associated with it, the outdoors and exercise, and his faith. He did indeed achieve what he had hoped for when he wrote in his diary at the beginning of 1892 that he "would be content if he got plenty of exercise, had a jolly time in general, and everything continued to run smoothly".

But he did much more than this. His life was very different from that of the country parson leading "a humdrum existence in which one day is the same as another, and nothing happens from year's end to year's end to break the monotony of daily life", a fate he feared in his 1892 diary entry. He was adventurous, energetic and intelligent, and left a mark in both England and Southern Africa. He had intellectual curiosity and artistic sensibilities and talent. He loved both humanity and nature. His was decidedly an accomplished and eventful, as well as a jolly, life.

---

196 *The Net,* December 1930.

INDEX

BV - #0036 - 070721 - C74 - 254/203/17 - PB - 9781861519764 - Gloss Lamination